Classics

from

The New Yankee Workshop

Norm Abram

with Tim Snyder

Little, Brown and Company

Boston Toronto London

FIRST EDITION

Illustrations: David Dann
Photographs: Richard Howard

LIBRARY OF CONGRESS CATALOGING-IN-PUBLICATION DATA

Abram, Norm.
    Classics from the New Yankee workshop/by Norm Abram with Tim
Snyder. — 1st ed.
        p. cm.
    A companion guide to the second season of public television's
popular series the New Yankee workshop hosted by Norm Abram.
    ISBN 0-316-00456-1.—ISBN 0-316-00455-3 (pbk.)
    1. Furniture making. 2. Cabinet-work. I. Snyder, Tim. II. New
Yankee workshop (Television program) III. Title.
TT194.A24 1990
684.1′042 — dc20   90-34765
                                                            CIP

10 9 8 7 6 5 4 3 2 1

RRD OH

Published simultaneously in Canada
by Little, Brown & Company (Canada) Limited

Printed in the United States of America

Rodale Press, Inc., publishes AMERICAN WOODWORKER™, the magazine for the
serious woodworking hobbyist. For information on how to order your subscription,
write to AMERICAN WOODWORKER™, Emmaus, PA 18098.

Contents

With love to my wife, Laura, whose sacrifice,
understanding, and silent support made it possible for me to get through
the intense schedule that was necessary to make this book a reality.

Acknowledgments

Many forces have converged to produce this book, and I want to express gratitude to everyone who's had a hand in the undertaking. Russell Morash's ingenuity and vision conceived the New Yankee Workshop; the support of David Liroff, station manager at WGBH Educational Foundation, has made it a reality. Associate producer Nina Sing's tireless efforts keep the show's production running smoothly.

Tim Snyder distilled each woodworking project into prose and selected the accompanying photos. Photographer Richard Howard stood by my side in sawdust to capture each step of the process and, with the help of Kate Morash, the finished pieces as well. David Dann rendered the fine drawings detailing the construction process. Marian Morash's incomparable provender and good cheer kept our energy levels high. At Little, Brown and Company, William D. Phillips has championed the New Yankee Workshop from the beginning. Christina Ward coaxed and cajoled the book's many participants toward a united goal. David Coen's assiduous eye for detail, Barbara Werden's elegant design sense, and the heroic efforts of Ellen Bedell and Donna Peterson have shaped both the process and the end result of the book's editing and production. Our literary agent, Don Cutler, has bolstered the spirit and substance of the endeavor from first to last.

Abiding thanks go to our series underwriters, the Parks Corporation, makers of Carver Tripp wood-finishing products, and the Square D Company, makers of electrical distribution and control equipment. Their financial support has made the series and the book possible.

Finally, the New Yankee Workshop owes its very inspiration to the craftsmen of yore whose work stands as a testament to their designs and techniques. Special thanks go to the helpful curators, directors, and staffs of Old Sturbridge Village in Sturbridge, Massachusetts; the Adirondack Museum in Blue Mountain Lake, New York; Kingscote House and the Preservation Society of Newport, Rhode Island; Beauport House and the Society for the Preservation of New England Antiquities; the Shelburne Museum in Shelburne, Vermont; Historic Deerfield in Deerfield, Massachusetts; the Crowninshield-Bentley House and the Essex Institute in Salem, Massachusetts; and Dr. Don Davidoff and Susan Tarlow, collectors of Mission and Craftsman-style furniture.

Classics from the New Yankee Workshop

Introduction

Tools and Techniques in the New Yankee Workshop

Safety

It's impossible to overemphasize the importance of safety in any workshop situation. To avoid injury, it's crucial to read, understand, and follow the instructions that come with each tool in your workshop. This is especially important when using power tools, since they move cutting surfaces at high speeds and involve electrical current. Always wear safety glasses when using power tools, and observe basic electrical safety procedures.

It takes time to develop skill in using woodworking tools. If a tool or technique is new to you, practice on some scrap stock before you work on a piece of wood that will go into the project. Even for experienced furniture-makers, test runs are standard procedure to make sure that a technique will work or that a power tool's setup is correct.

In terms of general shop safety, a first-aid kit and a fire extinguisher should be close at hand. Good ventilation is necessary for areas where finishes are applied. It's also worthwhile to have some system for collecting sawdust, wood shavings, and wood scraps. In my workshop, I have a heavy-duty shop vacuum that can be hooked up to outfeed shoots on several power tools.

Even with a good dust-collection system, a considerable amount of sawdust can remain airborne as wood is cut, milled, and sanded. Sawdust from teak, mahogany, and other tropical hardwoods has been known to cause allergic reactions in some people. I always keep a supply of disposable filter masks in the shop to use in dusty conditions or when I'm applying finish.

Apart from skill, patience, and safety concerns, the formula for a successful workshop is simple: you need good tools and as much room as possible to use them. In this introductory chapter, I'll discuss some of the basic tools and techniques that you'll see repeatedly throughout the book. If your workshop isn't equipped the same way mine is, don't worry. The good thing about woodworking is that there are at least several ways to perform most operations. Nevertheless, some tools are truly indispensable, and furniture-making projects would be unnecessarily difficult and time-consuming without them. Care taken in organizing and equipping a workshop promotes safety, precision, and the satisfaction of doing high-quality work.

I'm fortunate to have a separate "painting room" off the east end of my workshop. This enables me to apply finish in an area where no woodworking is done. There's no sawdust in the air or on the floor, and I keep the room clean by vacuuming it regularly.

If you have to apply finish coats in your workshop, take care to eliminate as much dust as possible before any finish is applied. Once you're done with final sanding, use a shop vacuum to clean sawdust from floor, tool, and work surfaces. Go over the furniture piece thoroughly with a tack rag to clean off loose sawdust. If possible, let airborne dust settle for a night before applying finish. Give the piece a final once-over with a fresh tack rag, and avoid activities in the shop that might raise dust before the finish has a chance to dry.

As for the workshop itself, I really appreciate its open plan (*see photo opposite page 1*). Thanks to a steel I-beam that runs just beneath the building's ridge, the 26-ft by 36-ft space isn't broken up by columns or partition walls. The cathedral ceiling gives me plenty of headroom (16 ft beneath the I-beam) for moving material around. I've divided the shop into different workstations and storage areas, which I'll describe in the following pages.

A good wood supply is important to any furniture-making operation, and quite a bit of space is devoted to storing wood. I've built a lumber rack designed to hold boards of varying lengths (*photo I-1*). Next to it is a tall, narrow compartment for storing sheet goods — plywood, hardboard, and solid wood panels (*photo I-2*). Smaller compartments hold off-cuts and scrap pieces that are always useful when jigs or small parts have to be made.

For furniture-making, wood needs to be dry, with a moisture content of 7 to 12 percent. This can be specified when wood is ordered, but it's also important to store wood in a dry place.

Wood is usually ordered in nominal dimensions, which differ from actual dimensions except in terms of length. Thus, a 12-ft 1x6 board will actually measure 3/4 in. thick, 5½ in. wide, and 12 ft long. A chart comparing nominal and actual dimensions is shown on page 3.

Comparing Nominal and Actual Dimensions

Nominal size Thickness & width	Approximate actual size (in inches) Thickness & width
1x2	3/4 x 1½
1x4	3/4 x 3½
1x6	3/4 x 5½
1x8	3/4 x 7¼
1x10	3/4 x 9¼
1x12	3/4 x 11¼

Thickness	Thickness
4/4	3/4
5/4	1⅛
6/4	1⁷⁄₁₆
8/4	1⅞
10/4	2⅜
12/4	2¾

I-1 (*below left*) A wood-storage rack with several tiers makes good use of space in the workshop. It also promotes air circulation between and around boards.

I-2 (*below*) Plywood, hardboard, and other sheet goods get their own storage section in the form of a vertical bin with several partitions.

I-3 The table saw gains great versatility with the 2 accessories that can be used in place of a saw blade. The molding head, at left, can be fitted with molding-knife sets to mill different profiles. The twin-blade dado cutter at right can be adjusted to cut dadoes with widths from 1/4 in. to 13/16 in.

In addition to space for wood storage, a workshop should have plenty of shelves to hold hardware, bits, screws, nails, portable power tools, books, hand tools, and countless other small items. In the New Yankee Workshop, there's a full wall of shelves that includes a countertop work surface with a broad shelf below it. This storage area is close to my workbench, so portable power tools are always within easy reach when I'm working at the bench.

Power Tools

The table saw is the most important power tool in my workshop. Project for project, it does more work than any other tool. For this reason, it's worthwhile to buy the best table saw you can afford. Buy a professional-quality saw with belt drive and a well-machined cast-iron table. The saw's rip fence and miter gauge should work smoothly and lock securely. A 220-volt motor, rated at 2 HP or more, is advisable.

For general cutting on the table saw, I use a carbide-tipped combination blade. To complete many of the projects in this book, you'll need a couple of accessories for the table saw: a dado head and a molding head. I use a carbide-tipped, wobble-type dado, but multiple-blade dado sets will also give good results. The molding head cutter is available as a kit that includes several different 3-knife sets for milling different profiles in wood (*photo I-3*).

The panel cutter is a shop-made jig that I use frequently on the table saw. This jig consists of a rectangular piece of 3/8-in.-thick plywood with an oak runner fastened underneath it. The runner fits in the miter-gauge groove milled in the tabletop. A 1x2 lip is fastened along the front edge of the jig to hold the front edge of the stock being cut. With the panel cutter, I can square-cut large panels with ease and accuracy (*photo I-4*).

I-4 The panel cutter is a shop-made jig that enables me to cut wide stock very accurately on the table saw. The stock rests on a piece of 3/8-in.-thick plywood and against a straightedge. Fastened underneath the plywood at a right angle to the straightedge, a 3/4-in.-wide hardwood strip guides the jig in the miter slot.

While the table saw excels at straight cutting and milling operations, the band saw and portable jigsaw are ideal for making curved cuts. The jigsaw is less expensive but also less powerful than the band saw. I don't like to use my jigsaw to cut material thicker than about 1½ in. because the jigsaw blade tends to wander slightly, reducing the accuracy of the cut.

The portable drill is another mainstay of the workshop. Variable speed control and a reversing switch are important features, and the drill should have a 3/8-in. chuck. If you use a cordless drill, as I often do, make sure that you have a spare battery or a backup corded drill to use if one battery runs down.

I use my portable drill most often for predrilling screw holes and driving bugle-head screws. For this work, you need a set of combination countersink/counterbore bits (for predrilling, countersinking, and counterboring) and a supply of #2 Phillips-head bits (for driving). Both types of bits are meant to be used in electric drills.

When screws won't be visible in the finished piece of furniture, I usually countersink them so that the flat heads are flush with the wood surface. When I don't want screws to show, I can counterbore the holes simply by driving a little deeper with the countersink/counterbore bit. After the screw is driven, a shallow hole remains that I fill with a round wood plug (*photo I-5*). I make the plug long enough to protrude beyond the wood surface, then glue it in place. Once the glue has dried, I sand the plug flush with the belt sander.

My drill press has the power and precision that the portable drill lacks. By adjusting the smoothly machined drill-press table relative to the chuck, I can bore holes precisely and at any angle. The drill press is a great tool for roughing out mortises by drilling a series of overlapping holes. I can also make square-edged mortises using a hollow-chisel mortising attachment in the drill press. Using a plug-cutting bit, I can make short dowel plugs for filling counterbored screw holes. With a sanding drum chucked in the drill press, I can smooth out saw marks and other irregularities in curved work.

There are a few other important tools that make up what I call a "core" workshop. Some of these are used to make panels, as described below. Other tools will be discussed as they're used in different projects.

Making Panels

Most of my furniture-making projects call for 3/4-in.-thick solid wood panels. They're used for tabletops, bench seats, cabinet sides, countertops, and other broad or large parts. I make panels by gluing up narrower boards — usually 1x6s or 1x8s.

The first step in making panels is selecting the boards to be

I-5 It's traditional to hide screws by driving them into counterbored holes, which are then filled with wood plugs. The plugs are glued into place and allowed to stand proud so that they can be sanded flush after the glue dries.

glued together. Boards that are warped, twisted, checked, or otherwise flawed aren't good panel candidates. I try to choose flat, sound boards that have similar color and grain. Clear, or knot-free, stock is important for tabletops, countertops, and other horizontal surfaces. Rough-sawn boards have to be run through the thickness planer before you can get a good idea of grain pattern and color. I also use the thickness planer to reduce the thickness of stock, or to plane a number of boards to a uniform thickness.

After selecting the boards that will be glued up to make a panel, I place them together on the workbench to get an idea of what the completed panel will look like. This is the time to rearrange boards until you're satisfied with the overall appearance. It's also the time to check the end-grain orientation of adjacent boards. To make the panel more warp-resistant, the end-grain pattern should alternate from one board to the next. If one board shows its end grain curving up, the adjacent board (or boards) should show end grain curving down. When boards are in their final position, I witness-mark them so that they can be replaced easily after board edges are jointed.

Straight, square edges are important when gluing up a panel. Without them, irregularities along a board's edge will create small gaps along a glue joint. Even though these gaps normally fill with glue, the resulting joint won't be as strong as it should be. And a visible glue line really detracts from the appearance of a finished piece of furniture.

You can't expect good edges on boards that come straight from the lumberyard. To mill straight, square edges in the workshop, I run stock through my 4-in. jointer (*photo I-6*). The heart of this power tool is a heavy, high-speed cutter head with 3 sharp blades. The edge of a board is fed into the cutter head on a smooth, flat infeed table that can be minutely adjusted for different planing depths. The face of the board is guided by an equally smooth fence. To plane a square edge, the fence is adjusted so that it's 90 degrees from infeed and outfeed tables.

If you don't have a jointer in your workshop, there are other ways to get straight, square edges. Portable power planes work very much like jointers, except that they're compact enough to move along the edge of a board, as shown in photo I-7. When using a portable power plane to joint a board's edge, the board should be clamped firmly in place with its edge facing up. An accessory fence, attached to the plane, should be used to keep the cutter square with the edge.

It's also possible to joint the edge of a board using a long-bodied hand plane like a jack plane or jointing plane (*photo I-8*). But hand planes, lacking the benefit of a powered cutter head or a fence, are especially difficult to use for jointing work. A more reasonable option (if you don't have a jointer or a portable power plane) is a good table saw fitted with a high-quality combination

I-6 The jointer excels at transforming wavy edges into edges that are straight and square. The fence can also be adjusted as a guide for milling beveled edges.

I-7 A portable power plane, fitted with an edge guide, is a good alternative to the jointer.

I-8 With a steady grip and a long-bodied plane, it's possible to joint the edges of a board by hand.

I-9 If one edge of a board is fairly straight, the opposite edge can be ripped straight and square on the table saw, using the rip fence to guide the stock.

I-11 The centerline on the tool is lined up with the layout line on the board before plunging the carbide-tipped blade into the edge of the board. The removable black fence on the biscuit joiner is designed to align the tool parallel with the edge of the board.

I-10 A short pencil mark across the edge-to-edge joint is all the layout work required when using a biscuit joiner to make panels. I like to place a biscuit every 6 to 8 in. The biscuits, made from compressed beechwood, are shown next to the biscuit joiner.

I-12 I spread glue on edge-to-edge joints and on the biscuits. Wetting the biscuits with glue causes them to swell slightly, so that they fit tightly in their slots. For this reason, it's best to assemble joints quickly.

I-13 The biscuits align as well as strengthen joints.

or ripping blade. If you have a fairly straight edge to run against the rip fence, you can rip an opposite edge to an extremely straight line (*photo I-9*).

Once their edges are straight and square, boards can be glued up to make a panel. Thanks to the high bonding capacity of modern wood glues, edge-to-edge joints can be made exceptionally strong. Sometimes, however, I use a power tool called a biscuit joiner to cut crescent-shaped grooves joining pieces. The grooves hold football-shaped splines made from compressed beechwood. These splines align joining pieces and also add considerable strength to the joint (*photos I-10–I-13*).

I prepare for glue-up by covering my workbench with paper. This way, glue that squeezes out of the joints will collect on the paper instead of on the bench surface. On top of the paper I place my pipe clamps. Pipe clamps or bar clamps are indispensable for gluing up panels, and they have many other uses for furniture-making and general carpentry. A good selection of pipe clamps will include several different lengths (*photo I-14*). Other clamps you'll see used in my workshop are shown in photo I-15.

With the boards placed on top of at least 2 pipe clamps, I use a special glue applicator to spread glue evenly over adjoining edges (*photo I-16*). If you don't have an applicator like mine, a small brush will also work well. I avoid spreading glue with my fingertips, since this usually results in glue being smeared unnecessarily onto wood surfaces and clothes.

When gluing up a panel, it's important to exert even clamping pressure across the full length of the panel. This usually requires at least 3 pipe (or bar) clamps — 2 underneath and one on top. Placing clamps alternately under and over the stock helps to produce even pressure. If the panel won't be trimmed to width following glue-up, I place scrap-wood "cushions" between panel edges and the steel feet of the clamps (*photo I-17*). I tighten the

I-14 Pipe clamps prove their worth on nearly every furniture project, and it's important to have a good selection of clamps in different lengths.

I-16 A glue applicator bottle equipped with a roller head does a quick, clean job of spreading glue along the edge of a board.

I-15 Other members of the clamp arsenal include wooden hand-screw clamps, aluminum straightedge clamps, spring clamps, C-clamps, and short bar clamps.

I-17 Scrap paper catches glue squeeze-out before it gets to my workbench. Alternating pipe clamps under and over the panel helps to prevent the panel from bowing across its width. Scrap-wood pads cushion panel edges from steel clamping feet.

clamps gradually, using glue squeeze-out and tightening effort together to gauge clamping pressure. When tightening clamps, it's important to remember that the goal is to hold joints together rather than to compress them. I check to make sure that the undersides of all boards rest flat against the lower pipe clamps, tapping them down with a mallet if necessary.

As soon as the clamps are secured, the panel can be lifted off the bench and set aside until the glue dries. When beads of squeeze-out along joint lines are hardened, clamps can be removed. I then take the panel back to the workbench and scrape off all the hardened glue along joint lines (*photo I-18*). The next step is to go over the entire panel with a belt sander. I usually use a 120-grit aluminum oxide sanding belt for this work. With light to moderate pressure on the belt sander, I go over the entire panel (*photo I-19*). It's important not to apply heavy pressure, since this can cause gouges, especially in pine and other softwoods.

Using Patterns

In the series of projects presented in the following chapters, there are quite a few furniture pieces with curved parts. In building pieces like the rocking horse (Chapter 1) or the kitchen cupboard (Chapter 4), I've had the luxury of making full-scale patterns for curved parts directly from an antique "original." By carefully taking measurements and making patterns, I'm able to duplicate the pleasing proportions that give some antique furniture pieces such timeless appeal.

The patterns for curved parts provided in this book have been reduced in size, with a grid superimposed over each pattern. It takes a little time, but it's not difficult to use a scaled-down pattern to make a full-scale pattern from which the curved part can be cut.

Each square in the grid that overlays a given pattern represents a square inch at full scale. To enlarge the pattern, you'll need to make a grid of squares at full scale. Some art-supply stores sell 1-in. grid paper. If you can't find any, make a single large sheet that can be photocopied (at full scale) to make multiple sheets. These can be taped together to enlarge patterns of all sizes.

When enlarging a pattern, it's best to draw the straight and square sections (if any) first. Then curved sections can be filled in, working square by square. A section of a curve that passes through a square at the reduced size shown in the book should pass through the corresponding square at full scale, in exactly the same way. Referring to the scaled-down grid, check measurements at different points on the full-scale pattern. If the full-scale version looks good, it can be cut out. Keep in mind, however, that a paper cutout isn't easy to trace against, nor is it very durable. After enlarging a pattern on grid paper, I prefer to glue the paper onto a scrap piece of hardboard or wood; then I cut out the pattern using the jigsaw or band saw. This makes a more permanent pattern that's also easier to trace against.

I-18 After the glue has dried, I remove the panel's clamps and use a scraper to scrape off glue that has hardened along joint lines.

I-19 I spend a few minutes going over each side of the panel with the belt sander, taking down high spots and removing hardened glue. I keep the sander moving to avoid gouging the wood, aiming for a smooth surface that's ready to become part of a piece of furniture.

Chapter One

Rocking Horse

THESE days, most children's toys seem to have short lives. It's difficult to find something that offers enjoyment and durability enough to last through several childhoods. In search of a more timeless toy, we took a trip to Old Sturbridge Village, a living museum of early American life in central Massachusetts. There, among carved animals, dolls, miniature houses, and other antique objects, we found a friendly rocking horse. With its graceful lines, solid structure, and well-crafted appearance, this horse can take generations of hard riding and still rest comfortably among a roomful of furniture.

The people at Sturbridge were kind enough to let me take some careful measurements of their rocking horse, so my design is very close to the original in shape and size. The original horse is made of pine, but I chose ash for my horse. Harder and heavier than pine, ash is also especially resilient. This makes it a good furniture wood, but ash is also widely used for tool handles and baseball bats.

The joints in my horse are held fast with glue and bugle-head screws that are counterbored. Screw heads are covered with wood plugs that are sanded flush with the surrounding wood surface. (For more on counterboring screws, see the Introduction).

Making the Sides

With their curved bottoms and pointed ends, the sides are close to 13 in. wide and over 33 in. long (*drawing 1-B*). So my first job in this project is to glue up some 3/4-in.-thick ash panels. I make a pair of panels, using two 4-ft 1x8 boards for each panel. From each of these panels, I'll be able to cut a side as well as a front or back crosspiece.

Before gluing up the panels, I joint the long edges of all 4 boards on my jointer; then I make sure to orient the paired

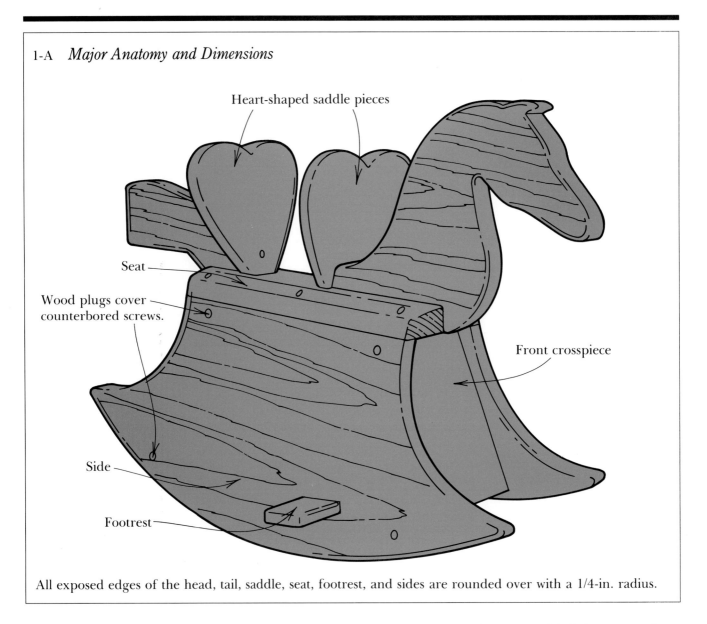

Heart-shaped saddle pieces

Seat

Wood plugs cover
counterbored screws.

Front crosspiece

Side

Footrest

All exposed edges of the head, tail, saddle, seat, footrest, and sides are rounded over with a 1/4-in. radius.

boards so that end-grain patterns alternate. This is important because it helps to counteract any tendency toward warping. To clamp up each panel, use 3 or 4 pipe clamps. I always alternate pipe position under and over the panel to exert even clamping pressure.

Once the glue is dry, I use a scraper to remove hardened squeeze-out. Then I spend a few minutes belt-sanding the panels using a 120-grit sanding belt. With both sides of each panel sanded smooth, I can take a close look at grain patterns and other characteristics. This is the time to select the best-looking sides and to make sure that they'll end up facing out in the finished piece. I place the panels back-to-back, with good sides facing out. Then I witness-mark the good faces, delineating left from right and front from back. These marks will get sanded off when the rocking horse is assembled, but for now they're good insurance that each piece will be cut and fit with the proper orientation.

1-B *Side Pattern*

1 square = 1 sq. in.

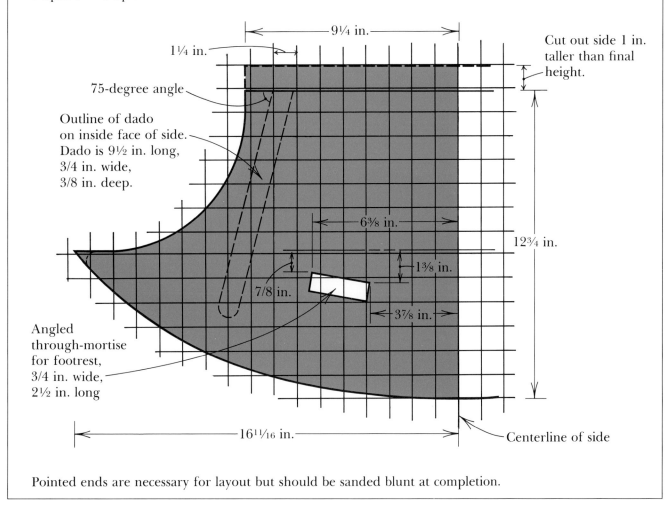

9¼ in.

1¼ in.

75-degree angle

Outline of dado
on inside face of side.
Dado is 9½ in. long,
3/4 in. wide,
3/8 in. deep.

Cut out side 1 in.
taller than final
height.

6⅜ in.

12¾ in.

1⅜ in.

7/8 in.

3⅞ in.

Angled
through-mortise
for footrest,
3/4 in. wide,
2½ in. long

16¹¹⁄₁₆ in.

Centerline of side

Pointed ends are necessary for layout but should be sanded blunt at completion.

Next, I trace the side pattern onto an outside face (*photo 1-1*).
You can use drawing 1-B to make a full-scale side pattern identical to mine. Leave an inch of waste above the top edge, as shown in the drawing. This will be trimmed off later. For the time being, it's useful as a place where 2 bugle-head screws can be driven to hold both panels together while the sides are cut.

Before moving to the band saw, I cut off what excess I can on the radial-arm saw. You could also do this work on the table saw, or with a circular saw. With the paired panels cut down to manageable size, I make all the curved cuts on the band saw, feeding the wood into the blade with slow, steady pressure (*photo 1-2*).

From the band saw, I go directly to the drill press, where I have a drum sander chucked and ready for smoothing the curved edges of the sides. The medium-grit paper in the drum sander does a good job of removing saw marks and other irregularities along the curved edges (*photo 1-3*). It's also good for rounding

Making the sides

1-1 Using a cardboard pattern, I trace the shape of the sides onto a glued-up panel of 3/4-in.-thick ash.

1-2 By temporarily screwing 2 panels together, I can cut out both side pieces at the same time on the band saw.

1-3 A drum-sanding attachment, chucked in the drill press, does a good job of removing saw marks and other irregularities along the curved edges of the rocking horse sides. At this stage, both sides remain screwed together.

1-4 To set the mortise angle for the footrest, I hold the square against the edge of my workbench at a 12½-degree angle. Then I set the bevel gauge against the angle and tighten the thumbscrew.

1-5 To drill out the angled mortise, I keep the 1/2-in. spade bit parallel with the bevel gauge. The gauge should be positioned at a right angle to the mortise layout.

over the pointed ends on the sides. It's important to round these points so that they won't hurt anyone.

With the sides still fastened together, I lay out the through-mortise for the footrest in each side, making sure that the mortises will be exactly opposite each other. When the layout is done, the sides can be separated.

The footrest is actually a crosspiece that extends through the horse, protruding through each side's mortise to become a resting place for the rider's feet. Because each side of the rocking horse angles outward 12½ degrees, the cheeks of each mortise must also be angled to keep the footrest level. Cheek angle is 77½ degrees, or 12½ degrees from a right-angled mortise.

These mortises are first drilled out then finished up with a jigsaw. A bevel gauge makes a good guide in situations like this, when you need to drill at an angle. To adjust the gauge, I use the angle scale on my square. With the square held against the edge of my workbench at a 12½-degree angle, I set the gauge against the angle and tighten the thumbscrew (*photo 1-4*).

I use a 1/2-in. spade bit to make a hole at each end of the mortise, approximately centered between the layout lines for the cheeks. With the bevel gauge positioned near the mortise layout (bevel arms should be at right angles to the layout), I guide the drill bit parallel with the gauge to make both holes (*photo 1-5*).

Once the holes are done in both side mortises, I switch to the jigsaw. The jigsaw base needs to be adjusted so that the blade will cut at a 12½-degree angle. This is easy to do with the bevel gauge. When the angle is set, I use the saw to cut along the mortise layout lines. Connect the holes first, then "nibble" away at the

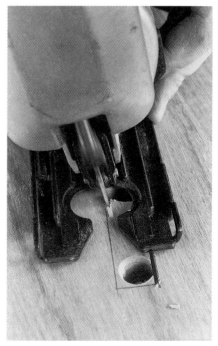

1-6 I cut out the mortise using my jigsaw, with the jigsaw base adjusted for a 12½-degree cut. After connecting the holes, I "nibble" away at any waste that remains.

waste that remains (*photo 1-6*). Once I've done as much as possible with the base angled one way, I readjust the base to angle 12½ degrees on the opposite side of 0 to finish up the mortises. If necessary, I clean up each joint with a sharp chisel.

Next, each side gets 2 dadoes, cut with a router, to hold front and back crosspieces. Dado width needs to match the thickness of the crosspieces; depth is 3/8 in. As shown in drawing 1-B, each dado begins 1¼ in. from the top corner of the side and extends about 9½ in., angled at 75 degrees from the top edge of the side.

Instead of using a 3/4-in. straight bit to cut the dadoes, I elected to use a 1/2-in. straight bit, making 2 passes to complete each dado. Because it removes less wood, the smaller bit is easier to control in a hardwood like ash. Precision is another reason to use a smaller bit. If your stock thickness doesn't exactly match the diameter of a 3/4-in. bit, you can get a more precise dado by making 2 passes with a smaller bit.

To guide the base of the router as each pass is made, I screw a guideboard, or straightedge, to the inside face of each side. The straightedge must be parallel to the dado layout lines and offset so that the bit will travel exactly within them. After making the first 1/2-in.-wide, 3/8-in.-deep cut with the router, I move the straightedge over slightly to guide the router for the second pass (*photo 1-7*). I use the same technique to complete the 3 remaining dadoes.

The last cuts to complete the sides are done on the table saw, with the blade tilted at a 12½-degree angle. The top edge of each side needs to be beveled to this degree so that the seat will fit flat along both edges. Set up the rip fence to guide the flat "waste" edge of each side, as shown in photo 1-8.

1-7 The sides are dadoed to receive the crosspieces, using a straight-edged board to guide the base of the router. The board is temporarily screwed against the inside face of the side. I complete the dado in 2 passes, using a 1/2-in. straight bit.

1-8 On the table saw, I bevel the top edge of each side. The blade is tilted at a 12½-degree angle, and the rip fence is set up to guide the flat "waste" edge of each side.

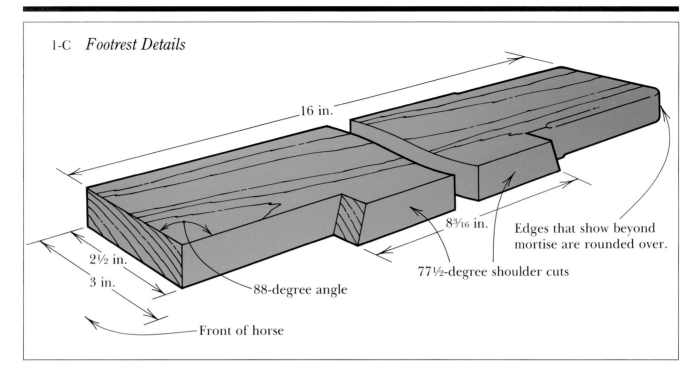

1-C *Footrest Details*

16 in.

8³/₁₆ in.

Edges that show beyond
mortise are rounded over.

77½-degree shoulder cuts

2½ in.

3 in.

88-degree angle

Front of horse

Footrest and Crosspieces

Now I turn my attention to the footrest. This part is made
from a piece of ash that's 3/4 in. thick, 3 in. wide, and about 17
in. long. In the finished horse, the footrest tilts slightly to better
accommodate the rider's feet. To remain parallel with the sides,
footrest ends need to be cut off at an 88-degree angle, or 2 degrees off square. Once these end cuts are made, the front edge of
the footrest should measure 16 in. long.

The ends of the footrest need to be ripped down to a finished
width of 2½ in. to fit through the side mortises. Two angled
shoulders, cut in the back edge of the footrest, effectively lock it
in place between the sides. I lay out the angled shoulders as
shown in drawing 1-C. Between shoulders, the inner bottom edge
of the footrest should measure 8³/₁₆ in. long. Once this layout
work is completed, I rip the ends of the footrest to width on the
table saw, using the rip fence to guide the stock (*photo 1-9*). I push
each end into the blade just far enough to cut to the shoulder
line, or slightly past it. Clamping the footrest in my bench vice, I
cut both shoulders with a backsaw.

To finish up the footrest, I round over the edges that will show
outside the mortises, using a 1/4-in. roundover bit in my router.
To stop me from running the bit too far along the footrest edges,
I test-fit each end of the footrest in its mortise and lay out stop-
ping points where it intersects with the outside face of the rocking
horse sides. Then I remove the footrest from the mortise and
rout to the layout marks.

With the roundover bit in the router, this is a good time to go
over both side pieces to ease all the corners that will be exposed

1-9 Using the rip fence to guide
the front edge of the footrest, I
rip the footrest ends to a width of
2½ in.

in the finished horse. Using my friction pad to hold each side in place, I round over the curved edges on each piece. Only the beveled top edges are left as is.

Front and back crosspieces are identical. I use my radial-arm saw to cut out each crosspiece, adjusting the arm to match the 12½-degree angle of the crosspiece sides. You could also cut these parts out on the table saw, or with a circular saw.

Each crosspiece starts out 9½ in. wide along its bottom edge. But the bottom corners need to be notched to cover the ends of the dadoes in the side pieces (*drawing 1-D*). I lay out the cutting lines for these notches with the crosspiece snugged up near the end of the dado (*photo 1-10*). The depth of the notch should match the depth of the dado. To be on the safe side, I make the notch about 1/4 in. longer than the distance between the end of the dado and the bottom edge of the side. To cut out the notches, I clamp each crosspiece in my bench vise and use a dovetail saw (*photo 1-11*).

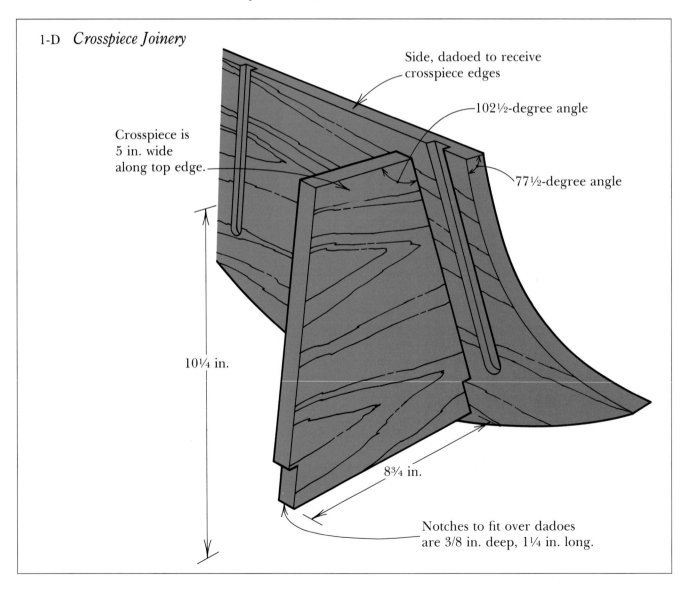

1-D *Crosspiece Joinery*

Side, dadoed to receive crosspiece edges

102½-degree angle

Crosspiece is 5 in. wide along top edge.

77½-degree angle

10¼ in.

8¾ in.

Notches to fit over dadoes are 3/8 in. deep, 1¼ in. long.

1-10 (*far left*) The depth of the notch at each bottom corner of the crosspiece can be marked with the crosspiece snugged into its dado.

1-11 (*left*) I use a dovetail saw to cut out each notch.

Side and Crosspiece Assembly

Before the body of the horse goes together, the sides, crosspieces, and footrest all need a good sanding. Using my orbital sander, I start with medium-grit paper, going over corners, edges, and flat areas. I finish up with fine-grit sandpaper. At this point, it's a good idea to dry-fit all the parts together. This way, you can be sure of a good fit before applying glue to the joints.

As shown in photo 1-12, the footrest must be slipped into its mortises as sides and crosspieces are joined together. Using a small brush, I start the assembly by spreading glue in both dadoes of a single side. Then I fit front and back crosspieces into these dadoes, taking care to align the top edges of all 3 parts. To snug up each joint, I drive a pair of 1⅝-in. bugle-head screws into the

1-12 The ends of the footrest are slipped into their mortises as dadoed sides are fit over crosspieces.

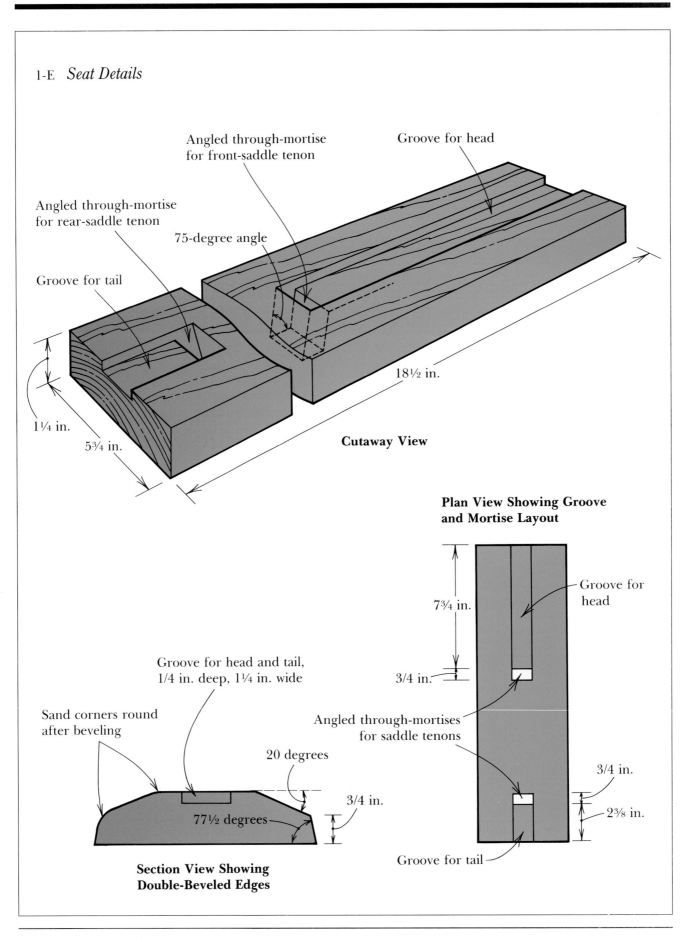

Angled through-mortise
for front-saddle tenon

Groove for head

Angled through-mortise
for rear-saddle tenon

75-degree angle

Groove for tail

1¼ in.

5¾ in.

18½ in.

Cutaway View

**Plan View Showing Groove
and Mortise Layout**

7¾ in.

3/4 in.

Groove for
head

Angled through-mortises
for saddle tenons

3/4 in.

2⅜ in.

Groove for tail

Groove for head and tail,
1/4 in. deep, 1¼ in. wide

Sand corners round
after beveling

20 degrees

3/4 in.

77½ degrees

**Section View Showing
Double-Beveled Edges**

crosspiece edge from the outside face of the side. Screws are driven in predrilled, counterbored holes that I make with a combination countersink/counterbore bit (*photo 1-13*). Where screws are driven into a dado, counterbore depth shouldn't be greater than 3/16 in. Otherwise, counterbore depth can be 3/8 in.

Making the Seat

Like the head and tail of the rocking horse, the seat is made from 1¼-in.-thick stock. Seat width should match the distance across the top edges of the assembled sides. On my horse, this comes out to 5¾ in. Seat length is 18½ in.

The seat has grooves to hold head and tail pieces, as well as through-mortises to hold a pair of heart-shaped saddle pieces. Lay out mortises and grooves following the plan view shown in drawing 1-E.

I cut the mortises before the grooves. Each mortise is 3/4 in. wide, 1¼ in. long, and extends all the way through the seat. In order to give the saddle pieces their outward tilt, the mortises need to be angled at 15 degrees. I rough out the angled mortises on the drill press. With a 3/4-in. Forstner bit chucked in the drill, I adjust the table to a 15-degree tilt and clamp a piece of scrap wood over the table surface. The scrap wood enables me to bore all the way through the seat without hitting the steel table of the drill press. Centering the bit between the mortise layout lines, I bore 2 overlapping holes to complete the roughing-out process for each mortise (*photo 1-14*).

To finish the mortises, I use a sharp 3/4-in. chisel. As I remove the waste that remains inside the mortise, I'm careful to maintain the 15-degree angle of the mortise. The bevel side of the chisel should face into the mortise (*photo 1-15*).

The grooves come next. For this work, I turn again to my router, making several passes with a 1/2-in straight bit to complete

1-13 To pull the crosspieces tight in their dadoes, I drive 1⅝-in. bugle-head screws into the joint from the outside face of the side. Screw holes should be counterbored.

1-14 (*far left*) The drill-press table needs to be tilted to a 15-degree angle for boring out the mortises in the seat. I use a 3/4-in. Forstner bit to drill 2 overlapping holes inside the layout lines of each mortise.

1-15 (*left*) I finish each mortise with a sharp chisel. It's important to maintain the 15-degree angle of the mortise as you pare away the waste that remains inside the layout lines.

1-16 With the seat positioned upside down on the table saw, I rip a 12½-degree bevel along both long edges.

1-17 To cut a second bevel along each edge, the blade is tilted to a 20-degree angle and the rip fence is positioned about 3/4 in. away from the blade. I use the rip fence to guide the bottom of the seat when making each cut.

each groove. Depth of cut should be adjusted to 1/4 in. To guide the router for successive passes, I use the adjustable fence that's available as an accessory for the tool.

This completes the joint-cutting work for the seat. Now I have to make some angled cuts to give the seat a more comfortable profile. First I tilt the blade on my table saw to a 12½-degree angle. With the seat positioned upside down on the table, I set the rip fence up to bevel both long edges, removing a thin, angled piece of waste with each cut (*photo 1-16*).

Next, I tilt the blade to a 20-degree angle and move the rip fence over until it's about 3/4 in. away from the blade. With this setup, I can rip a second bevel along each side. To make these cuts, I run the stock on edge through the blade, as shown in photo 1-17. The rip fence is used to guide the bottom of the seat.

The seat's double-beveled edges will get additional attention later, when they will be rounded over more smoothly. But now it's time to join the seat to the body subassembly. After spreading glue over the top edges of the sides, I set the seat down on these surfaces. Holding the seat in position, I predrill holes for 6 bugle-head screws — 3 in each side (*photo 1-18*). As with the sides, these screw holes are counterbored, leaving a 3/8-in.-diameter hole that needs to be filled with a wood plug.

To cover the screws and fill the holes left by counterboring, I need to use 3/8-in.-diameter wood plugs. Plugs are often cut from a length of dowel rod, but it's difficult to find dowel rod that's made from ash, the wood used for the rest of the rocking horse. So instead of using dowel rod, I cut my own plugs from scrap pieces of ash using a plug cutter. Designed to be used in a drill press, the plug cutter works like a bit, except that its cutting edges leave a short cylinder of wood after the bit is plunged into the stock (*photo 1-19*). As plugs are cut on the drill press, I free them from their holes using a thin, straight-blade screwdriver.

With a thin coating of glue spread on them, the ash plugs can be tapped into counterbored holes. Plugs should stand proud of the surrounding wood surface so that they can be sanded flush after the glue has dried.

Saddle, Head, and Tail

Like the other curved parts of the horse, the saddle pieces are made from a pattern (*drawing 1-F*). Both heart-shaped pieces are cut out on the band saw and the edges smoothed with the drum sander.

The square-shouldered tenons on the saddle pieces won't fit flat against the seat because of the angled mortises. To mark an

1-18 The seat is glued and screwed to the top edges of the sides. Screw holes should be counterbored.

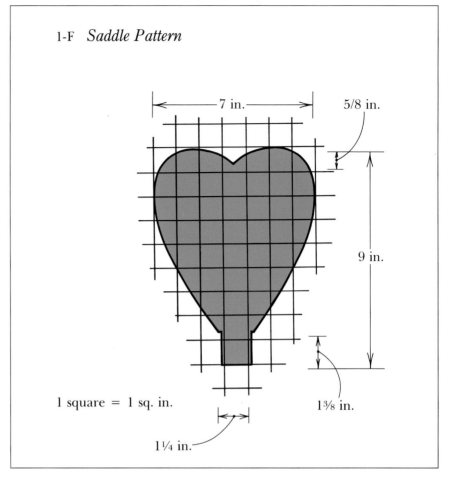

1-F *Saddle Pattern*

7 in.

5/8 in.

9 in.

1 square = 1 sq. in.

1⅜ in.

1¼ in.

1-19 I make my own wood plugs from a scrap piece of ash, using a plug-cutter bit in the drill press. Plugs can be broken loose from the holes with a screwdriver.

1-20 With the saddle tenon placed in its mortise, I use a pair of dividers to lay out an angled shoulder cut that will make the saddle fit squarely against the seat.

angled shoulder line on the saddle pieces, I fit them in their mortises and then transfer the angle using a pair of dividers, as shown in photo 1-20. Clamping each saddle in the bench vise, I use a dovetail saw to cut the shoulders at just the right angle. This finishes the saddle pieces for the time being.

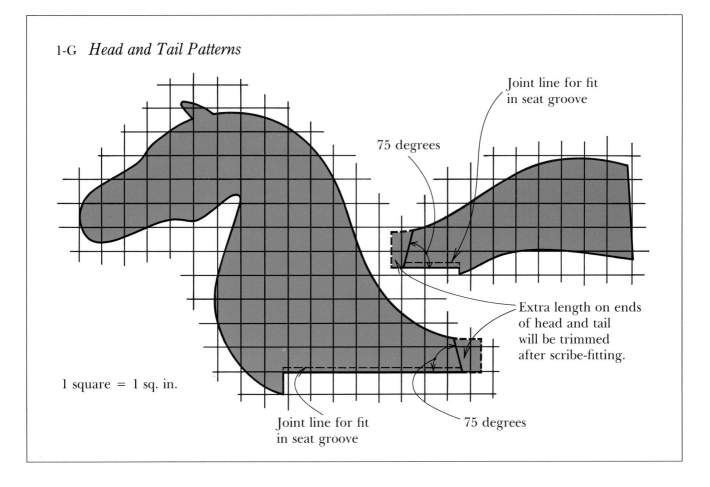

1-G *Head and Tail Patterns*

Joint line for fit in seat groove

75 degrees

Extra length on ends of head and tail will be trimmed after scribe-fitting.

1 square = 1 sq. in.

Joint line for fit in seat groove

75 degrees

1-21 Using the dividers again, I can scribe-fit the head to the angled face of the saddle piece.

The head and tail are cut from 1¼-in.-thick stock. Patterns for both pieces are shown in drawing 1-G. The drawing also shows that about an inch of waste should be left where head and tail pieces meet the saddle. This excess leaves room for scribe-fitting both parts against the saddle pieces. After cutting the parts out on the band saw, I spend a few minutes at the drill press, using the drum-sanding attachment to smooth all the curved edges that it can reach. To get at the contours that are too tight for the drum sander, I work by hand, using a fine rasp and some sandpaper.

Scribe-fitting the head and tail needs to be done with the saddles set in their mortises but not glued in place. First, I set the head in its slot and slide it against the saddle. Then I take a pair of dividers and adjust them to measure the distance between the front of the seat and the notch at the bottom of the head piece. With this distance set, I can scribe the head piece to the saddle (*photo 1-21*). Moving to the power miter box, I trim the waste, cutting exactly to the scribe mark. Then I use the same technique to fit the tail to the back of the saddle.

Saddle pieces, head, and tail are nearly ready to install. Using a 1/4-in. roundover bit in the router. I go over all these pieces carefully, rounding over edges that will be exposed on the finished horse. Front and back edges of the seat also get this treatment.

By this time, the wood plugs that I glued into counterbored screw holes are ready to be sanded flush. This is a job for the belt sander, using a medium-grit sanding belt. I also use the belt sander to round over the sides of the seat. Finally, everything gets a good smoothing with fine-grit sandpaper. It's much easier to sand the body and the remaining parts now, before everything is joined together.

I glue and screw the head and tail in place next, using 2-in. bugle-head screws. I predrill and countersink the screw holes.

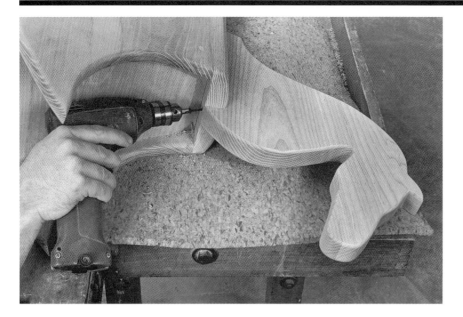

1-22 The head and tail of the horse are fastened by driving 2-in. bugle-head screws up from underneath the seat. Screw holes should be countersunk.

There's room for a single screw outside the crosspieces, just under each end of the seat (*photo 1-22*). From inside the horse, I drive a couple more screws into the head and tail pieces,

Saddle pieces go in last. These pieces are bound to get tugged on as the horse is used, so I make sure to apply a liberal amount of glue on saddle tenons and on the angled edges of the head and tail that join the saddle pieces. To further reinforce these connections, I drive a 1⅝-in. bugle-head screw through each saddle piece (just above the tenon) and into the head or tail (*photo 1-23*). As on the rest of the horse, these screws should be counterbored, with both holes filled with wood plugs that are sanded flush.

1-23 Saddle pieces are glued into their mortises and against angled edges of head or tail. A single 1⅝-in. screw, driven just above each tenon, adds strength to these joints. After screws are driven, I fill counterbored holes with wood plugs that will later be sanded flush.

Chapter Two

Adirondack Chair

PROJECT PLANNING
Time: 1 day

Special hardware and tools:

1⅝-in. and 1¼-in. "exterior" bugle-head screws with hot-dipped galvanized coating

(10) 1/4-in.-diameter, 2-in.-long galvanized carriage bolts with nuts and washers

4d finishing nails with hot-dipped galvanized coating

Wood:

The wood I used for this chair was 3/4-in.-thick cypress. If you have trouble finding cypress lumber, clear grades of redwood or cedar will also do well outdoors. My cutting list breaks down as follows (nominal dimensions):

(2) 8-ft 1x6s

From one 1x6, cut 2 side members plus the lower-rear cross-piece and the curved rear seat slat. The second 1x6 yields 2 arms and the upper-rear cross-piece.

(2) 10-ft 1x4s

From one 1x4, cut both legs, both brackets, the front cross-piece, and a single short back slat. The second 1x4 yields the remaining 4 back slats.

(1) 10-ft 1x3

Seat slats

It's smart to make and use patterns for a project like this. There are quite a few curved parts, and with a set of patterns you'll have no trouble duplicating your first chair over and over again.

N AMED after the mountains of northern New York, where it first graced the porches of hunting lodges and vacation cabins, the Adirondack chair is a true American classic. Countless versions of this chair exist, including one that my father built over 35 years ago. With peeling paint and a slightly rickety stance, this well-worn object is rich in memories but increasingly poor in structure and comfort. I brought it back to the New Yankee Workshop to help me in designing a new model. I also took time to examine a couple of other Adirondack chairs that are available at furniture stores or through mail-order outlets.

One of the interesting things about these chairs is that they manage to be comfortable, elegant, and exceptionally strong in spite of the most basic joinery details. You won't find any dovetail or mortise-and-tenon joinery here, but there are a few crucial curves and important proportions. In my design, I retained the curved back of the chair but raised the level of the seat slightly. I also kept the arms wide and made them level to hold drinks or even a dinner plate.

Good Wood

Adirondack chairs really belong outdoors — either on the porch or in the yard. It's important for the chair to be designed and built to endure all kinds of weather. Plenty of Adirondack chairs are made from oak and pine, but these woods don't do well outdoors, even with regular coats of paint or preservative. I chose cypress for my chair. Cypress once grew plentifully in swampy or lowland areas in many parts of the country. Today, most new cypress boards come from trees harvested in the southeastern United States. Exceptionally resistant to rot, mildew, and insect infestation, cypress is an ideal outdoor wood. It's also a joy for any carpenter to work with. Seasoned cypress has a tawny color

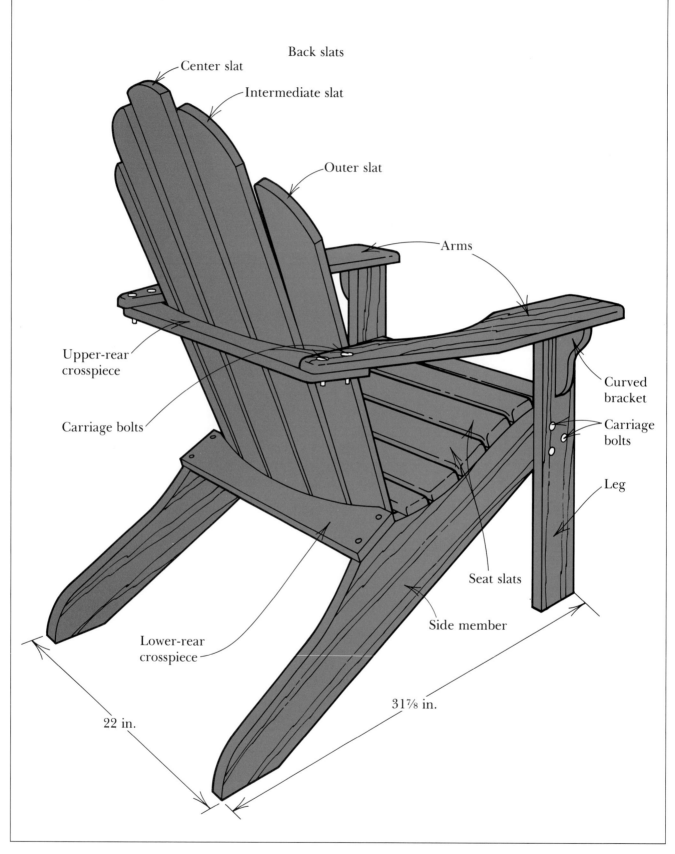

Back slats

Center slat

Intermediate slat

Outer slat

Arms

Upper-rear crosspiece

Carriage bolts

Curved bracket

Carriage bolts

Leg

Seat slats

Side member

Lower-rear crosspiece

22 in.

31⅞ in.

and a lively grain with very few knots. The wood is a pleasure to cut, mill, or sand.

The lumber dealer where I buy most of my hardwood didn't have any new cypress in stock, but he was able to locate some old wood salvaged from a brewery. The boards he supplied were nearly a full inch thick, with a waxy coating on one side and a very distinctive smell. I wanted to make my chair from nominal 1x stock, which actually measures 3/4 in. thick. So I used a scraper to remove the wax from the boards, then I ran the stock through my thickness planer. With each pass through the planer, I removed 1/32 in. of wood. When thicknessing stock like this, it's important to plane from both sides of each board. This way, you're sure to expose an even amount of fresh wood, which will help to prevent warping or cupping.

Side Members

The first parts to cut and assemble are the side members. These 2 pieces are joined to the legs at the front of the chair, hold the seat slats, and extend back to rest on the ground. The top edge of each side member is curved, while the bottom edge is straight, with angle cuts at each end. It's a complex shape, and the best way to ensure uniformity from one chair to the next is to preserve the shape in a pattern. Use drawing 2-B to make a full-size pattern for the side members. A scrap of piece of wood or a section of hardboard makes fine pattern stock.

Use a piece of wood at least 34⅜ in. long and 5¼ in. wide for each side member. After tracing the side-member pattern onto the stock, I cut out both pieces on the band saw (*photo 2-1*). To smooth out the curved edges on both side members, I go over to the drill press and tighten a 2-in.-diameter drum-sanding attachment in the chuck. For this type of smoothing operation, medium-grit sandpaper works well on the drum. Turning on the machine, I sand the curved sections of each piece, exerting just enough pressure against the sanding drum to remove the saw marks (*photo 2-2*).

Once the side members are complete, they can be joined together by attaching the front crosspiece and the lower-rear crosspiece. The front crosspiece is 3½ in. wide and 22 in. long. I clamp a side member in my bench vise, with its front edge facing up. This enables me to hold the front crosspiece in position while predrilling and countersinking the holes for a pair of galvanized 1⅝-in. bugle-head screws (*photo 2-3*). With their rough, rustproof coating and coarse thread pattern, these screws have excellent holding power in wood.

After joining the front crosspiece to the side members, the lower-rear crosspiece can be made and attached. This curved piece is 22 in. long and 3⅞ in. wide at its broadest points. Again,

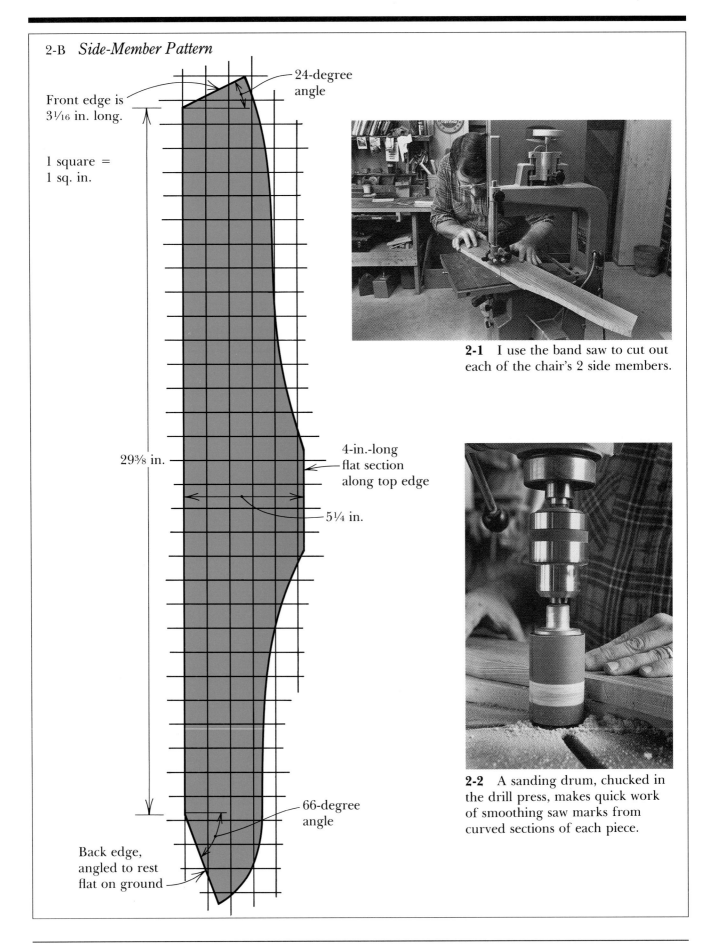

2-B *Side-Member Pattern*

24-degree angle

Front edge is 3 1/16 in. long.

1 square = 1 sq. in.

29 3/8 in.

4-in.-long flat section along top edge

5 1/4 in.

66-degree angle

Back edge, angled to rest flat on ground

2-1 I use the band saw to cut out each of the chair's 2 side members.

2-2 A sanding drum, chucked in the drill press, makes quick work of smoothing saw marks from curved sections of each piece.

2-C *Lower-Rear Crosspiece Pattern (including rear seat slat)*

1 square = 1 sq. in.

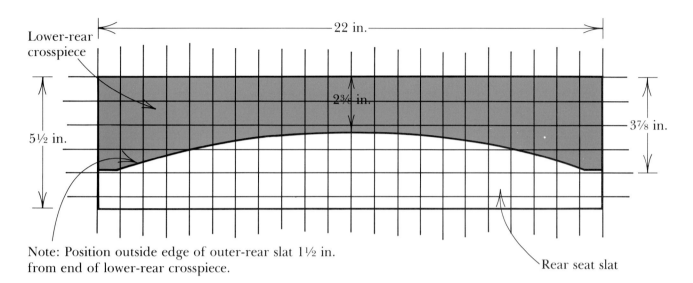

Lower-rear
crosspiece

22 in.

2¾ in.

5½ in.

3⅞ in.

Note: Position outside edge of outer-rear slat 1½ in.
from end of lower-rear crosspiece.

Rear seat slat

I used a pattern to trace the cutting lines onto a length of 1x6
stock (*drawing 2-C*), then I cut the piece out on the band saw.
Be sure to save the "waste" side of the 1x6 that remains after the
lower-rear crosspiece is cut. This outward-curving board will become the rear seat slat, a perfect match for the curve created by
the lower-rear crosspiece.

   The wide ends of the lower-rear crosspiece get screwed down
on the flat sections along the to edges of the side members (*photo
2-4*). Locate each end of the crosspiece so that its back edge is 19
in. from the upper corner of the side member. I use 2 screws per
joint, predrilling and countersinking the screw holes.

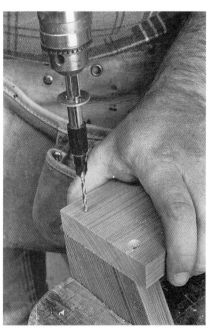

2-3 With the side member
clamped in my bench vise, I hold
the front crosspiece in place while
predrilling and countersinking
holes for 1⅝-in. bugle-head
screws.

2-4 The broad ends of the lower-
rear crosspiece are fastened to the
flat sections along the top edges of
the side members.

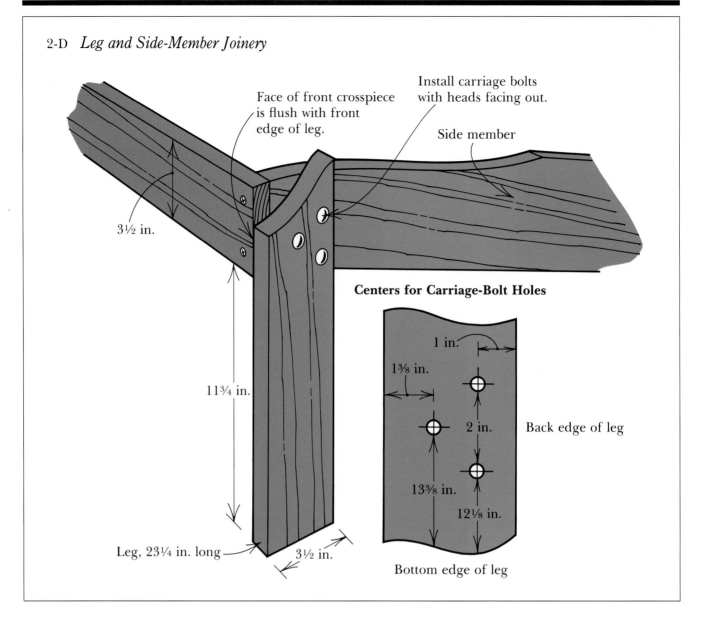

Face of front crosspiece is flush with front edge of leg.

Install carriage bolts with heads facing out.

Side member

3½ in.

11¾ in.

Leg, 23¼ in. long

3½ in.

Centers for Carriage-Bolt Holes

1 in.

1⅜ in.

2 in.

Back edge of leg

13⅜ in.

12⅛ in.

Bottom edge of leg

Legs and Arms

The legs for the chair are 23¼ in. long and 3½ in. wide. The connection between each leg and the side member it joins is important for the strength and stability of the chair. I set up the assembly on my workbench, using spring clamps to help position legs against side members. The bottom of the front crosspiece should be 11¾ in. from the bottom of each leg. The front edges of both legs should be flush with the front face of the crosspiece. This should place the ends of the side members squarely on the ground. Drawing 2-D shows crosspiece and leg position.

With the legs and side members clamped in their proper position, I drill holes for 2-in.-long carriage bolts. Just to make sure that these joints stay solid, I use three 1/4-in.-diameter bolts per joint. The smooth, round heads of the bolts show on the outside of the leg, so I space the bolt holes evenly, as shown in drawing 2-D. When you install carriage bolts, the drill-bit diameter should match the diameter of the bolt, and a washer should always be used between the nut and the wood. As the nut is tightened and the joint pulls together, the short, square shank section just beneath the bolt head seats in the wood, preventing the shank from turning as the bolt is fully tightened (*photo 2-5*).

I attach the arm-support brackets next. My brackets are 6⅝ in. long and 3 in. wide, cut in a gentle curve on the band saw. For the bracket pattern, see drawing 2-E. The straight inside edge of each bracket is centered on the outside face of the leg it joins. The top edge of the bracket needs to be flush with the top edge of the leg. Holding the bracket in position against the outside face of the leg, I drive a 1⅝-in. bugle-head screw through the inside face of the leg and into the thick section of the bracket near the top of the leg. Then I drive a 1¼-in. bugle-head screw through the leg and into the thinner lower section of the bracket (*photo 2-6*). Both these screw holes should be predrilled and countersunk.

2-5 I use 3 carriage bolts to fasten each leg to its side member. Bolts are installed in 1/4-in. diameter holes, with heads facing out. The square shank section just beneath the bolt head seats in the wood as the nut is tightened with a wrench.

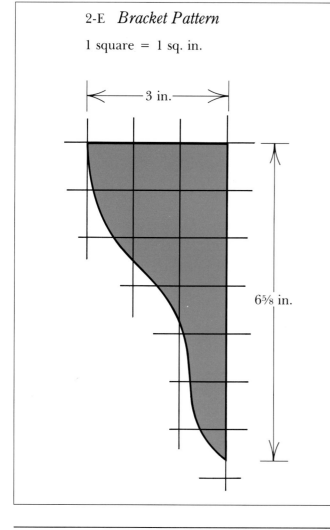

2-E *Bracket Pattern*

1 square = 1 sq. in.

3 in.

6⅝ in.

2-6 Each leg gets a small curved bracket attached against its outside face. The top edge of the bracket should be flush with the top edge of the leg. To install the bracket, I drive 2 screws through the inside face of the leg and into the edge of the bracket.

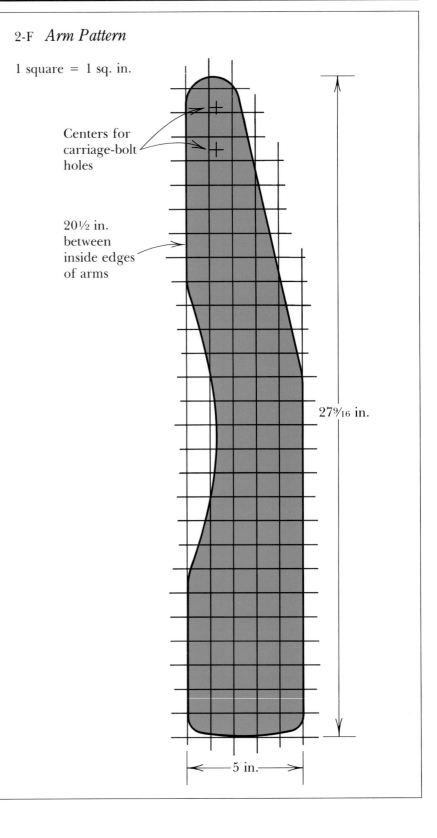

2-F *Arm Pattern*

1 square = 1 sq. in.

Centers for carriage-bolt holes

20½ in. between inside edges of arms

27⁹/₁₆ in.

5 in.

2-7 After cutting the arms out on the band saw and smoothing them on the drum sander, I round over their top edges with the router and a 3/8-in. roundover bit. The foam pad on the workbench keeps the arm from shifting as I work my way around its edge.

2-8 Arms are fastened to legs and brackets with 3 screws, installed in a triangular pattern.

The arms come next. Using a pattern (*drawing 2-F*), I trace the arm shape onto two 1x6 boards, then cut the arms out on the band saw. The sawed edges need to be smoothed, and I do this work on the drill press, using the drum sander with medium-grit sandpaper.

Next, I use a 3/8-in. roundover bit in my router to mill a round top edge on each arm. After milling the first arm, make sure that the correct face of the second arm is facing up — it should be an exact opposite of the first arm. Otherwise, you might round over a pair of right arms, or a pair of lefts. I rout these edges using a special foam pad that holds the stock in place while I work my way around it (*photo 2-7*). When using the router, make sure to rout from left to right as you face the work. This way, you're milling against the rotation of the bit, so cutting action will be safer and smoother.

Finally, while the arms are still "free," I take this opportunity to give them a good sanding with some fine-grit sandpaper. The remaining square edges should be "eased" slightly so that they won't catch on hands or clothes once the chair is in use.

Attaching the arms to the legs and brackets is a little tricky. A slight alignment error at the front end of the arm will be magnified several times near the back of the arm, where the upper-rear crosspiece and slats are attached. Drawing 2-G shows a plan view

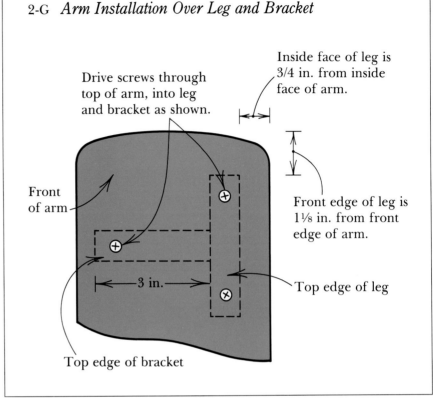

Drive screws through top of arm, into leg and bracket as shown.

Inside face of leg is 3/4 in. from inside face of arm.

Front of arm

Front edge of leg is 1⅛ in. from front edge of arm.

3 in.

Top edge of leg

Top edge of bracket

of the clearances for fitting the left (if you are sitting in the chair) arm. The inside edge of the arm should overlap the inside face of the leg by exactly 3/4 in. The front edge of the arm should overlap the front edge of the leg by 1⅛ in. I use 3 screws to fasten each arm to its leg (*photo 2-8*). A triangular screw pattern will provide good holding power, with one screw driven near the outer edge of the bracket and the other 2 driven into the top edge of the leg. Screw holes should be predrilled and countersunk, as usual.

Structural Slats

On this chair, the back slats actually help to support the arms. The slats are fastened to the lower-rear crosspiece, which connects the side members, and to the upper-rear crosspiece, which connects the backs of the arms.

Before the back slats can be installed, the upper-rear crosspiece must be cut and attached. This small but crucial member is not only curved but it's also beveled along its "inside" edge, where the back slats will fit. Bevel angle is 27½ degrees (*drawing 2-H*). Using a pattern, I trace the curved shape of the crosspiece onto a length of 1x6 stock. While the band saw is still set up for a 90-degree cut, I cut the 2 curved ends of the crosspiece. Then I tilt the saw table 27½ degrees and carefully cut the curved and bev-

1 square = 1 sq. in.

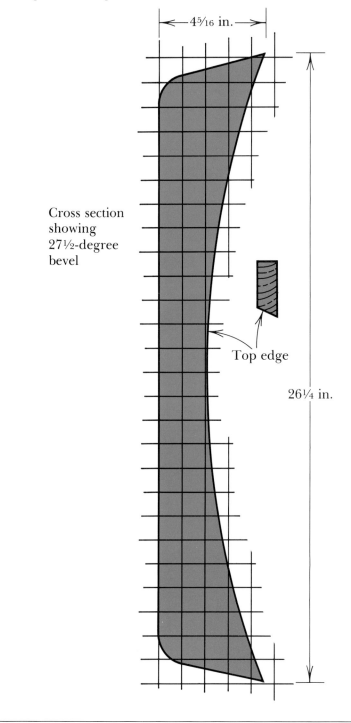

←—4⁵⁄₁₆ in.—→

Cross section
showing
27½-degree
bevel

Top edge

26¼ in.

2-9   The upper crosspiece is challenging to cut because one edge is beveled as well as curved. The band saw table is adjusted for a 27½-degree bevel cut.

eled edge (*photo 2-9*). It's difficult to cut a curve and bevel at the same time, so don't be upset if the saw blade wanders slightly off the cutting line. You can smooth out these irregularities by using a drum sander fitted with some medium-grit sandpaper.

The upper-rear crosspiece fits underneath the backs of the arms. When fitting the crosspiece, it's important to maintain a 20½-in. distance between the backs of the arms. Given this distance, the back-outside edge of each arm should overlap the outside edge of the crosspiece by about 1/4 in. The wide ends of the crosspiece are curved to follow the curved narrow ends of the arms. This gives me room to use a pair of 1/4-in.-diameter carriage bolts at each connection; both locations are shown in drawing 2-F. Using two bolts per joint ensures that this structurally important part of the chair won't do any shifting, no matter who's sitting down.

Spring clamps do a good job of holding the crosspiece in place under the arms while you drill 1/4-in.-diameter holes for the bolts (*photo 2-10*). As soon as one bolt is installed at each connection, you can remove the clamp and drill the second hole. Install the 2-in.-long bolts with heads facing up. Be sure to use a washer between each nut and the wood.

I cut the back slats from 1x4 stock. There are 5 in all — a center slat 30¾ in. long, a pair of outer slats 25¼ in. long, and a pair of intermediate slats 29⅝ in. long. Curving the slat tops is really a matter of personal taste. The center slat needs a symmetrical curve. The remaining 4 slats should be curved pairs that match on either side of the center slat. The 3 slat curves I use are shown in drawing 2-I.

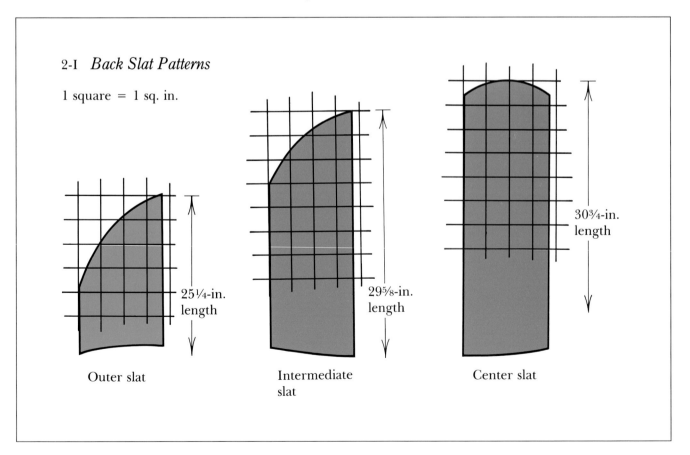

2-I *Back Slat Patterns*

1 square = 1 sq. in.

25¼-in. length

Outer slat

29⅝-in. length

Intermediate slat

30¾-in. length

Center slat

After cutting the curves on a band saw and sanding the curved edges smooth with the drum sander, I place all 5 slats on the workbench, orienting them as they'll be installed in the chair. This ensures that the rounding-over process will happen along the correct edges of each piece. It's the side and curved edges facing the front of the chair that need rounding over. I use a 1/4-in. round-over bit in my router to mill these edges. Again, I use a special foam pad beneath each slat to hold the slat secure as I work my way around 3 of its edges.

There are several steps to installing the slats. Driving a single screw near the bottom of each slat (and along the slat centerline), I first fasten the slats to the lower-rear crosspiece. Screw holes should be predrilled and countersunk, as usual. Screw the center slat in first, making sure that it is centered on the lower-rear crosspiece. The bottoms of the end slats can be screwed down next. The outer edge of each slat should be located 1½ in. from the outer edge of the lower crosspiece. Last to go in are the inter-

2-11 Back slats are installed with the aid of a 13¾-in.-long measuring stick. Wedged between the back edges of upper and lower crosspieces, the stick keeps these members correctly spaced while I nail the back slats with a pneumatic nail gun.

2-12 The front seat slat should be installed so that it overhangs the front crosspiece by 1/4 in.

mediate slats. I space these 2 slats by eye, centering them in the openings left between center and end slats.

The next step is to fasten the slats to the upper-rear crosspiece. While screws are fine along the bottoms of the slats (they'll be partially hidden by the rear seat slat), I don't like a line of screws showing along the back of the chair. So instead of driving screws through the slats and into the upper-rear crosspiece, I use a pneumatic nail gun and 4d galvanized finishing nails. It's possible to drive these nails by hand, but with a nail gun I can brace the slat with one hand and operate the gun with the other. This saves time, and the nail is driven so quickly that the chair stays put instead of shifting around after each hammer blow.

The 2 outer slats are the first to be fastened to the upper-rear crosspiece. The outer edge of each outer slat should butt against the edge of the arm. Vertical alignment between slats and the upper-rear crosspiece is also important. Without it, this crosspiece might end up lower on one side of the chair than on the other. To make sure this doesn't happen, I hold a 13¾-in.-long measuring stick between the upper-rear crosspiece and the lower-rear crosspiece when nailing the outer slats (*photo 2-11*). In my design, the ends of the stick should just fit between the outer corners of both crosspieces. Once you've attached the outer slats using this technique, the remaining slats can be fastened to the upper-rear crosspiece without the aid of the measuring stick.

The center slat should be fastened to the center of the upper-rear crosspiece following the installation of the outer slats. The intermediate slats are nailed down last, again positioned by eye so that they're centered in their openings. Finally, as a precaution against cupping, I make sure that each slat/crosspiece connection gets 2 nails. If you're nailing by hand, it's a good idea to predrill the nail holes that flank the screws driven into the lower-rear crosspiece.

The Tail End

At this point, the seat slats are all that stand between me and a comfortable chair. The curved rear seat slat is the "waste" side I saved when cutting out the lower crosspiece. The remaining slats are all 1x3s (which actually measure 2½ in. wide), cut to a length of 22 in. Each slat, including the rear one, should have all 4 of its top edges rounded over. I use my router for this job, with a 1/4-in. roundover bit.

I fasten all the slats to the side members with 4d galvanized finishing nails. The front and rear slats should be installed first. I let the front slat overhang the front crosspiece by 1/4 in., as shown in photo 2-12. To promote good drainage, the rear slat should have about 1/4 in. of space between it and the back slats. Once the front and rear slats are down, the intermediate slats can be positioned across the side members. As an aid in spacing these slats, I place 1/4-in.-thick scraps of wood between slats (*photo 2-13*). A pair of nails at each end should be sufficient to hold each slat.

2-13 After the rear seat slat is installed, remaining slats are positioned using 1/4-in.-thick spacers. Each slat end gets a pair of 4d galvanized finishing nails.

Chapter Three

Butler's Table

PROJECT PLANNING

Time: 2½ days

Special hardware and tools:

(4 pairs) solid brass butler's table hinges, with brass screws. These traditional hinges have a spring at the back to keep the leaves of the table upright when the top is used as a tray.

Wood:

My table is made entirely from mahogany. Cherry is also a nice wood for this traditional piece.

(1) 6-ft 8/4 x 8/4

Legs

(1) 12-ft 1x6

Top

(1) 10-ft 1x6

Leaves

(1) 8-ft 1x6

Rails and stretchers. Waste from this piece is used to make cleats for underneath the top.

THIS traditional piece of furniture earned its name in aristocratic surroundings where beverages were prepared in the kitchen and delivered to guests in the living room or parlor. The butler's table is actually a large tray that can be lifted free of its base. The tray has 4 curved leaves that swing up instead of down, and the leaves have handles to make the tray easier to carry. The base consists of 4 legs that are connected by rails and also by stretchers that cross to form an X shape.

My butler's table was inspired by a fine antique butler's table found in the Kingscote House in Newport, Rhode Island. I used solid mahogany to build my table. The joinery is traditional mortise-and-tenon work, and the solid brass hinges are specially designed for a butler's table.

Panels First

As with many furniture projects, my first job is to glue up a panel, in this case for the tabletop . I use four 1x6 mahogany boards to make this panel. To allow some room for squaring up the panel, each board should be about 33 in. long. Shifting and flipping the boards on the workbench, I orient them so that end-grain patterns alternate. I also try to create a pleasing grain pattern on the "top" face of the panel. When I'm satisfied with the arrangement of boards, I straighten all joining edges on my jointer.

Simple butt joints would probably be fine for gluing up this panel, but extra strength can be provided by biscuit-joining the edges of the boards. The biscuit joiner is a very useful power tool designed to cut shallow, curved grooves into which specially made beechwood biscuits are inserted (see the Introduction). I cut grooves for 5 biscuits in each edge-to-edge joint, spreading glue

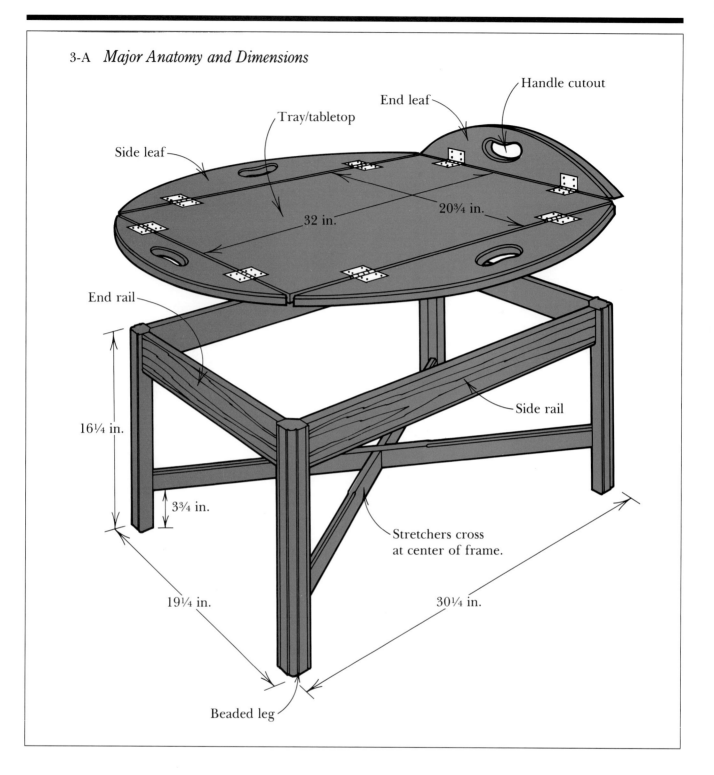

Handle cutout

End leaf

Tray/tabletop

Side leaf

32 in.

20¾ in.

End rail

16¼ in.

3¾ in.

Side rail

Stretchers cross
at center of frame.

19¼ in.

30¼ in.

Beaded leg

on the edges of the boards as well as on the biscuits. Then I close up the joints with pipe clamps (*photo 3-1*). While this glue is setting, I can work on the legs.

Making the Legs

Quite a bit of intricate work goes into the legs (*drawing 3-B*), but they start out square in section, with each side measuring 1⅝

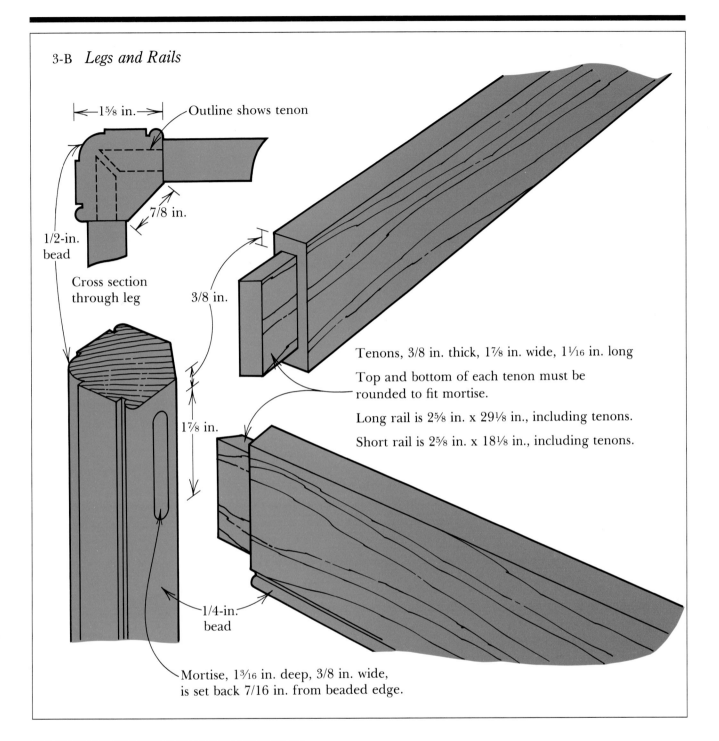

3-B *Legs and Rails*

←—1⅝ in.—→ Outline shows tenon

7/8 in.

1/2-in.
bead

Cross section
through leg

3/8 in.

1⅞ in.

1/4-in.
bead

Mortise, 1³⁄₁₆ in. deep, 3/8 in. wide,
is set back 7/16 in. from beaded edge.

Tenons, 3/8 in. thick, 1⅞ in. wide, 1¹⁄₁₆ in. long

Top and bottom of each tenon must be
rounded to fit mortise.

Long rail is 2⅝ in. x 29⅛ in., including tenons.

Short rail is 2⅝ in. x 18⅛ in., including tenons.

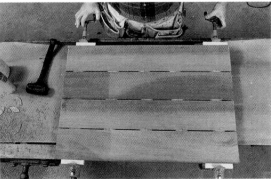

3-1 To make the top, I glue up 4
mahogany boards, using biscuit-
type splines to align and
strengthen the edge-to-edge joints.
Slots for the splines are cut with
the biscuit joiner.

3-2 To mortise each leg for its rail tenon, I use an overarm router with a 3/8-in. bit. Two stops, clamped to the fence of the tool, define the length of the mortise.

in. wide. Finished length is 16¼ in. As soon as the stock has been cut out and planed to these dimensions, I can start milling mortises.

Mortises can be cut in a variety of ways. For this project, I do the work with an overarm router. Basically, this power tool consists of a router mounted over a worktable that's equipped with a fence. The fence is adjustable relative to the location of the router bit, and the router can be plunged to different depths.

To mill the mortises for the rails, I chuck a 3/8-in.-diameter bit in an overarm router. The spiral-fluted straight bit I use is especially good for plunge-routing since the spiral flutes do a good job of removing waste as the mortise is cut. I adjust the fence on the table to be 1 in. from the center of the bit. Then I clamp stops to the fence to confine the movement of the leg so that the length of the mortise will be 1⅞ in.

Instead of attempting to mill the full 1³⁄₁₆-in. depth of the mortise in a single pass through the bit, I adjust depth of cut to about 5/8 in. Then, with the leg held against the fence and against one stop, I plunge the bit and slowly feed the leg into it until the other stop is reached (*photo 3-2*). Repeating this operation with a 1³⁄₁₆-in. depth of cut completes the mortise.

Using this setup on the overarm router, I can mill one of the 2 rail mortises on each leg. To mill the remaining mortises, the stops that are clamped to the fence must be reversed.

With mortises for the rails complete, I take the legs over to the table saw to trim off the inside corner of each leg on a 45-degree angle. In addition to giving the legs a more graceful appearance, this bevel cut will form a flat surface for the shoulders of the stretcher tenons. I tilt the blade to a 45-degree angle and adjust the rip fence to guide the leg so that the resulting bevel will be 7/8 in. wide, as shown in photo 3-3.

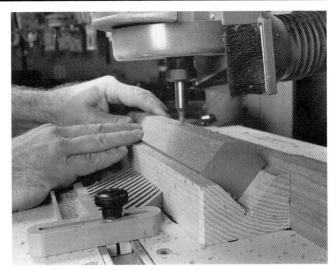

3-3 With the table saw's blade adjusted to a 45-degree angle, I trim off the inside corner of each leg.

3-4 To mill mortises for the stretcher tenons, legs need to ride in a cradle on the overarm-router table.

The next step is to mill the mortises for the tenons that will be cut on stretcher ends. Each leg gets a single mortise 1/4 in. wide, 3/4 in. high, and 1 in. deep. The bottom edge of the mortise starts 4 in. from the bottom end of the leg and is centered on the beveled inside edge.

The mortises for the stretcher tenons also get milled on the overarm router, using a 1/4-in. spiral-fluted straight bit. To orient the beveled inside edge of each leg perpendicular to the router bit, I use a shop-made jig that rests on the overarm router's table. As shown in photo 3-4, the jig is simply a cradle with a triangular cutout to hold the legs in the proper orientation. As with the rail mortises, I mill each stretcher mortise in 2 stages to reach a final mortise depth of 1 in.

Rails

The stock for my rails is 3/4 in. thick and $2\frac{5}{8}$ in. wide. Length of the 2 long rails, including tenons, is $29\frac{1}{8}$ in. The short rails measure $18\frac{1}{8}$ in., including tenons. I cut all these parts to size on the table saw and power miter box.

I also use the table saw to cut tenons on the rails. To fit their mortises, each tenon should measure 3/8 in. thick, $1\frac{7}{8}$ in. wide, and $1\frac{1}{16}$ in. long. I cut the shoulders first, starting with the blade raised 3/16 in. above the table. A gauge block, clamped to the rip fence, serves as a stop for the rail end, aligning the shoulder cuts. I use the miter gauge, adjusted to 90 degrees, to push each rail through the blade. The first 2 cuts in each end should be made with the stock held facedown on the table. (*photo 3-5*).

To cut the top and bottom of each tenon, I raise the blade 3/8 in. above the table and run the rails on edge through this setup. By making a series of passes through the blade, I can "nibble"

3-5 A gauge block, clamped to the table saw's rip fence, aligns the rail for its shoulder cuts. Blade height is 3/16 in.

3-6 With blade height adjusted to 3/8 in., I make successive passes to "nibble" away waste at the top and bottom of the tenon. Gauge-block setup remains the same.

3-7 Tenon cheeks are cut using a tenon jig accessory, designed to ride in the miter-gauge groove of the table. Each tenon requires a pair of cheek cuts.

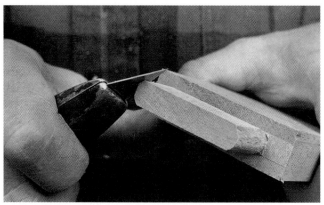

3-8 Using a sharp utility knife, I round over the ends of the tenons so they'll fit into their mortises.

3-9 On the motorized miter box, I miter tenon ends so that they won't hit each other where mortises meet inside the leg.

away the waste to expose the top and bottom of the tenon (*photo 3-6*).

Cutting the tenon cheeks is easy with the special tenon-cutting jig that's available as an accessory for my table saw. This heavyweight jig is designed to run in the table's miter-gauge slot, holding the stock vertically as you push it through the blade (*photo 3-7*). I raise the blade a full inch above the table and adjust the jig so that each pass through blade will remove 3/16 in. of waste, leaving the tenon 3/8 in. thick.

The tenon's square edges need rounding over to fit in their mortises. This takes a few minutes of whittling with a sharp utility knife (*photo 3-8*). Finally, tenon ends need to be mitered to clear each other inside the leg. I make these 45-degree cuts on the motorized miter box (*photo 3-9*).

Beaded edges are traditional on fine furniture, and rails as well as legs get this embellishment. To mill the beads, I replace the blade in my table saw with a molding head. In the head, I install a set of 3 knives designed to mill a triple bead. Two of these beads can be covered or "buried" in a wood auxiliary fence that's screwed to the rip fence. This leaves a single bead exposed to do the work.

When setting up a milling operation like this, it's always a good idea to run a scrap piece of wood through the setup to test the height of the cutter and the location of the rip fence. When I'm satisfied with this fine-tuning, I mill a bead along the outside bottom edge of each rail. Then I run each leg twice through the cutter, beading the two 90-degree corners closest to the bevel (*photo 3-10*). Given this decorative treatment, it wouldn't be right to leave the square outside corners of the legs untouched. Clamping each leg on my workbench, I use a router and a 3/8-in. beading bit to embellish these corners.

Legs and rails are now complete, and this is a good time to dry-fit the parts together. I assemble legs and rails on my workbench, checking to make sure that joints fit well. I also test the assembly for squareness by comparing diagonal measurements across opposite legs. In a square or rectangular frame, diagonal measurements will always be equal.

3-10 A wood auxiliary fence guides the leg as I mill a 1/4-in. bead along one edge. The table saw's blade has been replaced with a molding head fitting with beading knives.

Stretchers

The stretchers start out as 2 "sticks," each 5/8 in. thick, 1¼ in. wide, and 36 in. long. These narrow braces run diagonally, connecting opposite legs and crossing each other with a lap joint. On my table, the crossing angle for the stretchers (and thus the angle of the lap joint) is 62 degrees (*drawing 3-C*). It's a good idea to check this angle by positioning the stretchers across the top of the leg-and-rail assembly.

I cut both halves of the lap joint at the same time, using the radial-arm saw. Blade height should be adjusted so that depth of cut equals 5/8 in., or half the width of the stretchers. I complete the cut by making successive passes with the blade, "nibbling" away the waste inside the layout lines (*photo 3-11*).

To lay out the tenons on stretcher ends, I first dry-fit the 2 stretchers together on the workbench. Then I turn the leg-and-rail assembly (also dry-fit together) upside down and place it on top of the stretchers. Leg ends should rest on the top edges of the stretchers, with the beveled inside edge of each leg centered on a stretcher edge. It's also important for the lap joint where stretchers cross to be centered between legs and rails. This arrangement enables me to mark a shoulder line for each tenon where the inside bevel of each leg meets the stretcher (*photo 3-12*).

Using my combination square, I extend the shoulder line for each tenon around all 4 sides of the stretcher. Then with the end of the square's blade, I lay out the tenon cheeks perpendicular to

3-11 Holding both stretcher pieces together against the radial-arm saw's fence, I cut the lap joints by making multiple passes with the blade.

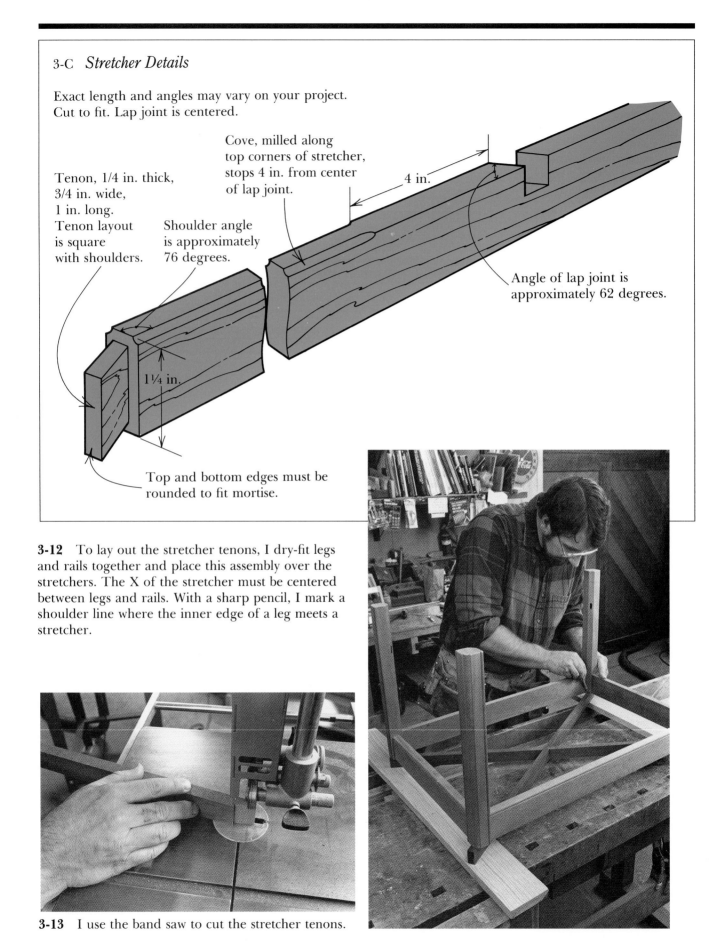

3-C *Stretcher Details*

Exact length and angles may vary on your project.
Cut to fit. Lap joint is centered.

Cove, milled along
top corners of stretcher,
stops 4 in. from center
of lap joint.

Tenon, 1/4 in. thick,
3/4 in. wide,
1 in. long.
Tenon layout
is square
with shoulders.

Shoulder angle
is approximately
76 degrees.

4 in.

Angle of lap joint is
approximately 62 degrees.

1¼ in.

Top and bottom edges must be
rounded to fit mortise.

3-12 To lay out the stretcher tenons, I dry-fit legs
and rails together and place this assembly over the
stretchers. The X of the stretcher must be centered
between legs and rails. With a sharp pencil, I mark a
shoulder line where the inner edge of a leg meets a
stretcher.

3-13 I use the band saw to cut the stretcher tenons.

the shoulder lines on the edges of the stock (*drawing 3-C*). Tenon thickness should be 1/4 in.

These tenons aren't square with the edges of the stock, so it's not practical to cut them on the table saw. Instead, I cut tenon cheeks and shoulders on the band saw (*photo 3-13*). This leaves 1/4 in. to be trimmed off the top and bottom of each tenon, yielding a 3/4-in. tenon width. I finish these cuts with my dovetail saw. To complete the tenons, I use my utility knife to whittle top and bottom edges round so that they'll fit into their mortises.

On the antique butler's table that inspired this one, I noted a delicate coved edge treatment along the top edges of the stretchers. The coves extend from the legs to within 4 in. of the lap joint (*drawing 3-C*). To duplicate this detail, I use the overarm router, with a 1/4-in. roundnose bit. I adjust the fence and the router's depth of cut so that the bit will remove a small cove of waste as the stock is pushed through the setup. Then I mill coves along each top corner, taking care to stop 4 in. shy of the lap joint (*photo 3-14*).

Now it's time to test-fit the entire base assembly. This is a final dry run before glue-up, so it's important to check individual joints as well as overall squareness and stability. If everything looks good, I disassemble legs, rails, and stretchers and start sanding. At this stage, it's tempting to bypass a thorough sanding in favor of gluing everything together. Unfortunately, it's always more difficult to sand certain areas once individual parts have been joined together.

It's challenging to glue up a frame like this one. There are plenty of joints involved, and assembly needs to happen before the glue starts to set. I use a small brush to give tenons and mor-

3-14 With a 1/4-in. roundnose bit in the overarm router, I mill a delicate cove along both top edges of each stretcher.

3-15 A band clamp does a good job of holding joints tight while glue sets.

tises a coating of glue, then start joining legs and rails. Instead of forcing these tenons tight in their mortises, I leave them loose at first. This allows the legs to swing back enough for the stretcher tenons to be fit into their mortises. As soon as all tenons are engaged, I tap joints together with a shot-filled mallet. Then I pull the entire assembly tight with a band clamp (*photo 3-15*).

Top

By the time I've built and assembled the base, the glued-up panel for the tray, or top of the table, is ready to scrape and sand. I give joint lines a quick once-over with my scraper to remove hardened squeeze-out. Then I go over both sides of the panel with the belt sander, using a 120-grit sanding belt.

Moving to the table saw, I cut the top to its finished width of 20¾ in. Then, with the panel cutter, I square one end of the top, flip the panel end-for-end, and trim it to a finished length of 32 in.

The next step is to cut hinge mortises in the top and in the 4 leaves. For mortise locations, see drawing 3-D. There are 8 hinges in all, so this means 16 separate mortises — quite a bit of work if

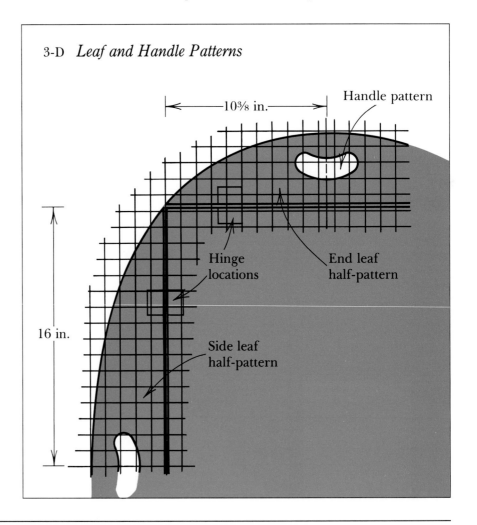

3-D *Leaf and Handle Patterns*

10⅜ in.

Handle pattern

Hinge locations

End leaf half-pattern

16 in.

Side leaf half-pattern

you plan to rely on a chisel. With these butler's table hinges, the mortises are even tougher to complete, since a small secondary mortise must be made to accommodate the spring on the back of each hinge.

A good way to cut mortises quickly and accurately is to use a router, a mortising bit, and a shop-made jig. Made from a scrap piece of plywood, the jig is basically a square frame that confines the base of the router as I remove waste for the mortise (*photo 3-16*). The dimensions of the frame, or cutout area of the jig, depend on 3 factors: the size of the router base, the diameter of the bit, and the dimensions of the hinges.

The jig I use for this mortising job was originally made to be used for a slightly larger hinge. A couple of thin pieces of wood, nailed to opposing inside edges of the jig, reduce the frame size just the right amount for the butler's table hinges. A 1x3 cleat, screwed to the underside of the jig, enables me to match the bit's depth of cut to the thickness of the hinge. The cleat also acts as a stop for the jig, registering against the edge of the top (or leaf) where the mortise layout aligns with the shoulders already cut in the cleat. Before using the jig on the top or leaves, it's a good idea to mill a test mortise on some scrap stock. Check the fit of the hinge in its mortise, and adjust the jig if necessary.

Working my way around the top, I clamp the jig securely to the top before routing out each mortise. Instead of depending on measurements alone to lay out the mortises in the leaves, I actually place each leaf board against the side or end of the top where it will eventually fit, then I transfer mortise layout from the top directly to the leaf. I also key each leaf to its side or end with witness marks or numbers. After completing this layout work, I use the jig to mill all the mortises in the leaves.

Squaring the corners of the mortises can be done quickly and easily with a corner chisel. The one I use is designed specifically for hinge mortises. The chisel itself is mounted in a small holder designed to align the tool using the existing shoulders of the mortise. A sharp tap with the hammer drives the right-angled cutting edges into the corner, leaving it perfectly square (*photo 3-17*).

As soon as the corners are squared, I can take on the small secondary mortises that need to be made inside the leaf mortises to accommodate the springs on the hinges (*photo 3-18*). With a pair of spacer strips tacked to 2 inside edges of the jig, I can again use the jig to guide the router as I mill these secondary depressions. The cleat can stay in the same position on the jig, and the procedure is the same.

Now it's time to cut the curved leaves. The curve for the end leaves has a tighter radius than the curve for the side leaves. Both patterns are shown in drawing 3-D. I do this cutting on the band saw; then I use the drill press and drum sander setup to smooth the curved edges.

3-16 With a shop-made jig clamped to the top, I mill a hinge mortise, using a mortising bit in the router. The jig's inside dimensions confine the router base, keeping the bit within the mortise layout.

3-17 I use a corner chisel to square the corners of the hinge mortises.

3-18 Mortises in the leaves need a secondary depression to accommodate the spring that's part of the butler's table hinge.

3-19 To mill the cove along the curved top corner of each leaf, I use a roller-guide attachment that's screwed to the router base. The bit is a 1/4-in. roundnose.

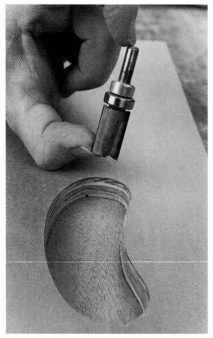

3-20 This bearing-over bit will be guided by a plywood template to cut out a handle in each leaf. After clamping the template to the leaf, I drill an access hole in the leaf so that the bit can be positioned to start the cut.

The curved top corner on each leaf gets a cove identical to those on the stretchers. To mill these coves, I use the same 1/4-in. roundnose bit, but I chuck it in my portable router instead of in the overarm router. A special guide attachment, shown in photo 3-19, can be adjusted to bear against the curved edge of the leaf, guiding the bit along the top corner of the stock.

Handles come next. Drawing 3-D shows the handle pattern I use for this for this table. I cut the pattern out, full-scale, in a piece of plywood. If necessary, the inside edges of the pattern should be smoothed with a drum sander. A smooth inner surface is important because the handles will be cut out using a bearing-over bit. As shown in photo 3-20, the bit's pilot bearing is located over the cutter. As the bearing rides against the pattern, the bit cuts out an identical shape in the stock positioned directly below the pattern.

I center the handle pattern in each leaf, then clamp it in place, taking care to position clamps so that they won't interfere with movement of the router base. Then I drill out an access hole inside the waste area of the leaf. The router's depth of cut must be adjusted to position the bearing against some portion of the pattern while allowing the cutter to be in full contact with the stock. Positioning the cutter carefully inside the access hole (so that the cutter isn't in contact with the wood) and holding the router firmly, I turn on the tool and slowly make my way around the pattern.

When all 4 handle-holes are cut, I replace the bearing-over bit with a 1/4-in. roundover bit. Then I use the router to round over both edges of each hole. This time, the bit's bearing is beneath the cutter and bears against the inside edge of the hole. Sanding is the final step before assembly. Using fine-grit sandpaper in my orbital sander, I go over flat areas thoroughly. Then I work by hand on all the curved sections, again with fine-grit sandpaper.

Assembly

First I install the hinges, joining the leaves to the top. Screw holes for the hinges should be predrilled to avoid the risk of splitting the wood. I wrap a piece of tape around my drill bit to make sure I don't drill through the 3/4-in.-thick stock.

When the top is put together, I place it upside down and then place the base over it, also upside down. Keeping the base centered on the top, I fasten 4 corner blocks to the underside of the top. The 45-degree-angle ends of these small pieces should align with adjacent rails, as shown in photo 3-21. To allow for expansion and contraction of the top, I leave 1/16 in. of space between the corner block ends and the rails. With a little help from gravity, the blocks lock the top in place on the base until the top is lifted free to become a tray (*photo 3-22*).

3-21 (*below left*) With the legs and rails centered on the top, I fasten corner blocks to the underside of the top.

3-22 (*below*) Hidden springs on the hinges keep the leaves upright when the table is being used as a tray.

Chapter Four

Kitchen Cupboard

PROJECT PLANNING

Time: 3 days

Special hardware and tools:

(1 pair) 12-in. Colonial-style T-hinges

Wood:

(1) sheet 1/4-in.-thick clear pine plywood

Cupboard back

(1) 32-in. x 18-in., 3/4-in.-thick plywood

Bottom shelf

(7) 10-ft 1x6s select pine

These boards will be used to glue up panels from which sides, top, countertop, and the 2 upper shelves will be cut.

(2) 12-ft 1x8s select pine

From a single 12-ft 1x8, cut top and lower rails, base and cornice molding pieces, the upper stile cleat, and the top beaded shelf. The second 1x8 will be used to make stiles, door, and vertical door stop.

(1) 6-ft, 1⅝-in x 3/8-in. window-stop molding, for the cornice

DURABILITY and convenience have always been important qualities in kitchen cabinetry. This cupboard is typical of the simple, functional furniture that graced many Colonial kitchens. The family's finest plates were often displayed on upper shelves, while the lower cabinet held more mundane items.

This cupboard is similar in design and proportion to an antique "original" that I found at Old Sturbridge Village in Massachusetts. The joinery work is fairly simple, and the only hardware required is a pair of Colonial-style T-hinges. Unlike an antique cupboard, my version has a back made from 1/4-in.-thick plywood. The plywood is a lighter, stronger, and more stable alternative to solid-wood backing, and it shouldn't look any different from solid wood in the finished piece.

Cutting Sides and Shelves

Each side of the cupboard is a 3/4-in.-thick pine panel that's 17½ in. wide and 73 in. long. I cut each panel from a glued-up blank that I make from three and a half 1x6 pine boards that are at least 74 in. long. I follow my standard procedure for panel glue-up, jointing board edges and orienting boards so that end grain shows an alternating pattern before applying glue and clamping pressure. In addition to making panels for the sides, I take the seven 1x6 cutoffs (which are each about 46 in. long) and glue up one panel 3 boards wide for the top and one panel 4 boards wide for the countertop. For thorough instructions on gluing up panels, see the Introduction.

Once the glue has dried, I use a scraper to remove hardened squeeze-out from around joints. Then I belt-sand both sides of

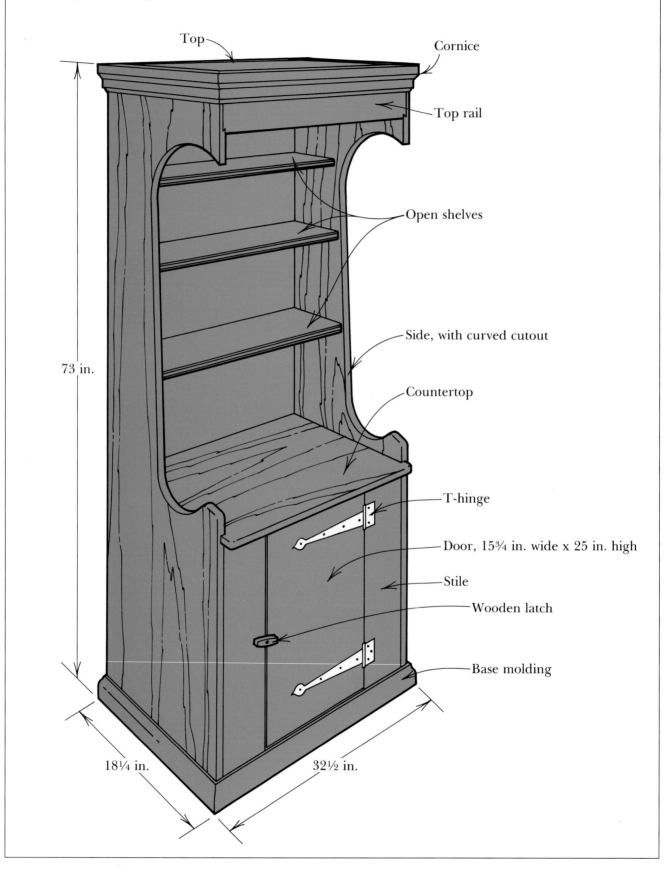

Top

Cornice

Top rail

Open shelves

Side, with curved cutout

Countertop

T-hinge

Door, 15¾ in. wide x 25 in. high

Stile

Wooden latch

Base molding

73 in.

18¼ in.

32½ in.

4-1 (*far left*) Using the table saw's rip fence as a guide, I rip a pair of 3/4-in.-thick pine panels to a width of 17½ in.

4-2 (*left*) Using the panel cutter, I square one end of each panel, then cut it to a finished length of 73 in.

each panel until all traces of glue are removed and the stock is uniformly smooth. After this, I turn to the table saw to cut the 2 side blanks into rectangular panels 17½ in. wide and 73 in. long. I rip the panels to width first (*photo 4-1*). Then I square them up and cut them to length with the panel cutter (*photo 4-2*).

This is a good time to examine the side panels and decide which faces look best and should face out in the finished cupboard. I mark outside faces and front edges. Then, using a cardboard pattern, I trace the curved cutout onto one side (*photo 4-3*). A scaled-down pattern for the side is shown in drawing 4-B.

Now I temporarily clamp both sides together. This will enable me to cut both sides at once from a single layout line. For this project, I use my jigsaw instead of the band saw to make the curved cutouts in the sides (*photo 4-4*). I save the 2 cutout pieces, since these will be used to make 2 of the upper shelves for the cupboard.

4-3 (*below left*) Cutouts for the cupboard's sides are traced from a pattern. Spring clamps do a good job of holding the pattern in place on the stock while I trace.

4-4 (*below*) Clamping both side panels together enables me to cut both pieces at the same time. A couple of spacer blocks, positioned between the workbench top and the stock, provide clearance for the jigsaw blade.

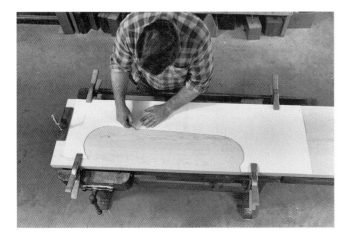

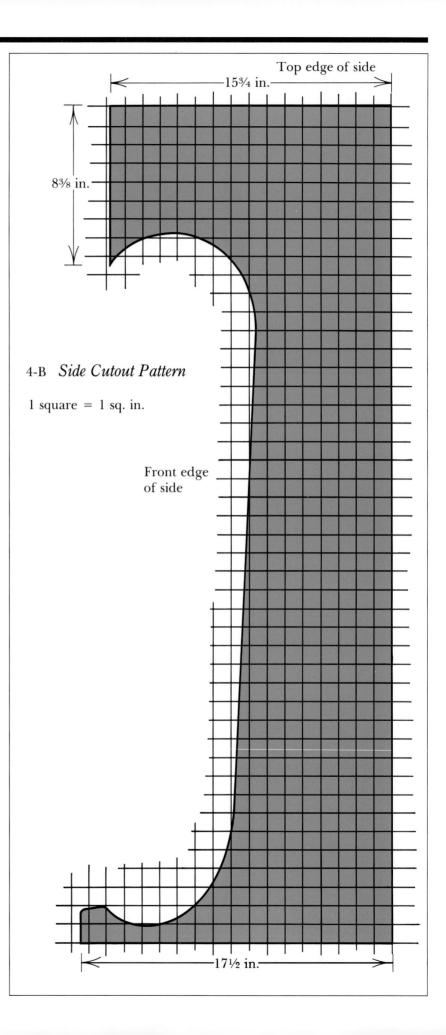

Top edge of side

15¾ in.

8⅜ in.

4-B *Side Cutout Pattern*

1 square = 1 sq. in.

Front edge
of side

17½ in.

After cutting with the jigsaw, I keep the sides clamped together for a few minutes so that I can drum-sand the cut edges. To smooth out the blade marks and other irregularities in the cuts, I use a drum-sanding attachment in my portable drill (*photo 4-5*). The important thing to remember when doing this smoothing is to keep the shaft of the sanding drum at a right angle to the sides' edges. Otherwise, these edges won't come out square.

When I'm done smoothing the edges, I separate the sides and trim the top of each side to its finished width of 15¾ in. This can be done on the table saw, using the rip fence to guide the back edge of each side.

While I'm at the table saw, I cut the countertop and shelves to their finished sizes. All these pieces share the same 30¼-in. length. The bottom shelf is 16⅜ in. wide. Top-shelf width is 15⅜ in., and the countertop is 18¼ in. wide. The 3 intermediate shelves have widths of 8 in., 7⅜ in., and 6¾ in.

This is a good time to sand the shelves, before the dadoes for the shelves are marked and cut in the sides. I give each shelf face a light sanding with my orbital sander, using fine-grit sandpaper. There's no need to sand the front edges of the shelves, since these will be beaded later.

Dadoes and Rabbets for the Sides

The top edge of each side is rabbeted to hold the cupboard's top shelf. All the remaining shelves, including the countertop, fit into 3/8-in.-deep dadoes milled in the sides. The dadoes for the countertop and bottom shelf run the full width of the sides. The 3 upper shelves fit into "stopped" dadoes that don't extend all the way through the front edges of the sides. The length of each stopped dado should be 1/2 in. less than the width of the shelf.

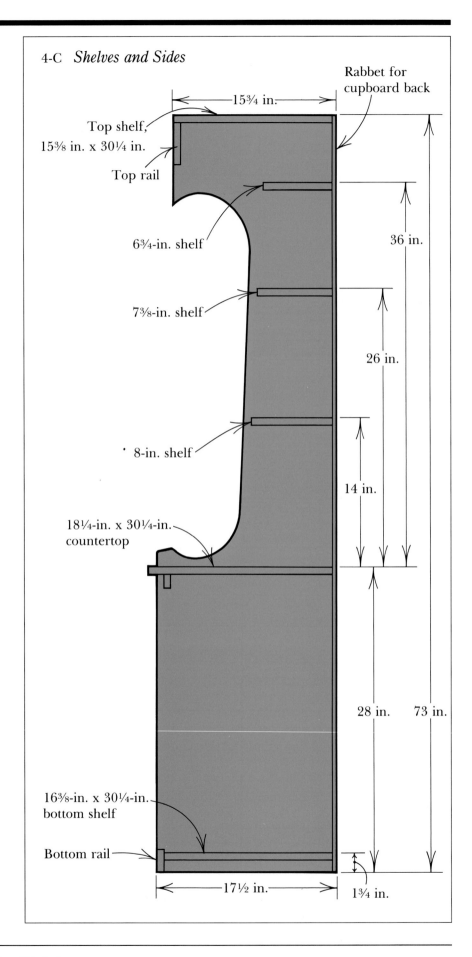

4-C *Shelves and Sides*

Rabbet for cupboard back

15¾ in.

Top shelf,
15⅜ in. x 30¼ in.

Top rail

6¾-in. shelf

7⅜-in. shelf

8-in. shelf

18¼-in. x 30¼-in.
countertop

16⅜-in. x 30¼-in.
bottom shelf

Bottom rail

36 in.

26 in.

14 in.

28 in.

73 in.

1¾ in.

17½ in.

4-6 The distance from the 1/2-in. straight bit to the edge of my router base measures 2⅞ in.

4-7 The straightedge clamp that guides the router should be positioned 2⅞ in. away from where the dado is to be located.

To plow the dadoes and the rabbet for the top of the cupboard, I use a 1/2-in. straight bit in my router, making 2 passes to complete each dado. I could use a 3/4-in. straight bit and cut each dado in a single pass, but my shelves aren't exactly 3/4 in. thick, so I can get a more accurate dado by making 2 passes with a smaller bit.

To lay out the dadoes, I mark the top edge of each dado, using the measurements given in drawing 4-C. I also mark the length of stopped dadoes, taking into account the 3/8-in.-wide rabbet that will be milled along the back edge of each side.

I use a special straightedge clamp to guide the base of the router when milling the dadoes and the top shelf rabbet. The straightedge must be parallel with the layout line, and at a distance that will let the bit cut right to the line. On my router, the distance between the outside edge of the bit and the edge of the router base is 2⅞ in. (*photo 4-6*).

Working against the straightedge, I plow a 1/2-in.-wide dado for one shelf after another, heeding the marks that show the ends of stopped dadoes (*photo 4-7*). To lay out the second pass that will complete each dado, I hold the top edge of a shelf against the top edge of its dado and mark where the bottom edge will fall (*photo 4-8*). Measuring 2⅞ in. below this line gives me the position of the straightedge that will guide the router for the second pass.

The top-front edge of each side needs to be rabbeted to hold a narrow top rail. The bottom of each rabbet ends in a half-dovetail that looks good and also locks the rail in place (*drawing 4-D*). It takes a couple of steps to cut this joint. First, I use my 1/2-in.

4-8 Holding the top edge of the shelf against the top edge of its dado, I mark the location of the bottom edge. This enables me to set up the second pass with the router that will complete the dado.

straight bit in the router to mill a rabbet 3/8 in. deep, 3/4 in. wide, and 4 in. long. A fence and guideboard, attached to the router base, help to guide the router for a pair of straight cuts.

To mill the half-dovetail end of each rabbet, I chuck a 1/2-in. dovetail bit in the router and adjust depth of cut to 3/8 in. Running the router base against a straightedge clamped across the top of the side, I mill the half-dovetail, taking care to let the bit travel the full 3/4-in. width of the rabbet (*photo 4-9*).

Finally, I finish the joinery work on the sides by rabbeting each side along its back edge (*photo 4-10*). For this work, I use a 3/8-in. rabbeting bit. The rabbet should be 3/8 in. deep and also 3/8 in. wide. This will allow the 1/4-in.-thick plywood back to sit slightly recessed.

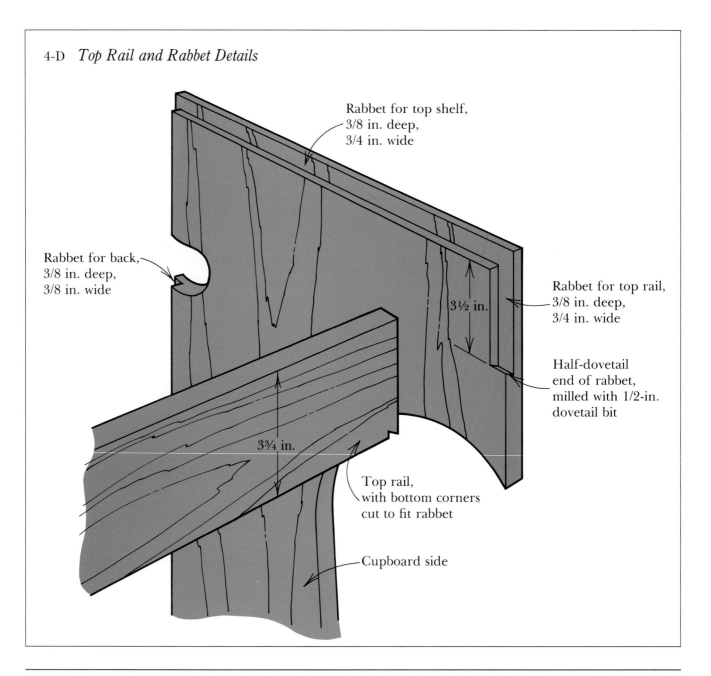

4-D *Top Rail and Rabbet Details*

Rabbet for top shelf, 3/8 in. deep, 3/4 in. wide

Rabbet for back, 3/8 in. deep, 3/8 in. wide

Rabbet for top rail, 3/8 in. deep, 3/4 in. wide

3½ in.

Half-dovetail end of rabbet, milled with 1/2-in. dovetail bit

3¾ in.

Top rail, with bottom corners cut to fit rabbet

Cupboard side

4-9 With a 1/2-in. dovetail bit in the router, I mill a half-dovetail at the lower end of the rabbet for the cupboard's top rail. The straightedge clamp guides the edge of the router base.

4-10 The back edge of each side is rabbeted to hold the plywood back. I use a 3/8-in. rabbeting bit and mill the rabbet 3/8 in. deep and 3/8 in. wide.

Shelves

The shelves need a little more work before they're ready to be installed. On the antique cupboard that inspired this design, all 3 upper shelves show a double bead along their front edges (*drawing 4-E*). The traditional way to reproduce this decorative edge detail is to work by hand, using a specially made molding plane fitted with a beading blade. Hand planes like this are difficult to come by and even more difficult to use. Fortunately, in the New Yankee Workshop I can reproduce the double bead using power equipment.

On the table saw, I replace the saw blade with a molding head cutter. This is an accessory that uses sets of 3 identical knives to mill various profiles in square-edged stock. One of the sets of knives I have is designed to cut a triple bead. But each intermediate shelf requires a single bead along top and bottom edges. I can use my triple-bead cutter to mill a single bead if I "bury" 2 beads in a wood auxiliary fence screwed to the saw's rip fence. This exposes a single bead on the knives.

The saw should be set up so that the top or bottom of a shelf runs against the wood auxiliary fence, while the front edge runs through the cutter. To mill the beads correctly, cutter height and fence position have to be just right. I run some scrap stock through the setup to make sure that no adjustments need to be made. Once the setup is right, it's quick work to mill the first bead on a shelf, then turn the stock end-for-end and mill the second bead (*photo 4-11*).

In order to fit into their dadoes, the intermediate shelves need to have their front corners notched. Each notch should be about 5/8 in. long. Notch depth should match the depth of the dado. To mark the depth of each notch, I temporarily fit each shelf into its dado and make a pair of layout lines at the front corner of the

4-11 To mill the 2 beads on the front edge of each upper shelf, I install a molding head on the table saw. The molding head is fitted with beading knives designed to mill a triple bead. In this setup, 2 beads are covered by the wood auxiliary fence, exposing a single bead to do the work. Two passes through the cutter complete each shelf.

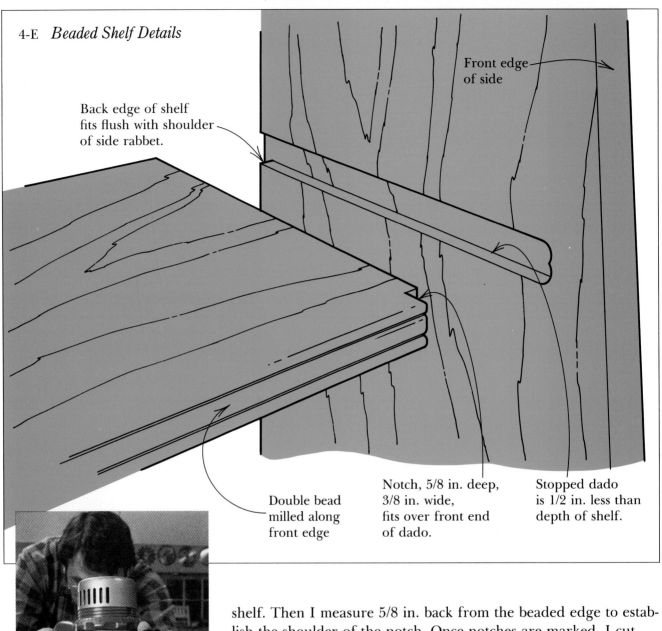

Front edge of side

Back edge of shelf fits flush with shoulder of side rabbet.

Double bead milled along front edge

Notch, 5/8 in. deep, 3/8 in. wide, fits over front end of dado.

Stopped dado is 1/2 in. less than depth of shelf.

4-12 With a 1/4-in. roundover bit in the router, I round the top and bottom edges of the countertop that will extend beyond the sides. The layout mark on the edge of the stock shows me where to stop milling.

shelf. Then I measure 5/8 in. back from the beaded edge to establish the shoulder of the notch. Once notches are marked, I cut them by hand, first clamping each shelf in my bench vise. A dovetail saw is good to use for this cutting work.

The countertop needs rounding over where it extends beyond the front edges of the sides. First, I round the corners slightly, giving them a very light touch with the belt sander and a fine-grit sanding belt. Then I chuck a 1/4-in. roundover bit in my router and go over the top and bottom edges of the countertop that will show beyond the sides. You should actually start milling on the left end of the countertop (as you face the cupboard), 1⅛ in. from the left-front corner. Similarly, finish the roundover treatment after turning the right-front corner and milling 1⅛ in. down the right side (*photo 4-12*).

Sanding is the final step before assembling sides and shelves. It takes me a good 20 minutes to give all the parts a thorough going-over. I take extra care with the inside faces of the cupboard sides, since these areas will be troublesome to sand once the cupboard is assembled.

Assembly

The countertop and bottom shelf are the first parts to be fastened to one of the cupboard's sides. After brushing glue in the dado for the countertop only, I assemble both joints. The back edge of the countertop and the back edge of the bottom shelf should both be flush with the shoulder of the rabbet that runs along the back edge of the side.

I use 4 pipe clamps to pull the countertop and the bottom shelf snugly into their dadoes. Then I nail through the dado for the countertop and into the countertop edge, using 4d finishing nails in my pneumatic nailer (*photo 4-13*). The bottom shelf can be screwed into its dado. I predrill and countersink holes for 1⅝-in. bugle-head screws. These screws will later be covered by the base molding. As soon as the countertop and bottom shelf are fastened to one side, the other side can be attached the same way.

The top of the cupboard is installed next. It fits into the rabbeted top edges of the sides. After gluing these joints, I secure them by driving 1⅝-in. bugle-head screws in predrilled, countersunk holes. Screws should be driven from the top as well as from the sides. The screw heads in the sides will later be covered by the cornice.

Now the upper shelves can be installed. I brush glue evenly in the pair of dadoes for each shelf, then I slide the shelf into posi-

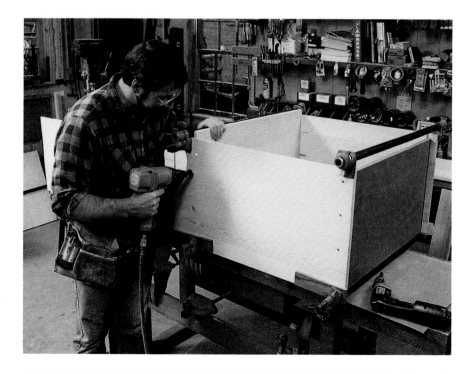

4-13 Pipe clamps force the sides tight against the countertop and bottom shelf as I nail through a dado joint and into the edge of the countertop. The bottom shelf should be screwed, but not glued, into its dadoes.

4-14 Upper shelves are coaxed into their dadoes with the shot-filled mallet.

4-15 Driving 1¼-in. screws in predrilled, countersunk holes, I fasten a cleat to the underside of the countertop. The cleat will act as a nailer for the stiles and also as a doorstop.

tion from the back. A few carefully placed blows from my shot-filled mallet help to coax the shelf forward, until its back edge sits flush with the shoulders of the rabbets in the sides (*photo 4-14*). If necessary, I use pipe clamps to pull the dadoed sides tight against the shelf edges before nailing the joints with the pneumatic nailer.

The back can go on next. Turning the cupboard over onto its front edges, I check the carcass for squareness by comparing diagonal measurements from opposite corners. Then I cut the 1/4-in-thick plywood to size and spread glue in the side rabbets and along each shelf's back edge. It's important to work carefully with the glue in this situation, since excess glue will squeeze out all over the inside of the cupboard. To fasten the back, I use my brad driver, a pneumatic nail gun that drives smaller fasteners — in this case, 1-in. brads. I fasten the back into side rabbets as well as into shelf edges.

With the cupboard now resting on its back, I screw a 3/4-in. by 1¼-in. cleat to the underside of the countertop. The cleat will act as a nailer for the lower cabinet stiles and also as a doorstop, so it should be positioned 3/4 in. back from the sides' front edges or 1⅞ in. back from the front edge of the countertop (*photo 4-15*).

Now the stiles can be installed. These 6¾-in.-wide pieces fit against the sides, against the upper cleat, and against the front edge of the bottom shelf (*drawing 4-F*). In cabinet construction, it's unusual for the sides' front edges to show at the front of the cabinet. Instead of trying to hide this joint, I use some fine-grit sandpaper to ease the corners where sides and stiles join. Then I install both stiles with glue and finishing nails.

When the stiles are in place, I glue and screw a 3/4-in. by 2-in. vertical doorstop to one stile. As shown in drawing 4-F, this stop should overlap the inside edge of the style by 3/4 in. To complete the door opening, I add a 3/4-in. by 2-in. bottom rail. This piece fits between the stiles and over the front edge of the bottom shelf, and it should be fastened down with glue and finishing nails.

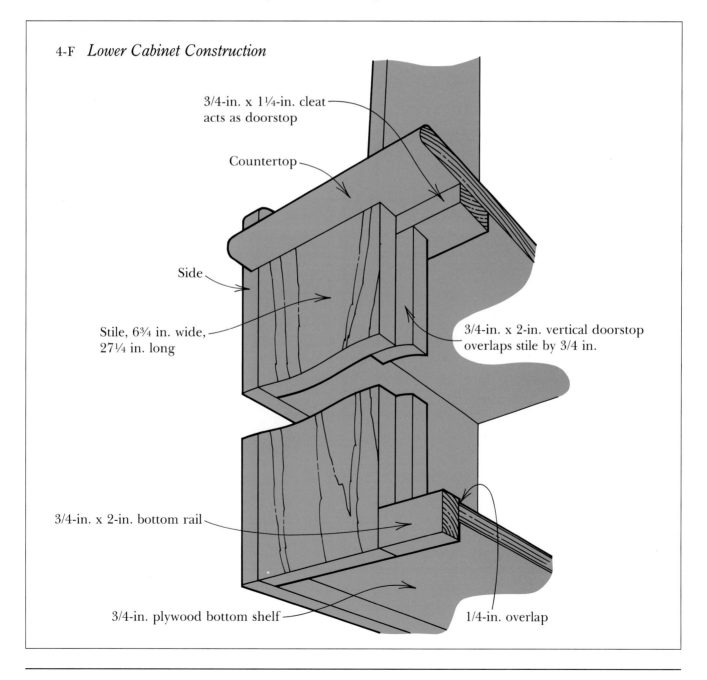

4-F *Lower Cabinet Construction*

3/4-in. x 1¼-in. cleat acts as doorstop

Countertop

Side

Stile, 6¾ in. wide, 27¼ in. long

3/4-in. x 2-in. vertical doorstop overlaps stile by 3/4 in.

3/4-in. x 2-in. bottom rail

3/4-in. plywood bottom shelf

1/4-in. overlap

4-16 Using the router table and a 1/4-in. ogee bit, I mill the cupboard's base molding from 1x2 stock.

4-17 The base molding is installed in 3 pieces, with miter joints at the corners.

Trim Work and Door Installation

The base molding for the cupboard starts out as clear 1x stock (actual measurements: 3/4 in. thick, 1⅞ in. wide). I use a 1/4-in. ogee bit in the router table to mold the top edge of the 1x2 (*photo 4-16*). Since I'll be removing quite a bit of wood to make the molding, I do the job in 2 passes. The first pass takes away most of the waste, while the second pass removes only about 1/8 in., leaving a smooth ogee curve.

The base molding is installed in 3 pieces, with miter joints at the front corners of the cupboard (*photo 4-17*). I use my power miter box to cut the miter joints and also to make the square cuts at the back of the cupboard. I only apply glue on the miter joints. Otherwise, the molding is fastened with 4d finishing nails.

Now I turn my attention to the top of the cupboard. Before the crown, or cornice molding, can go on, the top rail has to be fitted and installed. I start with a 1x pine board that's 3¾ in. wide and 30¼ in. long. The bottom corners of this rail need to be cut to fit in the half-dovetails that terminate the rabbet joints in the sides (*drawing 4-D*). I lay out these small angled cuts with the rail held up against the rabbet. Then I clamp the rail in my bench vise and cut the half-dovetails with a dovetail saw. These joints might need a little trimming with a sharp chisel to fit just right. I spread glue in both joints before fastening them (*photo 4-18*).

The cornice for a cupboard like this should be simple and modest in scale to match the style and proportions of the overall piece. I build my cornice up from 3 different profiles (*drawing 4-G*). Each profile is installed in 3 pieces, with miter joints where side pieces meet the front piece.

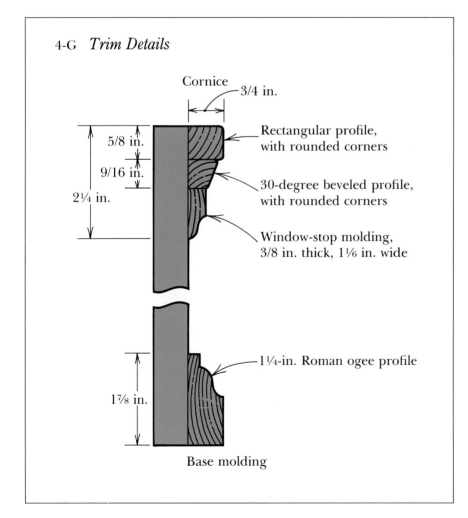

4-G   *Trim Details*

Cornice
3/4 in.

5/8 in.

9/16 in.

2¼ in.

Rectangular profile, with rounded corners

30-degree beveled profile, with rounded corners

Window-stop molding, 3/8 in. thick, 1⅛ in. wide

1¼-in. Roman ogee profile

1⅞ in.

Base molding

4-18 A half-dovetail locks the sides and the top rail together.

4-19 I make the second profile for the cornice on the table saw, with the blade tilted at a 30-degree angle.

4-20 Rectangular in section, the top cornice pieces are installed last. All corner joints are mitered.

The first profile to install is made from standard window-stop molding. The molding I use is 1¹⁄₁₆ in. wide. If yours is wider, you can rip it down to this width on the table saw. The bottom edge of the molding should be 2¼ in. down from the top edge of the cupboard. I use my brad driver to fasten the molding to the cupboard's sides and top rail. The second profile is easy to make on the table saw, with the blade set at a 30-degree angle (*photo 4-19*). As shown in drawing 4-G, the bevel faces down and should show a slight reveal above the window stop. Before installing these 3 pieces, I ease the edges slightly, sanding by hand with fine-grit sandpaper. This creates a delicate shadow line. The last profile is rectangular in section but should also have eased edges. It extends about 1/8 in. beyond the profile below it, creating another shadow line. Like the 2 profiles below it, this one is mitered at the corners (*photo 4-20*).

The door comes last and is easy to install. Cut from a glued-up panel, its width and height should be 1/4 in. less than the width and height of the opening. This allows for 1/8 in. of space around the door, a clearance that you'll appreciate if humid weather causes the wood to swell.

I screw the T-hinges to the door first (*photo 4-21*). The centerline for each strap should be 3½ in. from the top and bottom edges of the door. To start these screws, I use a self-centering punch. The tapered end of the punch fits in the holes of the leaves, positioning a spring-activated awl at the center of the hole.

A tap with the hammer causes the awl to punch a small starting hole in the wood (*photo 4-22*).

When the straps are screwed down, I position the door in its opening, using a few nails as spacers to keep the door centered. Then I fasten the hinge leaves against the stile, again using the self-centering punch to start screw holes (*photo 4-23*).

The last step calls for the smallest piece. Starting with a pine scrap 2½ in. long, 1/2 in. wide, and 1/2 in. thick, I make a simple latch that pivots on a 1-in.-long brass round-head screw, fastened to the stile. I use a sharp knife and some sandpaper to taper and smooth the latch before screwing it in place.

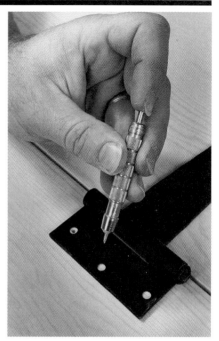

4-22 To start screw holes for hinges, I use a self-centering punch, which has a spring-activated awl and a tapered tip.

4-21 The T-hinges are screwed to the door first.

4-23 Using finishing nails as spacers, I center the door in its opening before screwing the hinges to the stile.

Chapter Five

Hearthside Settle

PROJECT PLANNING

Time 2 days

Special hardware and tools:

(1) 22-in. long, 1½-in. brass-plated piano hinge, with screws

Biscuit joiner and beechwood biscuits

Wood:

Select pine

(1) 10-ft 1x6
(1) 14-ft 1x6

Sides and upper-front nailer

(2) 10-ft 1x6s

Seat

(1) 10-ft 1x8

Upper crosspiece, front part of bottom shelf

(1) 12-ft 1x10

Baseboard backer piece, back part of bottom shelf

#2 common pine

(2) 12-ft 1x4s
(3) 12-ft 1x6s
(2) 12-ft 1x8s

Baseboard, beadboard for back and front

THIS hearthside settle was designed to make the most of the fireplace that served as the sole source of heat in early Colonial homes. With its high back and long form, the settle deflected the drafty chills of winter, while helping to contain the warmth of the fire. In size and function, the settle acted as a sort of room divider. This explains the decorative beads that show on both sides of the settle's tongue-and-groove back.

This particular settle is unusual because of its curved form. In proportion and style, it's identical to a beautiful old pine settle I found at the Beauport House, north of Boston. There are just a few subtle differences between my settle and the antique that inspired it. I chose to close in the bottom of my settle to make it more stable and also to create an underseat storage compartment. Providing access to this compartment, a hatch at the center of the seat swings open on a piano hinge. Colonists weren't able to enjoy the comforts of a foam-filled cushion, an accessory I definitely recommend for this piece.

Cutting Curves

The most challenging part of this project is making the curved pieces. There are 5 in all: seat, upper crosspiece, baseboard backer piece, bottom shelf, and front nailer. All the curves relate to one another, so the best way to ensure a precise fit is to cut one curved piece and use it as a master in laying out the 4 remaining curved pieces. I use the curved seat as the master. Edge and end cuts for all remaining pieces are generated from the seat's dimensions. To facilitate aligning these different parts as curves and end cuts are laid out, it's important to mark the centerline that runs across the width of each piece before it's cut out.

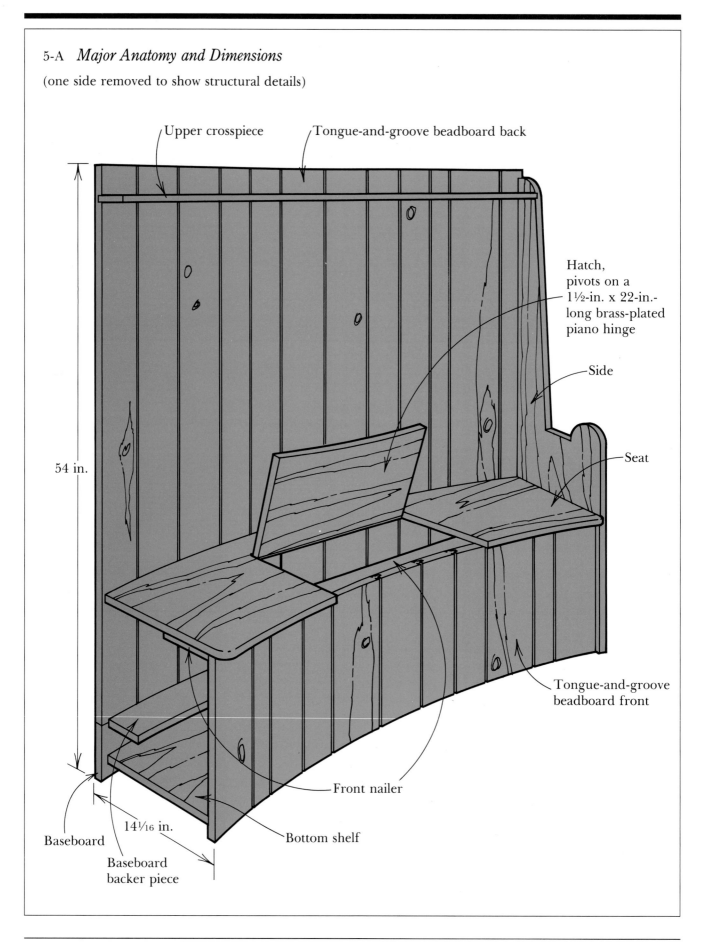

5-A *Major Anatomy and Dimensions*

(one side removed to show structural details)

Upper crosspiece

Tongue-and-groove beadboard back

Hatch,
pivots on a
1½-in. x 22-in.-
long brass-plated
piano hinge

Side

Seat

54 in.

Tongue-and-groove
beadboard front

Front nailer

Baseboard

14¹/₁₆ in.

Baseboard
backer piece

Bottom shelf

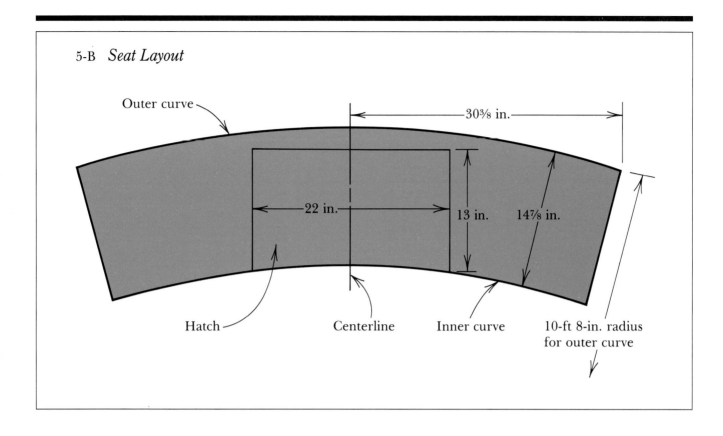

5-B *Seat Layout*

Outer curve

30⅜ in.

22 in.

13 in.

14⅞ in.

Hatch

Centerline

Inner curve

10-ft 8-in. radius
for outer curve

The seat is the largest curved piece, and is cut from a 3/4-in.-thick panel that I make by gluing together four 1x6 boards. Edge-to-edge joints in the panel are reinforced using the biscuit joiner and beechwood biscuits, as described in the Introduction. Each of the 10-ft 1x6s used for the seat will yield a single 59-in. board and a single 61-in. board. The 2 boards nearest the back of the seat should be 61 in. long. The 2 front boards should be 59 in. long. As soon as the glue has dried on the panel, I remove the clamps and scrape off any hardened squeeze-out. Then I give the panel a good sanding using my belt sander and a 120-grit sanding belt.

The seat's size and layout are shown in drawing 5-B. To lay out the 2 curved cuts for the seat, I set up a large compass in the shop. The panel rests on my workbench. The center for the arc that I trace is a screw, driven into a 12-ft-long 1x board that is temporarily screwed to the underside of the seat blank. The centerline that runs along the length of the 1x should align with the centerline that runs across the width of the seat blank and should be at a right angle to it. I use the table saw to support the bottom end of this "T" setup.

The radius for the outer, or back, curve of the seat should be 10 ft 8 in. I take care to position the screw on the 1x so that there will be a minimum of waste on the seat blank outside of the arc. To swing the arc, I use a pencil tied to string or cord that won't stretch (*photo 5-1*). A tape measure could also be used.

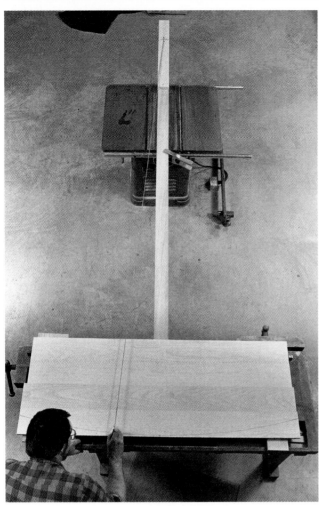

5-1 To lay out the curved cuts for the settle's seat, I set up a large compass, using a piece of string (one that won't stretch), a pencil, and a pivot point set in a long board. The radius for the outer curve of the seat is 10 ft 8 in.

5-2 The string compass is also used to lay out the end cuts for the seat. With the string held tightly over the back corner of the seat, I mark the intersection point on the inner curve. Then I use a straightedge to mark the cutoff line for the end of the seat.

When the seat's outer curve is marked, I shorten the radius on the pencil end of the arc by 14⅞ in. to trace the inner curve. With front and back edges of the seat marked, I can lay out the end cuts. At its longest point (in a straight line between back corners), the seat measures 60¾ in. I mark each back corner by measuring 30⅜ in. from the centerline that runs across the width of the seat. As shown in drawing 5-B, this measuring line should be at a right angle to the centerline. Another right angle, at the end of the measuring line, intersects the outer curve to give me each back corner of the seat.

Holding the string of my compass over each back-corner point, I mark where the string intersects the inner curve of the seat (*photo 5-2*). Then I use a straightedge to connect the corner points. This completes the layout for the seat's end cuts.

By securing a 1x8 board beneath the back edge of the seat

panel, I can cut the outer curve for the upper crosspiece at the same time as the outer seat curve. A couple of 1¼ in. bugle-head screws, driven in waste areas, hold the panel and 1x8 together. It would be too difficult to cut stock this large on the band saw, so instead I rely on my jigsaw. I use a few scrap boards to elevate the stock above the workbench, creating clearance for the blade as I cut first the outer curve (*photo 5-3*), then the inner one. When both cuts are made, I witness-mark the top faces of both parts before separating them. Then I cut the ends of the seat with a circular saw.

Now the upper crosspiece needs to be cut to its finished width of 2¾ in. I could lay out the inner curved cut for this piece by hand, but it's faster to simply set up the band saw to make this concentric cut. First I secure the fence to the band saw table so that it's 2¾ in. away from the blade. Then I use a piece of tape to mark a line on the fence that's 90 degrees from the front edge of the blade. I can now cut the inner curve by guiding the stock against the fence, taking care to keep the outer curve in contact with the fence at the tape line (*photo 5-4*).

To mark the end cuts for the upper crosspiece, I lay the crosspiece underneath the seat, just as it was when both pieces were screwed together. Then I use the ends of the seat to guide the pencil in marking the ends of the crosspiece. These cuts can be done with the circular saw.

Next, I cut out the baseboard backer piece. The outer curve for this piece is cut first, using the seat as a pattern (*drawing 5-C*). I use the jigsaw to make this cut, then turn to the band saw to cut the inner curve. The taped-fence technique is the same as

5-3 By clamping a 1x8 beneath the seat blank, I can cut the outer curve of the upper crosspiece and the outer curve of the seat at the same time. Scrap boards, placed beneath the seat blank and 1x8, provide clearance for the jigsaw blade.

5-4 A piece of tape on the band saw's rip fence, positioned 90 degrees from the front of the blade, provides an index mark for cutting a concentric inner curve on the upper crosspiece.

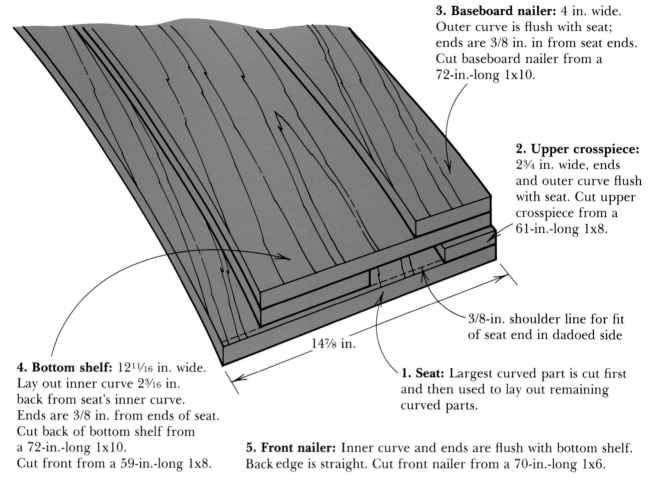

3. Baseboard nailer: 4 in. wide. Outer curve is flush with seat; ends are 3/8 in. in from seat ends. Cut baseboard nailer from a 72-in.-long 1x10.

2. Upper crosspiece: 2¾ in. wide, ends and outer curve flush with seat. Cut upper crosspiece from a 61-in.-long 1x8.

3/8-in. shoulder line for fit of seat end in dadoed side

14⅞ in.

4. Bottom shelf: 12¹¹⁄₁₆ in. wide. Lay out inner curve 2³⁄₁₆ in. back from seat's inner curve. Ends are 3/8 in. from ends of seat. Cut back of bottom shelf from a 72-in.-long 1x10. Cut front from a 59-in.-long 1x8.

1. Seat: Largest curved part is cut first and then used to lay out remaining curved parts.

5. Front nailer: Inner curve and ends are flush with bottom shelf. Back edge is straight. Cut front nailer from a 70-in.-long 1x6.

for the upper crosspiece, except that the fence is positioned for a 4-in.-wide cut.

To lay out the end cuts for the baseboard backer piece, I place it on top of the seat. Back edges and centerlines for both pieces should line up. The backer pieces will butt against the sides, instead of being dadoed into the sides as the seat is. Consequently, the ends of the backer piece should be marked 3/8 in. in from the ends of the seat, as shown in drawing 5-C.

The bottom shelf comes next. On my settle, this piece is 12¹¹⁄₁₆ in. wide and can be made by gluing up a 1x10 and a 1x8. Again, I mark and cut the outer curve first, using the outer curve of the seat as a pattern. The inner curve can be marked using the inner curve of the seat as a reference line. First, I trace the inner curve of the seat onto the shelf blank. Along this line, I place the salvage piece that's left over after cutting the inner curve of the seat. Then I adjust as pair of dividers to measure 2³⁄₁₆ in. Using the curved salvage piece to guide the dividers, I mark the cutting line for the inner curve of the shelf exactly 2³⁄₁₆ in. in from the inner curve of the seat. To mark this line accurately, the compass should be held at 90 degrees to curve.

The front nailer has a straight edge that faces inside the underseat compartment. The nailer's other long edge is curved, and the curve matches the inner curve of the bottom shelf. So it makes sense to cut both of these curves at the same time, temporarily screwing the bottom shelf to the 1x6 that will become the front nailer. When aligning the 1x6 beneath the bottom shelf, I take care to position it so that after the curve is cut the front nailer's width at its center (also the center of the seat) will be about 1¾ in. After cutting these curves with the jigsaw, I lay out the end cuts, again measuring off the seat as shown in drawing 5-C. End cuts can be made with both pieces together, using the circular saw.

All the curved parts for the settle are now complete, except for a few edges that need sanding, since they'll be visible in the finished settle. Using the drum sander in my drill press, I smooth the seat's front edge, as well as the front edge of the upper crosspiece and the front edge of the upper baseboard backer piece.

Sides

To make each side, I start by gluing up a panel, using a single 5-ft-long 1x6 and two 2-ft-long 1x6s. Once the glue has dried and both panels have been scraped and sanded smooth, I lay out the shape of the side on one panel. Then I temporarily screw both side panels together in waste areas so that I can cut them out at the same time. Layout details for the sides are shown in drawing 5-D.

On the table saw, I rip the panels to a finished width of 13⅞ in. (*photo 5-5*). Then, with my circular saw, I cut the taper from the armrest to the top of the side. The remaining cuts I make with the jigsaw. After the cutting is done, I spend a few minutes at the drill press, using the drum-sanding attachment to smooth the cut edges.

Now each side gets a dado to hold the edge of the seat and a dado to hold the upper crosspiece. First I separate the sides and place them on the workbench symmetrically, with their back edges together. The "inner" side of each piece should be facing up. In this position, I witness-mark these inside faces and lay out dado locations (*photo 5-6*).

To plow the dadoes, I set up the wobble dado in the table saw, adjusting it for a 3/4-in.-wide cut and raising the cutter 3/8 in. above the table. The dadoes for the seat can be cut using the rip fence to guide the bottom edge of each side (*photo 5-7*). The fence should be set 14½ in. away from the cutter. With a wobble dado, it's a good idea to test this distance with a piece of scrap stock. To

5-5 Temporarily screwed together, the settle's sides are ripped to a finished width of 13⅞ in.

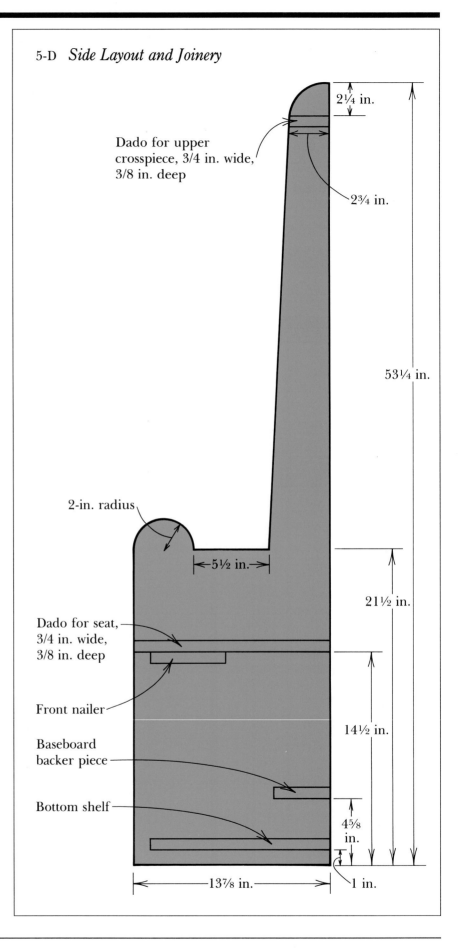

5-D *Side Layout and Joinery*

Dado for upper crosspiece, 3/4 in. wide, 3/8 in. deep

2¼ in.

2¾ in.

53¼ in.

2-in. radius

5½ in.

21½ in.

Dado for seat, 3/4 in. wide, 3/8 in. deep

Front nailer

14½ in.

Baseboard backer piece

Bottom shelf

4⅝ in.

13⅞ in.

1 in.

5-6 To lay out dadoes in the sides, I place both sides on the workbench with their back edges together.

plow the dadoes for the upper crosspiece, I use the miter gauge (set to 90 degrees) to guide the back edge of each side.

When the dadoes are done, I need to do a little more work on the seat and the upper crosspiece. First, I dry-fit seat and sides together in order to mark the front corners of the seat, where they protrude beyond the sides. To duplicate the antique settle, I knock off these corners, using my circular saw to cut off 2 small triangles of waste. The resulting edges get a quick touch with the orbital sander to round them slightly. Then I use a 1/4-in. round-over bit in the router to ease the top and bottom front edges of the seat (*photo 5-8*). I just want to ease these edges slightly, so I adjust the depth of cut on the router to expose only the lower 3/16-in. of the roundover bit to the stock. Using this same adjustment, I ease both front edges of the upper crosspiece, taking care to stop milling 3/8 in. from each end.

5-7 I plow the dado for the seat using the rip fence to guide the bottom edge of the side. The wobble dado blade is adjusted to cut 3/4 in. wide and 3/8 in. deep.

5-8 After trimming off the front corners of the seat, I ease both front edges, using a 1/4-in. roundover bit in the router. I just want to ease these edges slightly, so I adjust the router to show only 3/16 in. of the cutter below the base.

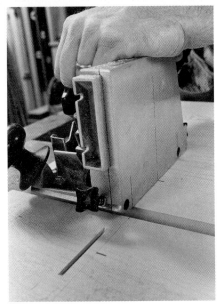

5-9 Holding the biscuit joiner's centerline against a layout line on a side, I mill a groove that will hold a biscuit-type spline for joining the baseboard backer piece to the side.

Biscuit-Aided Assembly

The bottom shelf and the baseboard backer piece butt against the sides as the settle is assembled. Thanks to the biscuit joiner, I can strengthen these connections and align them at the same time. First I have to mark up the sides with the layout for each joint. As shown in drawing 5-D, the bottom shelf is located 1 in. up from the bottom edges of the sides; back edges are flush. The baseboard backer piece should be located 4⅝ in. from the bottom edge of each side.

Holding the end of a curved member against its layout line on a side, I make a short alignment mark on both pieces. This enables me to center the biscuit joiner over both marks, making a pair of shallow grooves where a beechwood biscuit will fit (*photo 5-9*). Each bottom-shelf/side joint gets 4 biscuits. Each baseboard backer/side joint gets a pair of biscuits.

Now the seat, the bottom shelf, the baseboard backer piece, and the upper crosspiece can be joined to the sides. I start with the seat first, spreading glue in the sides' dadoes before fitting the joints and tapping them together with a shot-filled mallet. Using my pneumatic nail gun, I drive 4d finishing nails into both joints (*photo 5-10*).

5-10 With my pneumatic nail gun, I drive 4d finishing nails into the dado joint that holds side and seat together.

5-11 Biscuits help to strengthen the joints where the bottom shelf and baseboard backer piece meet the sides. Biscuits and butt edges are glued, then nailed.

5-12 The ends of the upper crosspiece fit into dadoes in the sides. These joints are also glued and nailed.

When the seat is secured, the bottom shelf and the baseboard backer piece can be installed (*photo 5-11*). I spread glue on the ends of these pieces and also on the biscuits. Then I join both pieces to one side and drive a single 4d finishing nail into each joint. This will help to hold these pieces together while I fit the joints into the opposite side. To pull all the joints tight, I use a pair of long pipe clamps, tightened across the sides. With the clamps secured and cranked down, I drive a few more nails through the sides and into the bottom shelf and the baseboard backer piece.

I install the upper crosspiece last (*photo 5-12*). The ends of the crosspiece are glued into their dadoes and then secured with 4d finishing nails. Once this is done, I set the assembly aside while the glue dries.

Beaded Boards

You can find beaded, tongue-and-groove boards at most lumberyards, but they're not like the beaded boards I mill in the workshop for the back and front of the settle. First of all, I start with a mixture of 1x4, 1x6, and 1x8 stock, which enables me to create a random-width pattern of boards, just like on the antique settle. Secondly, the boards are divided into pieces with double tongues and double grooves (*drawing 5-E, which includes beadboard milling list*). Only the double-tongue boards are beaded, and these beads are milled on both sides of the stock. This also duplicates the antique settle's detail.

Before I can begin milling tongues and grooves, the #2 common boards need some work. First I cut all the 12-ft-long boards in half so that I can work with 6-ft lengths. Then I go over each

**Milling List for
Random-Width Beadboard**

Boards that get double tongues	Boards that get double grooves
(2) 1x4s	(2) 1x4s
(3) 1x6s	(2) 1x6s
(2) 1x8s	(2) 1x8s

Bead, 1/4 in. wide

Groove, 1/4 in. thick, 5/16 in. deep

Tongue, 1/4 in. thick, 1/4 in. long

board to see if there are any knots that might cause problems as I mill tongues, groves, and beads. Small, tight knots are fine, but you don't want loose knots, or large knots right on the edge of a board. Knots on the edge of a board can be eliminated by ripping the board to narrower width on the table saw.

Now I run each board a couple of times through the thickness planer (*photo 5-13*). If you start with 3/4-in.-thick stock, planing 1/32 in. off both sides of a board should yield a finished thickness of 11/16 in. When I'm done planing, I turn to the jointer to make each edge straight and square (*photo 5-14*).

As a final preparation before milling begins, I stand the boards up vertically so that I can establish a random-width orientation. Every other board will either be double-tongued or double-grooved, except for a single 6-ft 1x6 that should be reserved as the baseboard.

I mill grooves and tongues on the router table, using a 1/4-in.-wide slot-cutting bit. For both milling operations, it's important to test the setup using a scrap piece of wood whose thickness matches that of the stock you plan to mill. The grooves get done first. I adjust bit height so that the slot will be centered exactly in the edges of my boards. The fence is positioned to allow for a groove that's 5/16 in. deep. A featherboard, clamped to the fence, helps me to prevent boards from riding up as grooves are milled. I can mill each groove with a single pass through the bit (*photo 5-15*).

It takes 2 passes to mill a tongue with a slot-cutting bit. After the first pass is made, the stock is flipped, end-for-end, and then a second pass is made. The bit must be lowered just the right amount to leave slightly less than a 1/4-in.-thick tongue after 2 passes. Also, the fence must be adjusted so that the depth of the tongue is 1/4 in. (*photo 5-16*).

5-13 The #2 pine boards I use to make the back of the settle benefit from a couple of passes through the thickness planer. I remove about 1/32 in. from each side.

5-14 I use the jointer to mill straight, square edges on each board.

5-15 Using my router table and a 1/4-in.-wide slot-cutting bit, I mill a groove in each long edge of this board. A shop-made featherboard, clamped to the fence, helps to hold the stock down against the table.

5-16 By changing the height of the slot-cutting bit, I can use it to mill tongues along edges that will join grooved boards. Completing each tongue requires 2 passes through the setup.

5-17 On the table saw, each "double-tongue" board receives 4 beads. The saw blade has been replaced with a molding head, fitted with beading knives. A wood auxiliary fence is positioned to guide the end of the tongue as the bead is milled along one edge of the board.

5-18 With glue, a clamp, and counterbored screws, I secure one end of the baseboard in preparation for bending it to the settle's curve. The overhanging end of the baseboard keeps the clamp out of the way and will be trimmed flush later.

All "double-tongue" boards now have to be beaded on both sides and both edges. In other words, each double-tongue board gets a total of 4 beads. I use the table saw for this work, replacing the blade with a molding head. The beading knives that go with my molding head are designed to mill 3 beads in a row, but I only need to mill a single bead at a time. To solve this problem, I attach a wood auxiliary fence to the table saw's rip fence. The wood fence covers one of the beads while guiding the end of the tongue as a single bead is milled along the board's edge (*photo 5-17*).

Installing the Back

The first back piece to install is the baseboard. This 5-in.-wide board follows the curve of the back and is fastened to the back edges of the sides, bottom shelf, and baseboard backer piece. Before installing the baseboard, I "back-bevel" its top edge just slightly — about 2½ degrees. This ensures a tight joint where the back's vertical boards butt against the baseboard. Back-beveling is easy to do on the jointer. I simply adjust the fence so that it leans in 2½ degrees from its usual 90-degree setting.

To install the baseboard, I start on one side of the settle and slowly work my way toward the opposite side, bending the baseboard to the curve of the back as I go. I glue and clamp one end of the baseboard to the side before fastening it in place with three 1⅝-in. bugle-head screws. It's a good idea to let the end run long, overlapping the side by about 2 in. (*photo 5-18*). It can be trimmed flush after the baseboard is completely installed. All 3 screw holes should be predrilled and counterbored. Wood plugs, glued in the counterbores, will be sanded flush later.

5-19 Using glue, clamps, and 4d finishing nails, I gradually bend the baseboard from one end of the settle to the other.

Once one end of the baseboard is securely fastened, I apply glue a little bit at a time to the back edges of the baseboard backer piece and the bottom shelf and use clamps to pull the baseboard against these edges (*photo 5-19*). As you install the baseboard, it's important to keep it centered on the baseboard backer piece, at the same time maintaining a 1-in. overhang where the baseboard meets the bottom shelf. I secure the baseboard to these edges with 4d finishing nails. Continuing to bend the baseboard, I apply more glue and advance the clamps to pull the baseboard into position before nailing it down. After repeating this sequence a few times, I'm ready to screw the other end of the baseboard down against the side.

After trimming the ends of the baseboard with a circular saw and sanding them smooth, I'm ready to install the tongue-and-groove beadboard back. I cut the 6-ft-long milled boards to length on the radial-arm saw. Each board yields a single back piece and a single front piece. As with the baseboard, it's best to work from one side to the other. I start with a tongued piece, ripping its outside edge square on the table saw. The square edge should be installed flush with the outside face of the side. This "starter" board should be glued and nailed to the back edges of the side, the upper crosspiece, the seat, and the baseboard backer piece (using 4d finishing nails). Successive tongued or grooved boards should be nailed, not glued (*photo 5-20*).

For a flush fit, the last tongued or grooved board will need to be ripped to width on the table saw. I dry-fit this board in place on the settle in order to mark its proper width. Then I adjust the table saw's rip fence so that this piece will be cut just a trifle wide. I'll belt-sand it flush after it's installed. Like the starter board, this last one should be glued and nailed in place.

5-20 Working from one end to the other, I nail the tongued or grooved boards for the back to the back edges of the seat, the baseboard backer piece, and the upper crosspiece.

5-21 The front nailer is fastened to the underside of the seat with 1¼-in. screws driven in predrilled, countersunk holes. The curved front edge of the nailer should be 2³⁄₁₆ in. back from the seat's front edge.

5-22 Tongued or grooved boards for the front of the settle are installed by driving nails into the front edge of the bottom shelf and into the front edge of the front nailer.

5-23 After starting the hatch cutout with the circular saw, I complete it by cutting out the back corners with the jigsaw.

5-24 The hatch swings on a brass-plated piano hinge, cut to the 22-in. length of the opening.

Finishing the Front

Before the settle's beadboard front can be installed, I have to screw the front nailer to the underside of the seat. The curved front edge of the nailer must be vertically aligned with the curved front edge of the bottom shelf. Positioning the nailer's edge $2\frac{3}{16}$ in. back from the seat's front edge should give you the proper alignment. I use $1\frac{1}{4}$-in. bugle-head screws to fasten the nailer to the seat, taking care not to drive screws where the hatch will be cut (*photo 5-21*).

Boards for the front of the settle can be fastened to the front nailer and bottom shelf, using 4d finishing nails. When installing the front, I start on the side where the first back board was installed. The order of boards is also the same, except that I start with the first grooved board (the second board to go on the back). One edge of this grooved board has to be ripped to create a square edge that butts against the inside face of the side. After this board is installed, I work my way across the front (*photo 5-22*). The last board will need to be ripped to fit snugly against the opposite side.

The hatch comes next. To lay out the 13-in. by 22-in. opening, see drawing 5-B. I start the 3-sided cutout with the circular saw. To make the two 13-in.-long cuts, it's important to match the circular saw's depth of cut precisely to the thickness of the seat. The cut near the back of the seat is a pocket cut. I make it by carefully lowering the blade in the seat and cutting along as much of the line as possible. To cut out the back corners of the seat, I use my jigsaw (*photo 5-23*).

The hatch swings on a 22-in.-long piano hinge that's fastened to the back edge of the opening. As soon as I've cut the hatch free, I temporarily attach the hinge to the back edge of the opening with a couple of screws. Then I place the hatch in the opening, butting its back edge against the "free" leaf of the hinge. In this position, I can see how much needs to be trimmed from the back edge of the hatch in order for its front edge to fit flush with the front edge of the seat. Several passes through the jointer do the trick. To install the hatch, it's easiest to screw the hinge to the hatch first, then screw the hinge to the back edge of the opening (*photo 5-24*).

Before a finish is applied to this piece, it needs a little more sanding. The hard, square edges along the top of the back should be eased. The hatch edges as well as the edges of the opening can also use some smoothing. Finally, sides and seat need a final going-over with fine-grit sandpaper.

This settle is much more comfortable with a seat cushion. A $3\frac{1}{2}$-in.-thick cushion is just about right. An upholstery shop, if provided with a paper pattern of the seat, will be able to turn out a foam-core cushion covered with the material of your choice.

Chapter Six

Pencil-Post Bed

PROJECT PLANNING
Time: 3 days

Special hardware and tools:

(4) 3/8-in.-diameter, 4-in.-long hanger bolts, with washers and nuts

(4) Bed bolt covers

Biscuit joiner and beechwood biscuits

Wood:

I used poplar to make my version of this bed. Poplar is strong, easily workable, and economical as woods go. It also takes a painted finish very well. For a bed with a clear or stained finish, choose a wood with more distinctive grain, like oak, ash, or cherry.

(4) 7-ft 12/4 x 12/4s
Posts

(1) 14-ft 6/4 x 8
Side rails and support cleats

(1) 12-ft 6/4 x 8
Head and foot rails

(1) 12-ft 1x8
Headboard

WHETHER it's among contemporary furnishings or in a restored farmhouse, the pencil-post bed never seems out of place. A marriage of graceful lines and functional design, this traditional piece has a truly timeless appeal. I designed my pencil-post bed after an antique bed found at Vermont's Shelburne Museum.

In designing my own version of this traditional piece, I wanted to duplicate the proportions and detailing found on a fine antique bed while adapting the frame to accommodate a modern box spring and mattress. Antique beds were built with a rope suspension that was meant to hold a mattress only. Today's bed frames need to support a box spring, which in turn supports a mattress. The combined thickness of these 2 items is about 16 in. For the mattress to be at a comfortable height, the rails need to be lowered slightly from their position on the original bed frame. Also, the headboard has to be raised so as not to be hidden by the mattress.

I modified the dimensions of my bed to fit a queen-size mattress and box spring. But all queen-size mattresses aren't the same. Depending on the manufacturer, size and thickness can vary. So it's best to buy your mattress and box spring first, before building the bed. You may have to adjust rail lengths and height, as well as headboard height.

The joinery work for this bed is fairly straightforward. Making the bedposts is the most difficult part of the project. The posts start out square in section. But after some careful layout and cutting work, only a small square section remains in each post, where the rails join it. Above and below the remaining square section, each post is tapered on all 4 sides. Tapered edges are chamfered,

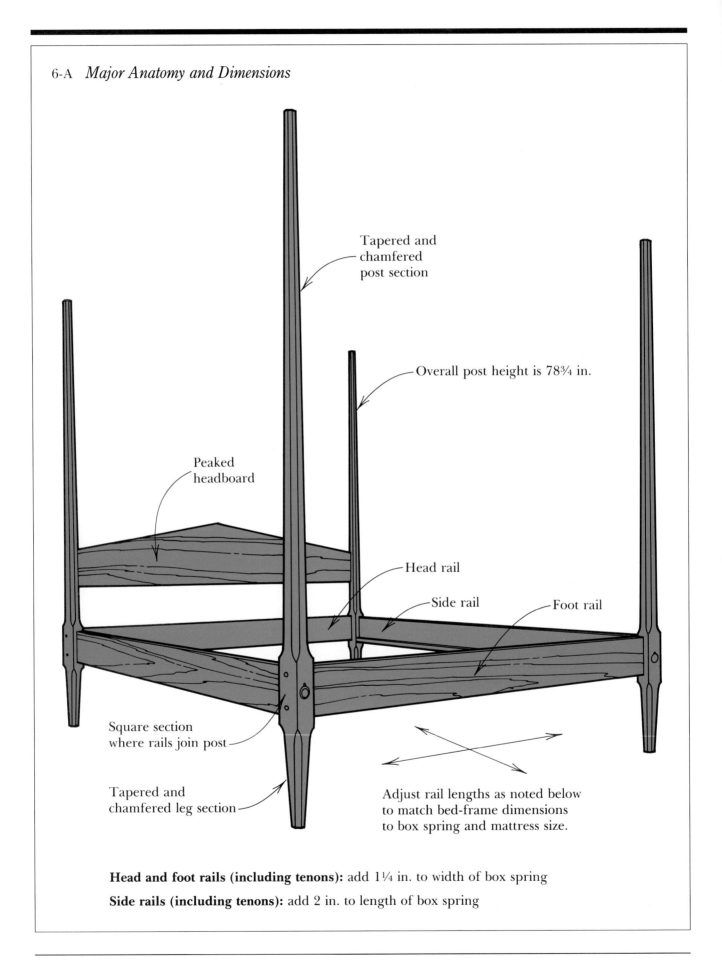

Tapered and
chamfered
post section

Overall post height is 78¾ in.

Peaked
headboard

Head rail

Side rail

Foot rail

Square section
where rails join post

Tapered and
chamfered leg section

Adjust rail lengths as noted below
to match bed-frame dimensions
to box spring and mattress size.

Head and foot rails (including tenons): add 1¼ in. to width of box spring

Side rails (including tenons): add 2 in. to length of box spring

resulting in an 8-sided cross section. Each chamfer ends at the square section of the post with a graceful scallop cut.

Taper Cuts on a Giant Jig

I make the bedposts from nominal 12/4 stock, which has an actual thickness of about 2¾ in. Using the table saw, jointer, and thickness planer, I dimension 4 posts that are straight, square in section (2½ in. on a side), and measure 78¾ in. in length.

Drawing 6-B shows the full finished profile of the posts. I begin my layout work with a square and a sharp pencil, marking the borders for the square sections, each of which starts 11 in. from the base of the post and ends 19 in. from the base. When the square sections are marked, I find the center point on every post end by crossing diagonals. Measuring from these center points, I lay out the dimensions that the post ends will have after all taper cuts have been made. The long upper tapers (which I call *post tapers*) will leave a square at the top end of the post that measures 1⅛ in. on a side. The short lower tapers (I call these the *leg tapers*) will leave a square "footprint" that measures 1⅝ in. on each side. Both square layouts are shown in drawing 6-C.

Thanks to the jig that will be used to cut tapers and chamfers, it's only necessary to lay out a single post taper and a single leg taper on one post. From these layout lines, the jig can be set up to make repetitive taper and chamfer cuts on all 4 posts.

I lay out the leg taper first. To do this, I extend one side of the "bottom" square to mark the end of a single taper cut on one face of the post. I connect this point with the nearest lower corner of the post's square section, as shown in drawing 6-C. This completes the lower, or leg-taper, layout. I lay out the long post taper the same way, except that I connect the top point to the nearest upper corner of the post's square section.

Cutting the tapers is a challenging job, involving the table saw and a large, shop-made jig. To keep the jig stable, I use 2 sets of guide rollers — one at the infeed side of the saw and one at the outfeed side.

The jig is essentially a large rectangular frame, made from scrap pieces of plywood or MDO board (medium-density-overlay plywood). On my jig, the inside dimensions where the blank for the post is held are about 14 in. by 79¾ in. One side of the jig is built in an inverted U shape to fit snugly over the saw's rip fence. This allows the jig to slide along the rip fence and table without wandering, remaining parallel with the saw blade at all times. To cut the tapers, the post blank is mounted at an angle inside the jig, while the layout lines for the tapers are parallel with the sides of the jig, which is also parallel with the saw blade.

I use a pair of shop-made hangers to mount the post blank in the jig. A 1x cleat, screwed to each hanger, allows the hanger to

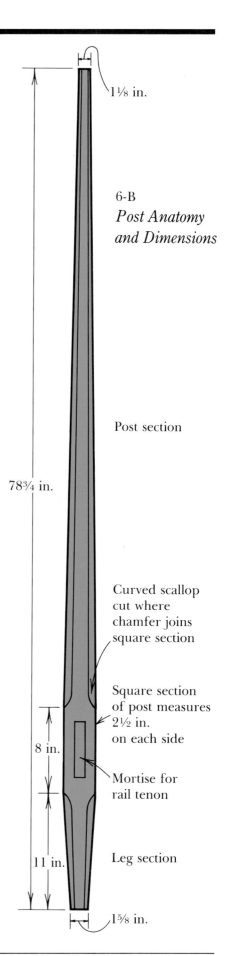

1⅛ in.

6-B
*Post Anatomy
and Dimensions*

Post section

78¾ in.

Curved scallop
cut where
chamfer joins
square section

Square section
of post measures
2½ in.
on each side

8 in.

Mortise for
rail tenon

11 in.

Leg section

1⅝ in.

rest on the crosspiece at each end of the jig, while aligning the bottom edge of the hanger flush with the bottom edge of the jig. After marking a vertical line on both sides of each hanger, I fasten the hangers to the ends of my post blank (the one with the taper layout marks) by driving a screw through each vertical line and into the center point of each end (*photo 6-1*). The screw should be driven 1¼ in. up from the bottom edge of the hanger for the taper cuts.

Once the hangers are attached to a post blank, the blank can be positioned inside the jig. I set up to cut the short leg tapers first. As mentioned earlier, the blank must be positioned at an angle inside the jig in order for the taper layout line to be parallel with the sides of the jig, and thus parallel with the saw blade. A good way to position the blank is to screw one cleat to its crosspiece and then shift the opposite end of the blank back and forth until the taper layout is parallel with the side of the jig that fits over the rip fence. I take measurements between the layout line

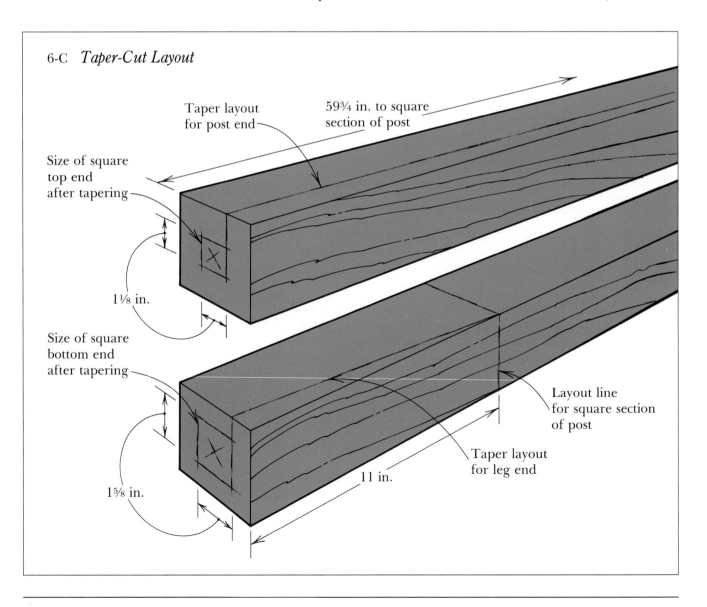

6-C *Taper-Cut Layout*

Taper layout for post end

59¾ in. to square section of post

Size of square top end after tapering

1⅛ in.

Size of square bottom end after tapering

1⅝ in.

11 in.

Layout line for square section of post

Taper layout for leg end

and the fence side of the jig at the top and bottom of the leg taper. When both measurements are equal, I screw the "free" cleat to its crosspiece.

Now that the blank is fixed at the proper angle in the jig, I shift the entire setup by moving the rip fence to line up the taper layout with the saw blade. The blade needs to be lowered just beneath the table surface while the rip fence is shifted. To check the jig's position, I slide it forward until the leg section is just beyond the blade. This enables me to sight down the blade and see clearly how it aligns with the taper layout on the blank.

When I'm sure the alignment is right, I move the jig back so that the blank is ready to enter the blade. Then I raise the blade just high enough to cut through the 2½-in.-thick blank. Turning on the saw, I advance the jig, moving the blank slowly and firmly through the blade until the first leg-taper cut is complete (*photo 6-2*). When cutting each leg taper, it's important to use a push stick to prevent the triangular waste piece from being caught by the blade.

To cut the remaining 3 leg tapers on the first blank, I lower the blade, pull the jig and post back behind the blade, and lift the jig slightly to rotate the blank a quarter turn. The rip fence and hangers remain in the same position. With an untapered side facing the blade, the second cut is made, followed by the third and fourth.

With the leg tapers complete on the first post blank, I mark both hangers' positions on the crosspieces of the jig before unfastening them — first from the jig, then from the blank. This enables me to reattach the hangers easily after they've been screwed to the ends of an untapered blank. For the remaining 3 post blanks, I repeat the procedure for attaching hangers first to ends of the blank and then to the jig. The cutting and rotating operations are also identical.

When the lower tapers are complete on all 4 blanks, I use the jig to make 4 chamfer cuts in each leg. First, I drill a second screw hole in each hanger, about 1/2 in. above the first screw hole. Then I attach the hangers to the post blank by driving a screw through each new hole and into the center of each blank end. The hangers are reattached to the jig in the same positions used for making taper cuts. The only difference in the chamfer-cut setup is that the blank is turned so that one corner of the blank aligns with a vertical line on the hanger that runs through both screw holes (*photo 6-3*). In this position, the sides of the blank are at a 45-degree angle to the saw blade — just the right orientation for a chamfer cut that follows the taper. A stop mark, made 1¼ in. down from the square layout on the blank, tells me when to withdraw the blade from the cut, so that the chamfer can be scalloped into the square section with a curved cut.

Cutting the chamfers is the same as cutting the tapers, once the

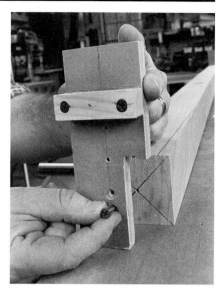

6-1 Two hangers are used to position the post inside a large jig designed for making taper and chamfer cuts. Each hanger is screwed to the center of a post end. A 1x cleat, fastened to the hanger, will fit over the top edges of the jig's crosspieces.

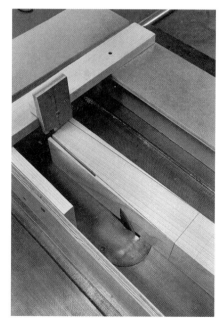

6-2 The first leg taper is cut as the jig is pushed forward. The post blank is held at an angle inside the jig's frame to keep the taper layout aligned with the saw blade. The broad side of the jig (top right) is built in an inverted U shape to slide snugly over the rip fence.

6-3 Chamfer cuts are made in the leg after taper cuts are complete. I raise the level of the posts in the jig slightly so that the post blank can be turned, aligning post corners with a vertical line on the cleat.

6-4 One leg-chamfer cut has already been made as I push the jig forward to complete a second. I stop each chamfer cut about 1¼ in. from the square section of the post.

post blank is in the jig. I turn on the saw and push the jig forward, letting the blade enter the blank to cut the chamfer (*photo 6-4*). When the blade reaches my stop mark, I lower the blade until it's free of the blank and withdraw the jig and blank together. Then I rotate the blank a quarter turn, raise the blade, and repeat the process for successive chamfer cuts.

The upper tapers and chamfers are also cut using the jig. The sequence of steps is identical, but the position of the blank in the jig is different because the tapers are more gradual. After attaching the hangers to the blank, I flip it end-for-end to put the leg at the back of the jig. The rear hanger can be fastened to the jig in the same position that was used when tapering the legs. On my jig, I move the front hanger (nearest the saw blade) about 2½ in. to the right. I also adjust the rip fence position slightly, again sighting along the blade to make sure the alignment is correct.

Post taper and chamfer cuts are made by sliding the jig and blank through the blade, just as when making these cuts in the legs (*photo 6-5*). When making the chamfer cuts, remember to stop each chamfer about 1¼ in. from the square section of the post.

With tapers and chamfers complete, I turn to the band saw to make the curved scallop cuts that will connect each chamfer with the square section of the post. Using a cradle with a 90-degree triangular cutout, I can keep the chamfers in line with the blade as I make each cut (*photo 6-6*).

Now the posts need a thorough sanding to smooth out saw marks along tapers, chamfers, and scallops. I go over tapers and chamfers with the belt sander, using a fine-grit sanding belt. To

6-5 An outfeed roller will help to support the front end of the jig as I complete a long taper cut.

6-6 Making a short, curved cut on the band saw, I scallop the post chamfers into the square section of the post. A cradle with a 90-degree triangular cutout helps me to steady the post as I make each scallop cut.

smooth the scalloped sections of each post, I use a sanding drum, chucked in the drill press. The same cradle I used on the band saw to steady the post comes in handy on the drill-press table (*photo 6-7*).

Mortises and Counterbores

Each post gets a pair of mortises to hold one side-rail tenon and one head- or foot-rail tenon. Mortise layout is shown in drawing 6-D. The 7/8-in.-wide mortises need to be centered in adjacent faces of each post and cut to a depth of 1 in.

I use the drill press and a 7/8-in.-diameter Forstner bit to rough out the mortises. After marking up each post with its mortise layout, I clamp a wood fence to the drill-press table. I position the fence so that when the square section of a post is butted against it, the bit will be centered between the layout lines for the mortise cheeks.

6-7 A sanding drum, chucked in the drill press, does a good job of smoothing the scallop cuts. I use the cradle shown in photo 6-6 to support the post on the drill-press table.

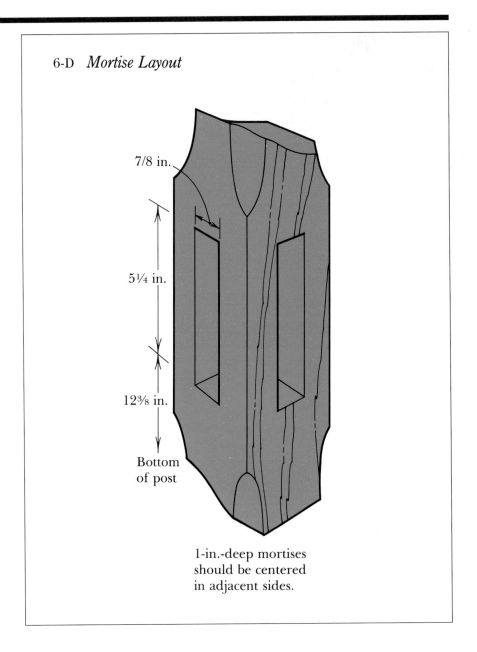

6-D *Mortise Layout*

7/8 in.

5¼ in.

12⅜ in.

Bottom
of post

1-in.-deep mortises
should be centered
in adjacent sides.

Using the stops on the drill press, I adjust the tool so that the bit will penetrate a full inch into the post. Then I bore a series of overlapping holes to remove as much waste as possible from inside the layout lines (*photo 6-8*). I finish up each mortise with a sharp chisel. With a hammer, I drive the chisel down against the layout lines to square the ends of a mortise. The cheeks of the mortise can be pared straight using hand pressure alone (*photo 6-9*). This work is best done with the bevel of the chisel facing into the mortise.

To finish up the posts, all that's left is to predrill and counterbore holes for screws and hanger bolts. To make the bed movable, side-rail tenons need to be detachable from their mortises. One way to make these take-apart joints is to use hanger bolts. A hanger bolt is "lagged" on one end, which means that it has a spiral thread, like a wood screw. On the opposite end are machine threads that take a hex-head nut. In the finished bed, each side-rail tenon will get a single hanger bolt, screwed into the end of the tenon so that the machine thread remains exposed. The free end of the hanger bolt will extend through the back of the mortise, protruding into a counterbore hole so that the nut can be attached. Tightening the nut (over a washer) effectively pulls the joint tight (*drawing 6-E*).

I drill out the counterbore holes for the hanger bolts first, using a 1⅛-in.-diameter Forstner bit in the drill press. The center for the hole, shown in drawing 6-E, will position the hanger bolt in the center of the tenon. Counterbore depth is 3/4 in. After drilling the counterbores, I chuck a 3/8-in.-diameter bit in the drill press. With this bit, I bore through the bottom of the counterbore hole and into the back of the mortise (*photo 6-10*).

Head and foot rails will be permanently fastened to posts with glue and 2½-in. bugle-head screws. A pair of screws will be driven into the end of each head or foot rail's tenon to pull it tight in its mortise. Centers for these screw holes are shown in drawing 6-F. I drill the counterbore holes for these screws using a 3/8-in.-diameter bit in the drill press. Counterbore depth is set at 1/2 in. After counterboring, I drill pilot holes that extend through the bottom of the mortise, using a 3/16-in.-diameter drill bit.

6-8 With a 7/8-in.-diameter Forstner bit in the drill press, I bore a series of overlapping holes to rough out 2 mortises in each post. Mortise depth is set at 1 in.

6-9 Using a sharp chisel, I pare away the waste that remains inside the layout lines for a mortise.

6-10 I drill a 3/8-in.-diameter hole for the hanger bolt after the 1⅛-in.-diameter counterbore hole has been made. The smaller hole should be drilled into the back of the mortise for the side rail.

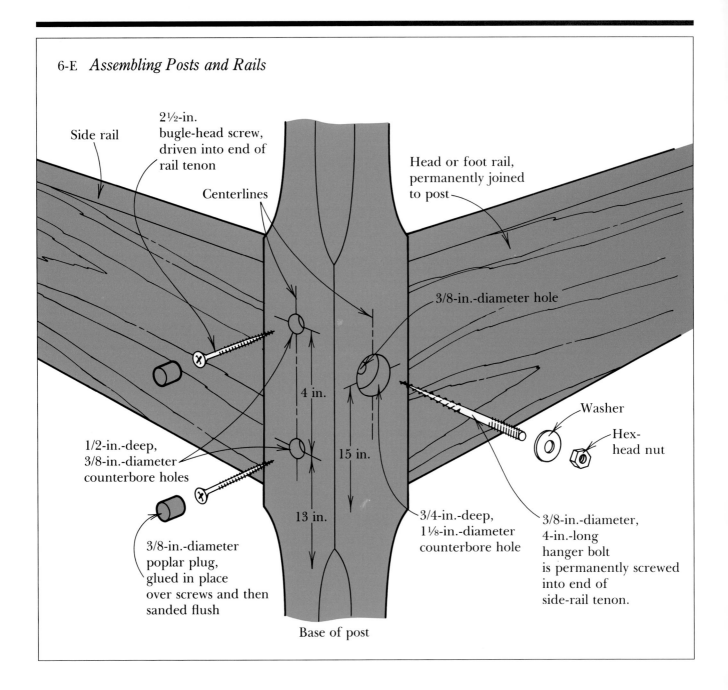

6-E *Assembling Posts and Rails*

Side rail

2½-in. bugle-head screw, driven into end of rail tenon

Centerlines

Head or foot rail, permanently joined to post

3/8-in.-diameter hole

4 in.

1/2-in.-deep, 3/8-in.-diameter counterbore holes

Washer

Hex-head nut

15 in.

13 in.

3/8-in.-diameter poplar plug, glued in place over screws and then sanded flush

3/4-in.-deep, 1⅛-in.-diameter counterbore hole

3/8-in.-diameter, 4-in.-long hanger bolt is permanently screwed into end of side-rail tenon.

Base of post

Rails and Rail Tenons

The rails for my bed are cut from 1¼-in.-thick stock. Finished width of the rails is 6 in. Head and foot rails are 61¾ in. long; side-rail length is 82½ in. Both these dimensions include a pair of 1-in.-long tenons on each rail. Tenon layout is shown in drawing 6-F.

Because of the size of the rails, it's easier to cut their tenons on the radial-arm saw, since this allows the stock to remain fairly stationary. I replace the radial-arm saw's blade with a dado head and adjust it for maximum width of cut. The height of the cutter above the saw's table is crucial, since it will determine the thickness of the tenons. Testing the setup on scrap stock, I adjust cut-

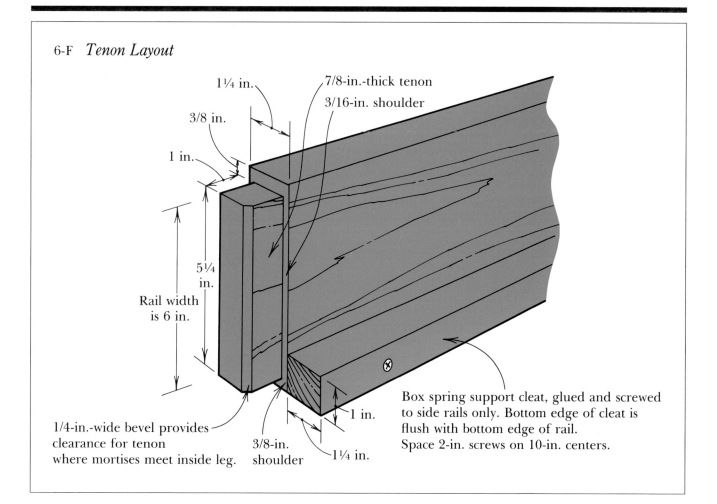

6-F   *Tenon Layout*

1¼ in.

7/8-in.-thick tenon

3/16-in. shoulder

3/8 in.

1 in.

5¼ in.

Rail width is 6 in.

1/4-in.-wide bevel provides clearance for tenon where mortises meet inside leg.

3/8-in. shoulder

1¼ in.

1 in.

Box spring support cleat, glued and screwed to side rails only. Bottom edge of cleat is flush with bottom edge of rail. Space 2-in. screws on 10-in. centers.

ter height until a 7/8-in.-thick tenon is left after passes on both sides of the stock.

When the cutter height is set, I screw a stop block to the saw table to line up the shoulder cuts for each tenon. When the rail is held against the saw fence, with its end butted against the stop block, the saw is set up to make the shoulder cut for a 1-in.-long tenon. After the shoulder cut is made, I slide the rail about 1/2 in. to the left prior to making a second pass with the dado cutter (*photo 6-11*). Repeating these 2 cuts on the opposite side of the rail gives the tenon its finished thickness.

To make each tenon 5¼ in. wide, I have to trim 3/8 in. from its top and bottom. To set up for this cutting operation, I raise the saw and install a high fence to keep each rail braced in a vertical position. Cutter height should be adjusted to remove just 3/8 in. of waste from the top (or bottom) of the tenon. It takes a couple of passes with the dado head to fully trim the top and bottom of each tenon (*photo 6-12*).

I finish off each tenon with a block plane. I use the plane to trim a 1/4-in.-wide bevel on the inside edge of the tenon, as shown in drawing 6-F. Removing these corners prevents tenons from hitting each other inside the post, where the mortises meet.

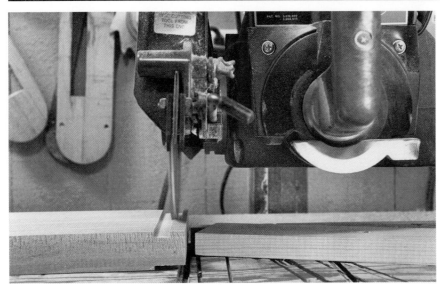

6-11 I use the radial-arm saw, fitted with a dado cutter, to mill a 1-in.-long tenon at each rail end. Cutting height must be carefully adjusted to leave a final tenon thickness of 7/8 in. after a couple of passes on each side of the rail. A stop block, screwed to the saw table, sets up the shoulder cut on each side of the tenon.

6-12 I raise the radial-arm saw to trim 3/8 in. from the top and bottom of rail tenons. A high fence, clamped in the table, helps to keep the tenon vertical while several passes are made with the dado cutter.

Headboard

The next step is to lay out and cut the headboard. I start with a glued-up panel made from a pair of 6-ft-long 1x8 boards. As shown in drawing 6-G, the headboard is straight along its bottom edge and has a peaked top edge. The 7-in.-wide ends of the headboard need to be cut at an angle that matches the taper of the posts. Measuring this angle is the most critical part of laying out the headboard cuts.

To get an exact measurement of the end cuts for the headboard, I have to dry-fit the head rail in its posts. I assemble the mortise-and-tenon joints, then pull them tight by driving bugle-head screws in their predrilled holes. I also fasten a temporary board across the tops of the posts to keep the assembly rigid and square. On my bed, the distance between center holes in the tops of the posts (the same holes where cleat screws were fastened) is 62¼ in.

The bottom corners of the headboard will join the posts 9 in. above the head rail. With my tape measure, I take an exact measurement between the posts 9 in. above the head rail and 16 in. above the head rail (*photo 6-13*). The 7-in. span accounts for the width of the headboard where it will join the posts. Using these measurements, I can lay out the angle of the end cuts, measuring from a centerline on the headboard blank that will intersect with the peak of the finished headboard.

Using my bevel gauge, I transfer the end-cut angle from the headboard blank to the radial-arm saw. By setting the wooden

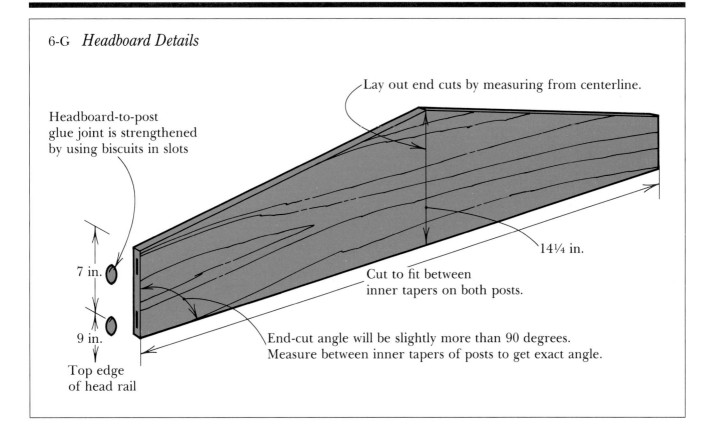

Lay out end cuts by measuring from centerline.

Headboard-to-post glue joint is strengthened by using biscuits in slots

14¼ in.

Cut to fit between inner tapers on both posts.

7 in.

9 in.

Top edge of head rail

End-cut angle will be slightly more than 90 degrees. Measure between inner tapers of posts to get exact angle.

handle of the gauge against the saw's fence, I can adjust the cutting angle so that the blade contacts evenly with the steel arm of the gauge (*photo 6-14*). Once the angle is set, it's quick work to cut both ends of the headboard. I use my circular saw to make the 2 top cuts for the headboard (*photo 6-15*). After completing both cuts, I dress both edges by running them through the jointer (*photo 6-16*).

6-13 Layout work for the headboard begins by measuring the distance between inner tapers where the ends of the headboard will join both "head" posts.

6-14 I use the bevel gauge to transfer the end-cut angle for the headboard to the radial-arm saw. With the wood handle of the gauge set against the fence, I adjust the cutting angle so that the blade makes full contact with the steel arm of the gauge.

6-15 To cut the peak of the headboard, I make 2 angled cuts with the circular saw.

6-16 A couple of passes through the joiner leaves the top edge of the headboard square and smooth.

6-17 To lay out the biscuit joints between headboard and post, I dry-fit the joints, taking care to center each headboard end on the inner taper of the post. I make a line where the edge of the headboard contacts the post, and 2 marks across the joint to locate biscuit centers.

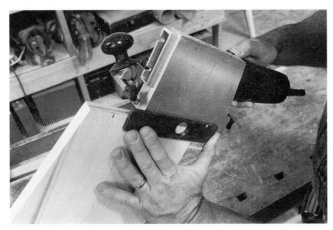

6-18 The black fence on the biscuit joiner helps center the slot on the headboard edge as I line up the centerline on the tool with the layout line on the stock.

6-19 To mill biscuit slots in the post, I remove the biscuit joiner's fence. This enables me to align and center the front edge of the tool against the layout marks on the inner taper of the post.

The next step is to test-fit the headboard between both "head" posts and make layout marks for the biscuit joiner. The football-shaped biscuits will fit in slots cut in the posts and in the ends of the headboard (see the Introduction for more on biscuit-joining). Using scrap pieces of wood to prop up the headboard, I center each headboard end on the inner taper of the post it will join. I mark a line where each headboard edge meets its taper. Then, with 2 short pencil marks that cross each joint, I lay out center marks for biscuits (*photo 6-17*).

To cut the slots in the headboard ends, the biscuit joiner is fitted with a fence that helps center the slot in the 3/4-in.-thick stock (*photo 6-18*). I remove the fence to cut slots in the posts, aligning the front edge of the biscuit joiner with the headboard-edge line marked on the post (*photo 6-19*).

Assembly

Before any joints get glued together, I take a few minutes to give posts, rails, and headboard a thorough sanding. This is the time to sand out layout marks and soften corners on posts, rails, and headboard. The orbital sander is good for this work, along with fine-grit sandpaper.

I assemble the bed in separate head and foot sections. The head section is more difficult to assemble, since it contains the headboard in addition to 2 posts and the head rail. I spread glue on rail tenons and also on biscuits and butt-joint areas where the headboard connects with the posts. Driving the screws into the rail tenons pulls them tight in their mortises, but a long pipe clamp is needed to close up the headboard-to-post joints (*photo 6-20*). On the drill press, I use a 3/8-in.-diameter plug-cutter bit to make poplar plugs for the screws' counterbore holes. I glue the

6-20 After spreading glue on rail tenons and on headboard ends and biscuits, I use a long pipe clamp to pull headboard ends snugly against posts.

plugs in the holes, letting them stand proud of the post surface so that they can be sanded flush later.

To install the hanger bolts in the side-rail tenons, I first have to fit the tenons in their mortises. With the 3/8-in.-diameter bit in the drill, I bore about 1 in. into the end of the tenon from the counterbore side of the joint (*photo 6-21*). Then I disassemble the joint, chuck a 1/4-in.-diameter bit in the drill, and complete the pilot hole for the hanger bolt by drilling another inch or so into the tenon. The hanger bolt can now be turned into the tenon. I tighten 2 nuts against each other near the end of the bolt, then I turn nuts and bolt together with a socket wrench (*photo 6-22*). When I've turned all but about 1⅛ in. of the bolt into the tenon, I remove the nuts so that the rail can be fit into the post.

I wait until the bed frame is assembled to install a pair of box-spring support cleats. These cleats, which measure 1 in. by 1¼ in. in section, are glued and screwed to side rails only. As shown in drawing 6-F, the 1¼-in.-wide bottom edge of the cleat should be flush with the bottom edge of the side rail. I predrill and counter-sink screw holes about every 10 in. along each cleat, then attach the cleat to its rail (*photo 6-23*).

6-21 (*top left*) Side rails need to be fit in their mortises to start the pilot hole for the hanger bolt. Using a 3/8-in.-diameter bit, I bore about 1 in. into the end of each side-rail tenon. Protruding wood plugs cover counterbored screws that are driven into the end of the foot rail. The plugs will be sanded flush later.

6-22 (*top right*) To install the hanger bolt, I turn a pair of nuts tightly against each other near the free end of the bolt. Then I use a socket wrench to turn the bolt into the pilot hole in the tenon. About 1⅛ in. of the bolt should show outside the tenon. With the nuts removed, the rail can be fit into its mortise and bolted tight.

6-23 When rails and posts are assembled, I cut and install a box-spring support cleat along each side rail. Cleats are glued and screwed to the rail, with the bottom edge of each cleat flush with the bottom edge of its rail.

Chapter Seven

Kitchen Worktable

PROJECT PLANNING

Time: 3 days

Special hardware and tools:

5/8-in.-diameter collar for router

Wood:

(1) 14-ft 5/4 x 10 cherry
(1) 14-ft 5/4 x 8 cherry

Each board is cut in half to make a 4-board panel for the top.

(1) 6-ft 5/4 x 2 cherry

Breadboard edge

(1) 12-ft 12/4 x 12/4 poplar

Legs

(2) 8-ft 1x8s poplar

Each board makes one short rail and one long rail

(2) 8-ft 1x6s poplar

Each board is ripped to a width of 3⅞ in. The 2 thin strips yield corner blocks and top-drawer guides. The two 3⅞-in.-wide pieces yield drawer fronts and sides. Sides should be planed to a 1/2-in. thickness.

(1) 10-ft 6/4 x 3 poplar

Drawer runner and support

(1) 10-ft 5/4 x 3 poplar

Stretchers

(2) 22-in. x 20-in., 1/4-in.-thick plywood

Drawer bottoms

T HE great thing about this table is its versatility. With its sturdy, widespread stance and storage drawers, this piece is ideal as a kitchen worktable, but it also makes a fine dining table or might serve as a desk in an office or study. In a broad hallway or dining room, it could even take the place of a sideboard.

The proportions for my table come from an antique at the Shelburne Museum in Vermont. The old table I found has a well-worn top made from a couple of wide pine boards. I decided to use cherry for my tabletop because it's harder than pine and should wear a little better. Cherry is also nice because of its naturally dark, well-figured grain.

Tapered legs contribute to the table's graceful proportions. Each leg is tapered on 2 sides only — the inside faces of the leg, which are mortised to hold rail tenons. A large table like this one needs stretchers for added stability. These members extend horizontally between the legs, several inches above the floor. The antique table that served as my model has 4 stretchers, each one connecting a pair of legs. While this configuration has a strong bracing effect on the table, the long stretchers make it impossible to slide chairs under the table. In my design, I retained the short stretchers (which run parallel to the end rails) but replaced the 2 long stretchers with a single stretcher that extends between the midpoints of the short stretchers (*drawing 7-A*).

Gluing Up the Top

I use 5/4 cherry to make the top of the table, which finishes out to be 32 in. wide and 78½ in. long, including a pair of bread-

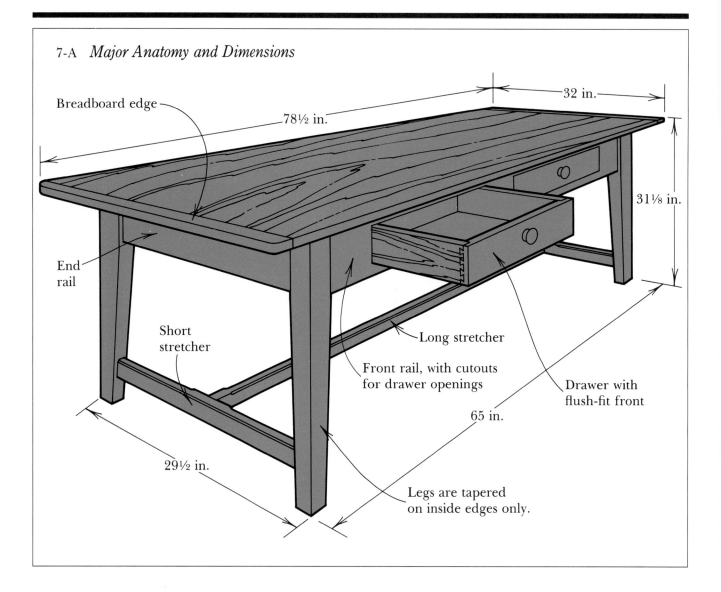

Breadboard edge

78½ in.

32 in.

31⅛ in.

End rail

Short stretcher

Long stretcher

Front rail, with cutouts for drawer openings

Drawer with flush-fit front

65 in.

29½ in.

Legs are tapered on inside edges only.

board edges at each end. The panel that I glue up contains two 9¼-in.-wide boards and two 7¼-in.-wide boards (see wood list for this project). I spend a few minutes examining all 4 boards, choosing the "good" sides that should face up in the finished top. Once this is done, I shift the boards around on the workbench, seeing which edge-to-edge arrangement looks best. I also try to orient the boards so that the end-grain pattern alternates across the width of the panel. Alternating the end grain in adjacent boards makes the entire panel more resistant to warping.

Next, I use my jointer to mill straight, square edges where boards join each other. Then I lay out marks for the biscuit joiner, which I use to cut short, shallow slots in joining edges of the boards. The slots will hold specially made beechwood biscuits that function like splines, strengthening as well as aligning the edge-to-edge joints in the panel (see the Introduction for more on biscuit-joining). The biscuit joiner will also come in handy later on in the project, when I install stretchers and drawer runners. After applying glue to joining edges, including slots and biscuits, I pull the panel together with pipe clamps. Then I set it aside until the glue dries.

Legs and Rails

The rails of the table join the legs with traditional mortise-and-tenon joints. I start working on the legs first. All 4 legs are cut from a single 12/4 board that's 12 ft long. I cut this board into 4 equal lengths on the radial-arm saw. Then I use my table saw to rip each blank to a square cross section that measures 2⅝ in. on a side. Moving to the thickness planer, I run all 4 sides of each blank through the planer knives. This yields a final cross section of 2½ in. Back on the radial-arm saw, I cut each blank to a finished length of 30 in.

As shown in drawing 7-B, the mortises for the rail tenons are 1/2 in. wide, 5½ in. long, and 1¼ in. deep. The top of each mortise starts 1/2 in. from the top of the leg, and the outside cheek of the mortise is 3/8 in. from the outside face of the leg.

To mill the mortises, I set up my plunge router with a 1/2-in.-diameter, spiral-fluted straight bit and a 5/8-in.-diameter collar. The collar, which extends below the router base, will ride snugly in the 5/8-in.-wide slot in the top of my shop-made mortising jig. The jig is essentially a 4-sided tunnel made from scrap pieces of MDO board (medium-density-overlay plywood). The 2½-in.-square leg fits inside the tunnel, with enough clearance on 2 sides for some wedges that I use to brace the leg firmly against the top and side of the tunnel (*photo 7-1*). The slot in the top of the jig is located to align the router bit with the mortise layout. A pair of

7-1 To mill leg mortises, I use my plunge router, a 1/2-in. straight bit surrounded by a 5/8-in.-diameter collar, and a shop-made jig. Using wedges, I position the leg in the square tunnel of the jig.

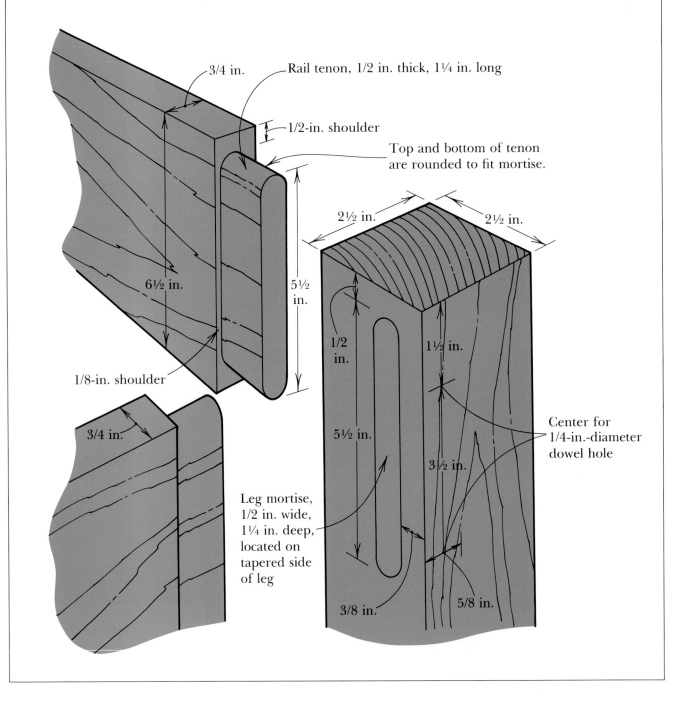

3/4 in.

Rail tenon, 1/2 in. thick, 1¼ in. long

1/2-in. shoulder

Top and bottom of tenon are rounded to fit mortise.

2½ in.

2½ in.

6½ in.

5½ in.

1/8-in. shoulder

3/4 in.

1/2 in.

1½ in.

5½ in.

3½ in.

Center for 1/4-in.-diameter dowel hole

Leg mortise, 1/2 in. wide, 1¼ in. deep, located on tapered side of leg

3/8 in.

5/8 in.

wood stops, screwed to the top of the jig at a right angle to the slot, confine the base of the router to keep the mortise 5½ in. long.

After wedging the leg blank in place, I adjust the router's plunge depth so that the bit will cut about 1/2 in. into the leg. Positioning the router so that the collar is in the jig's guide slot, I turn on the tool, plunge the bit into the leg, and mill the full length of the mortise, using slow, steady pressure (*photo 7-2*). I repeat this process with plunge depth adjusted to 1 in. (into the leg), and then 1¼ in. By milling the mortise in 3 stages, I don't risk forcing the bit or straining the router.

To mill the second mortise in each leg, I change the position of the leg in the jig. An adjacent face of the leg needs to face up, against the jig's slot, and the bottom of the leg needs to extend from the opposite end of the jig. Be sure to double-check the leg's position in the jig to make sure the mortise will be milled in the right place. The milling technique is the same. I use 3 separate depth adjustments on the plunge router, each time moving the router along the slot and between the stops on the jig. It takes me about 20 minutes to complete the mortises in all 4 legs.

Now I turn to the rails. First they have to be cut to size out of 1x8 stock. The end rails are 27 in. long and the side rails are 62½ in. long (including tenons). I rip and joint all 4 rails to a finished width of 6½ in. Rail tenons, which I'll mill next, need to be 1/2 in. thick, 5½ in. wide, and 1¼ in. long.

To mill the tenons, I use the router again, along with the same 1/2-in.-diameter straight bit I used to mill the mortises. The collar, however, should be detached from the router base. And instead of relying on a jig to hold the stock and guide the bit, I use a couple of special bar clamps. One clamp has double sets of feet. With this clamp, I can hold both side rails together (edge-to-edge, with their ends flush) and clamp them to the workbench at the same time.

7-2 The collar that extends below the router base rides in a 5/8-in.-wide slot as the bit is plunged into the leg to mill the mortise. Wood stops, screwed at a right angle to the slot, confine the router base to define the length of the mortise.

7-3 With 2 rails clamped together and to the work-bench, I use a straightedge clamp to guide the router base as I mill tenon cheeks on both rails. I use a 1/2-in. straight bit in the router, with bit depth adjusted to 1/8 in.

7-4 With the straightedge clamp positioned across the top edges of the rails and bit depth set at 1/2 in., I mill the shoulders that define the top and bottom of each tenon.

I attach the other clamp across both rails so that its straight, aluminum edge will guide the router base as I make shoulder and cheek cuts. I adjust bit depth to 1/8 in. and make my first pass near the end of the board. With the third pass, I make the shoulder cut, revealing the full cheek of the tenon (*photo 7-3*). I turn the rails over to make cheek and shoulder cuts on the opposite sides of both side-rail tenons. Then I give the end rails the same treatment.

The 1/2-in. shoulders at the tops and bottoms of the tenons can be cut with all 4 rails "ganged" together on their edges. Again, I use the straightedge clamp to guide the edge of the router base. With the clamp positioned across the top edges of the rails and bit depth set at 1/2 in., I make 3 passes (starting at the rail ends) to complete each set of shoulder cuts across all 4 rails (*photo 7-4*).

In order to fit into its leg mortise, the top and bottom of each tenon needs to be rounded over. I do this shaping with a rasp, test-fitting the tenons to make sure they mate well with the mortises.

The next step is to cut out 2 drawer openings in the "front" rail. As shown in drawing 7-C, each drawer opening is 3⅞ in. high and 21 in. wide. The openings begin 6 in. from either leg, or 6 in. from the tenon shoulders. Marking up the face of the rail, I lay out each opening so that its top edge is 1⅛ in. below the top edge of the rail.

A good jigsaw is a real asset when making straight, rectangular cutouts like these. But even with a good saw, I don't want to do this work freehand. I start by drilling a 3/8-in.-diameter access hole for the jigsaw blade. The hole should be just inside the layout lines, at the corner of the opening. This way, the blade will be aligned to start the first long cut (either the top or the bottom edge of the cutout). Now I screw a wood fence to the rail to guide the edge of the jigsaw base as I make the cut. I use my tape measure to make sure that the fence is parallel with the layout line. I also make sure to drive screws into the waste areas inside the cutout lines. Then I make the first long cut, taking care to keep the edge of the jigsaw base firmly against the fence. The remaining long cuts are made the same way, after repositioning the fence and drilling a new access hole for each cut (*photo 7-5*).

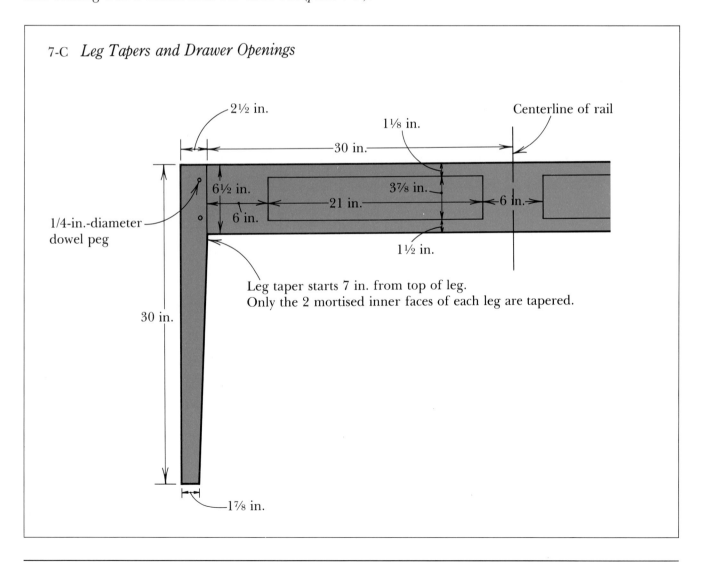

7-C *Leg Tapers and Drawer Openings*

2½ in.

1⅛ in.

Centerline of rail

30 in.

6½ in.

3⅞ in.

21 in.

6 in.

1/4-in.-diameter dowel peg

6 in.

1½ in.

Leg taper starts 7 in. from top of leg.
Only the 2 mortised inner faces of each leg are tapered.

30 in.

1⅞ in.

7-5 To make the long cuts for drawer openings in the front rail, I use a wooden straightedge to guide the base of my jigsaw. I screw the straightedge to the waste areas inside and parallel with the cutting line. To start each cut, I drill an access hole at the corner of the planned opening.

7-6 I start the end cuts for drawer openings in a corner access hole. To keep the cut square and straight, I use the edge of my square to guide the jigsaw base.

7-7 Leg sides with mortises are tapered. I cut the tapers on the table saw, using my taper jig. The jig is adjustable and designed to run against the saw's rip fence.

The short end cuts for each opening can also be made with the aid of a guide. Starting off in an access hole near a corner, I run the edge of the jigsaw base against the edge of my square, which I hold firmly against the rail (*photo 7-6*). After top, bottom, and end cuts are made, the opening will still need some cleaning up near the corners, where holes were located. After doing this work with the jigsaw, I go over the inside edges of both openings with a fine rasp and sandpaper to smooth out saw marks.

Now I taper the legs. As shown in drawing 7-C, only the 2 inside faces of each leg are tapered — the same faces of the leg that are mortised. Leg tapers start 7 in. from the top of each leg. The taper is very slight, leaving the bottom of the leg 1⅞ in. wide.

Tapered legs are fairly easy to cut on the table saw, using a taper jig. My shop-made jig has a fixed arm that runs against the saw's rip fence. Hinged to the fixed arm is an adjustable arm that holds the stock at an angle to the blade. I adjust the jig to make the taper layout line up parallel with the blade, then I tighten a thumbscrew on the adjustment arm to lock the arms in position. I also adjust the rip fence to align the blade with the taper layout. This setup stays the same as I make 2 taper cuts on each leg (*photo 7-7*). When all tapers have been cut, I use the jointer to clean up the freshly sawed edges. A single pass through the knives removes any saw marks, leaving a smooth surface.

Drawer Runners

Each drawer has 2 runners, located at the bottom corners of the drawer opening and extending horizontally between side rails (*drawing 7-D*). Made from 6/4 stock, each runner is 27½ in. long and has a rabbet 1/2 in. deep and 3/4 in. wide along one edge. The shoulder of the rabbet is positioned flush with the vertical edge of the opening. This guides the side of the drawer. The

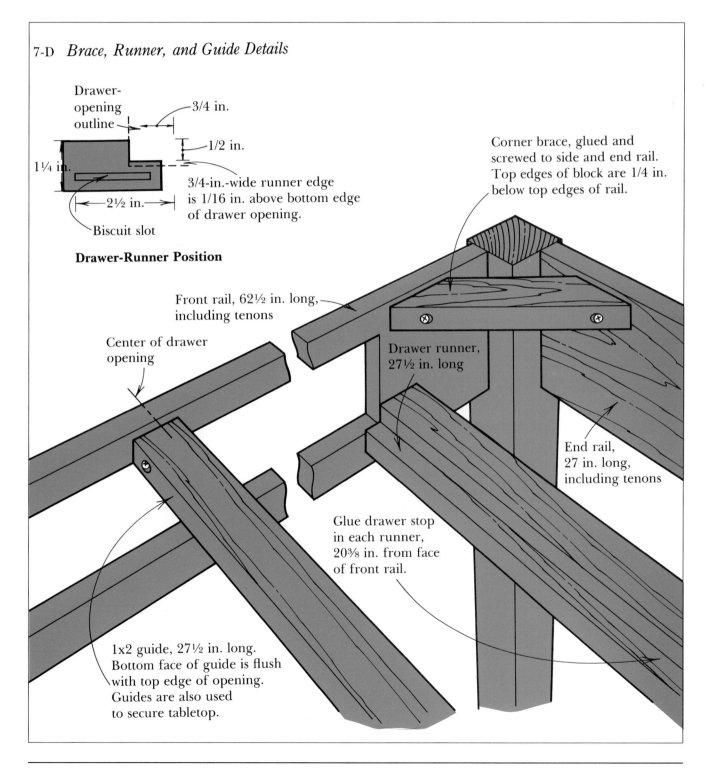

7-D *Brace, Runner, and Guide Details*

Drawer-opening outline

3/4 in.

1/2 in.

1¼ in.

3/4-in.-wide runner edge is 1/16 in. above bottom edge of drawer opening.

2½ in.

Biscuit slot

Drawer-Runner Position

Corner brace, glued and screwed to side and end rail. Top edges of block are 1/4 in. below top edges of rail.

Front rail, 62½ in. long, including tenons

Center of drawer opening

Drawer runner, 27½ in. long

End rail, 27 in. long, including tenons

Glue drawer stop in each runner, 20⅜ in. from face of front rail.

1x2 guide, 27½ in. long. Bottom face of guide is flush with top edge of opening. Guides are also used to secure tabletop.

7-8 (*left*)   Aligning the base of the biscuit joiner with layout lines on the inside face of the front rail, I mill a biscuit slot for the drawer runner.   **7-9** (*right*)   To mill slots in the ends of the drawer runners, I clamp each runner in the bench vise. Before making the slot, I position the centerline on the biscuit joiner's base even with the layout line on the runner.

horizontal edge of the rabbet sits 1/16 in. above the bottom edge of the drawer opening. This surface acts as a runner for the bottom edge of the drawer side, preventing the drawer from binding as it's opened and closed.

I use the table saw to cut the rabbets in the runners and the biscuit joiner to align and fasten the runners to the side rails. The runners are relatively small in section, so I use smaller biscuits to join them to the rails. To lay out biscuit locations, I carefully position the end of each guide against the drawer-opening rail, as noted above. Then I make a line across the joint as well as a line where the bottom edge of the guide meets the rail. I also make corresponding marks where each runner meets the table's back rail. This layout work shows me where to place the base of the biscuit joiner when milling the slots in the rail (*photo 7-8*) and in the runners (*photo 7-9*).

Assembly

Now it's time to join legs and rails and install drawer runners. The side rails are joined to the legs first. I spread some glue on both tenons of the drawer-opening rail, then fit the tenons in the leg mortises. A few taps with the shot-filled mallet gets each tenon partway into its mortise, then I snug up both joints with a long pipe clamp. Scrap pieces of wood, placed between the clamping feet and the legs, prevent the clamping feet from marring the legs.

I peg each tenon in its mortise with a pair of 1/4-in.-diameter dowels. Centers for dowel holes are shown in drawing 7-B. With a piece of tape wrapped around my 1/4-in. bit as a drill stop, I bore each dowel hole to a depth of 1¼ in. (*photo 7-10*). This ensures that the dowel will extend through the tenon and into the opposite cheek of the mortise, truly locking the joint fast. After dabbing some glue onto a 1½-in.-long dowel, I tap it into its hole (*photo 7-11*). The protruding 1/4 in. of dowel will be sanded flush with the leg after the glue dries. Once all 4 dowels have been driven into the subassembly (containing a side rail and 2 legs), I can remove the clamp and use it on the second subassembly.

When both side rails have been joined to their legs, I glue, clamp, and peg a single end rail to 2 legs. For this assembly sequence, the table base should be upside down, with legs pointing up. Now I turn to the drawer runners. Working quickly, I spread glue on the ends of one runner and on the biscuits I'll use to join it to the side rails. I install this runner in the location closest to the assembled end of the table. Then I spread some glue on the tenons of the "free" end rail and barely engage these tenons in their mortises. This leaves enough space between side rails for me to install the remaining runners, placing biscuits in slots to keep each joint aligned. When the final runner is in place, I clamp the legs firmly against the end rail (*photo 7-12*). I also install several

7-10 I use a pipe clamp to pull each end-rail tenon tight in its leg mortise while drilling out for a 1/4-in.-diameter dowel pin. A piece of tape on the drill bit reminds me to limit hole depth to 1¼ in.

7-12 I pull the final rail-to-post joints tight only after all the drawer runners have been glued and positioned between front and back rails.

7-11 Each mortise-and-tenon joint gets a pair of pegs. After spreading glue on each dowel, I drive it firmly into its hole. About 1/4 in. of the dowel should stand proud of the surface so that I can sand it flush after the glue dries.

pipe clamps across the side rails to pull these rails tightly against the drawer runners. Finally, I drill and peg the remaining mortise-and-tenon joints.

Stretchers

I cut and install the stretchers while the table base is still upside down on the workbench. There are 3 stretchers in all. The 2 short stretchers run parallel with the end rails, spanning the distance between legs. The long stretcher runs lengthwise, connect-

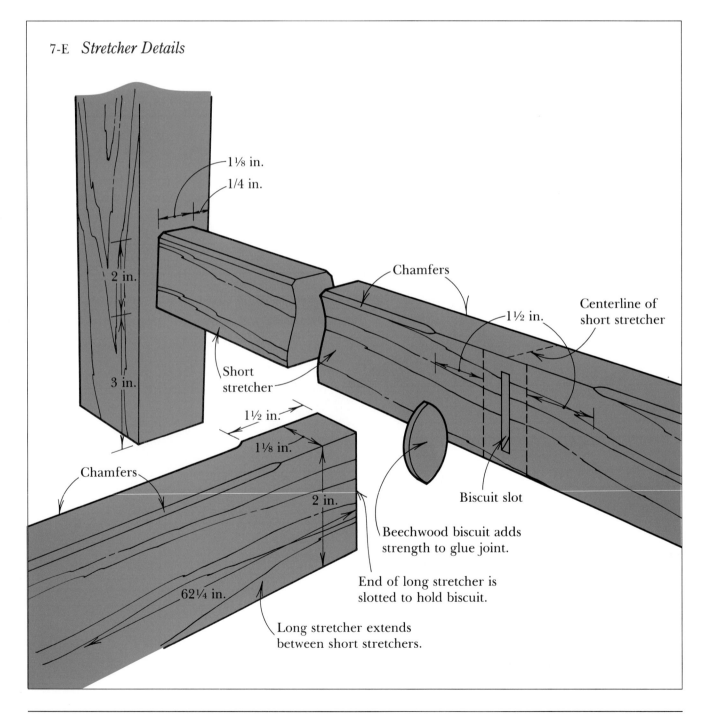

7-E *Stretcher Details*

1⅛ in.

1/4 in.

2 in.

3 in.

Short
stretcher

Chamfers

1½ in.

Centerline of
short stretcher

1½ in.

Chamfers

1⅛ in.

2 in.

62¼ in.

Biscuit slot

Beechwood biscuit adds
strength to glue joint.

End of long stretcher is
slotted to hold biscuit.

Long stretcher extends
between short stretchers.

ing both short stretchers at their midpoints. All 3 stretchers measure 1⅛ in. thick and 2 in. wide.

I cut the short stretchers to size first. As shown in drawing 7-E, these stretchers are positioned 3 in. up from the bottoms of the legs, and the outside face of each short stretcher is set 1/4 in. in from the outside face of each leg.

The ends of the short stretchers need to be cut at an angle that matches the inner taper of the legs. These cutoff lines can be marked by holding the stretcher across both legs, but before doing this, I check each end pair of legs to make sure that their outside edges (the untapered ones) are parallel. At rail level and at the bottom ends of the legs, the distance between outside edges should be identical. On my table, this measurement works out to 29½ in. A clamp, placed across the bottoms of the legs, keeps them parallel while I hold a stretcher in place and mark 2 cutoff lines (*photo 7-13*).

When both short stretchers have been marked, I make the end cuts on my motorized miter box. After adjusting the cutting angle (it works out to be about 1¼ degrees), I make a test cut just outside the layout line on the stretcher. This allows me to check the angle adjustment before cutting to the line.

When the short stretchers are cut, I position them between the legs, using clamps, if necessary, to hold them exactly in place.

7-14 With a stretcher piece placed on a nonskid pad, I chamfer its top edges, using the router and a chamfering bit.

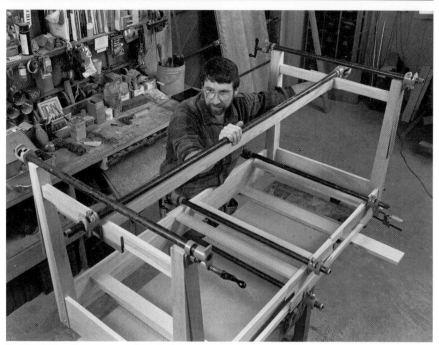

7-15 The long stretcher is installed after the 2 short stretchers are in place. Pipe clamps hold stretcher joints tight until the glue dries.

This enables me to measure the length of the long stretcher (62¼ in. on my table). This stretcher has right-angled end cuts that I make on the motorized miter box.

On many traditional tables, stretchers get some form of decorative treatment. Here, I chamfer the top corners of each stretcher, using a chamfering bit in the router (*photo 7-14*). As shown in drawing 7-E, chamfers stop 1½ in. shy of the intersection points between the short stretchers and the long stretcher.

I use biscuit joints to install the stretchers. While the short stretchers are in position, I lay out centers for biscuit slots on legs and stretcher ends. Because the stretchers are quite narrow, I adjust my biscuit joiner to mill short, shallow slots in legs and stretcher ends for the smallest-size biscuits. Once the slots are cut, I glue and clamp the short stretchers in place, then glue and clamp the long stretcher between the short stretchers (*photo 7-15*).

Corner Braces and Top Guides

Now it's finally time to turn the table base right-side up. There are just a few more parts to cut and install before I begin work on the drawers and tabletop. Each drawer needs a top guide to prevent the drawer from tipping downward as it's opened. These 2 guides also serve as additional fastening points for installing the tabletop.

Each 1x2 guide is centered along the top of its drawer opening. The bottom edge of the guide should be flush with the top edge of the opening (*drawing 7-D*). To install each guide, I pre-drill a pair of angled pilot holes near each end. Then I drive 1¼ in. bugle-head screws into the rails while holding the guide in position (*photo 7-16*).

The base also needs 4 corner braces. Connecting side and end rails, the braces stiffen the frame of the table, while also providing 4 more fastening points for the tabletop. When I install the top later, I'll simply center the base of the table on the underside of the top and drive a single 1⅝-in. screw through the bottom of each corner brace and into the top. I also drive 2 screws through each top drawer guide and into the top.

I cut the braces from 1x2 stock, making the 45-degree-angle end cuts on my motorized miter box. Braces should be long enough to just clear the inside corners of the legs, as shown in drawing 7-D. I install the braces with glue and 1¼-in. screws after predrilling pilot holes. The top of each brace should sit about 1/4 in. below the top edges of the rails. This will ensure that the tabletop gets pulled down tightly against the rails when it's installed.

Making the Drawers

The drawers for this table are designed so that drawer fronts will fit flush with their openings. Construction details are shown in drawing 7-F. The first thing I do is cut all the parts to their finished sizes. On the table saw, I rip the 3/4-in.-thick fronts and the 1/2-in.-thick sides to a width of 3¾ in. Then I adjust the rip fence so that it's 3¼ in. from the blade and rip drawer backs to width. Using the motorized miter box, I cut all these parts to their finished lengths: 20⅞ in. for the fronts, 20 in. for the sides, and 20⅜ in. for the backs. Drawer bottoms, cut from 1/4-in.-thick plywood, measure 20⁵⁄₁₆ in. by 19⅜ in.

7-16 I install the drawer guides by driving bugle-head screws at an angle in predrilled holes. The bottom face of the guide should be flush with the top edge of the drawer opening.

Next, I mill the half-blind dovetail joints used to connect the front of each drawer with its sides. My dovetail jig is designed so that the side pins can be milled at the same time as the front tails. Once the edges of a front and side piece have been positioned and clamped in the jig, I set up my router with a dovetail bit and with a collar that's matched to the fingers of the jig's template. Then I turn on the router and carefully guide the collar through the template to complete the tails and pins for a single joint (*photo 7-17*).

When all 4 joints are done, I go back to the table saw, replacing the blade with a wobble-type dado blade. Using the rip fence to guide each side and front, I mill 1/4-in.-wide, 1/4-in.-deep grooves for the drawer bottoms (*photo 7-18*). The groove should be located 1/4 in. from the bottom edges of these parts.

Next, I dado the sides to hold the back of the drawer. The wobble dado needs to be adjusted to make a 1/2-in.-wide cut. Depth of cut remains at 1/4 in. To line up the side so that the

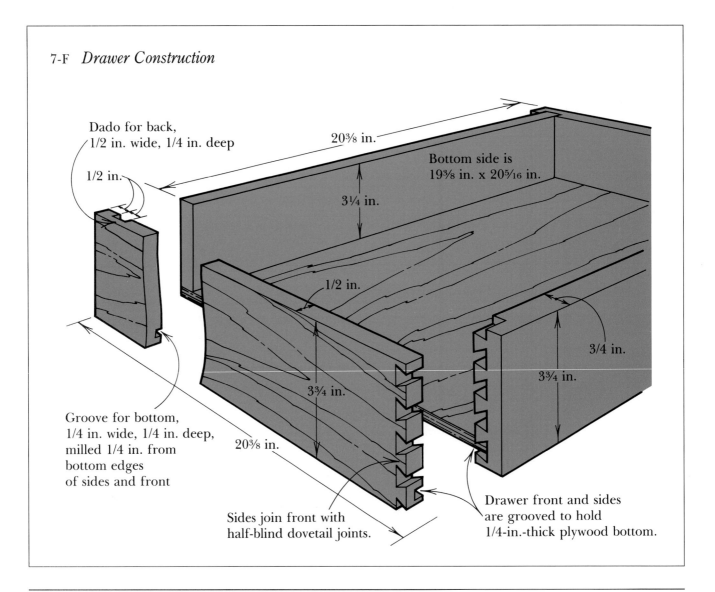

7-F *Drawer Construction*

Dado for back,
1/2 in. wide, 1/4 in. deep

1/2 in.

20⅜ in.

Bottom side is
19⅜ in. x 20⁵⁄₁₆ in.

3¼ in.

1/2 in.

3/4 in.

3¾ in.

3¾ in.

Groove for bottom,
1/4 in. wide, 1/4 in. deep,
milled 1/4 in. from
bottom edges
of sides and front

20⅜ in.

Sides join front with
half-blind dovetail joints.

Drawer front and sides
are grooved to hold
1/4-in.-thick plywood bottom.

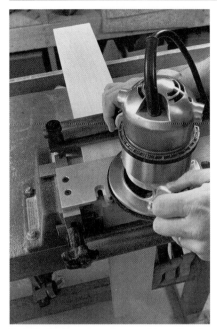

7-17 Using my dovetailing jig, I mill the pins in each drawer side at the same time as I mill the corresponding tails in the drawer front. The drawer front is held horizontally in the jig, while the side is held vertically.

7-18 I set up the dado blade in the table saw to mill a groove for the drawer bottom in each front and side piece. Blade width and height are both adjusted to 1/4 in., and the fence is set 1/4 in. from the blade.

7-19 With the dado blade adjusted for a 1/2-in.-wide, 1/4-in.-deep cut, I mill a dado in the drawer side that will hold the back of the drawer. I hold the edge of the side against the miter gauge and use a stop block, clamped to the rip fence, to align the cut.

dado will be cut 1/2 in. from its end, I clamp a gauge block to the rip fence on my side of the dado blade. Then I adjust the fence so that the gauge block is 1/2 in. away from the dado's cutting line. To make the dado cut in each side, I place the side with its end against the gauge block and its edge against the miter gauge (*photo 7-19*).

To assemble each drawer, I use a small brush to spread glue on dovetail joints, then I join the sides to the front of the drawer. The bottom goes in next. I don't glue it to sides or front. If the bottom can "float" in these grooves, it can expand and contract without stressing the rest of the drawer joinery. After spreading some glue in the side dadoes, I slide the back in place and nail through the dado joints with 1-in. brads. Then I turn the drawer upside down and use a framing square to keep the sides square with the front while I nail the bottom to the back (*photo 7-20*).

I don't worry about the drawer pulls until I've put the final coat of paint on the drawer. But now is a good time to drill a hole in each drawer front for the screw that will be used to install the knob. This is also the time to install some drawer stops, so that the drawers can't be closed beyond the point where their fronts are flush with the opening. The exact depth of your drawers will depend on the length of your sides and the depth of their dove-

7-20 To square drawer sides with the front, I hold a framing square against front and side edges as I nail the plywood drawer bottom to the back.

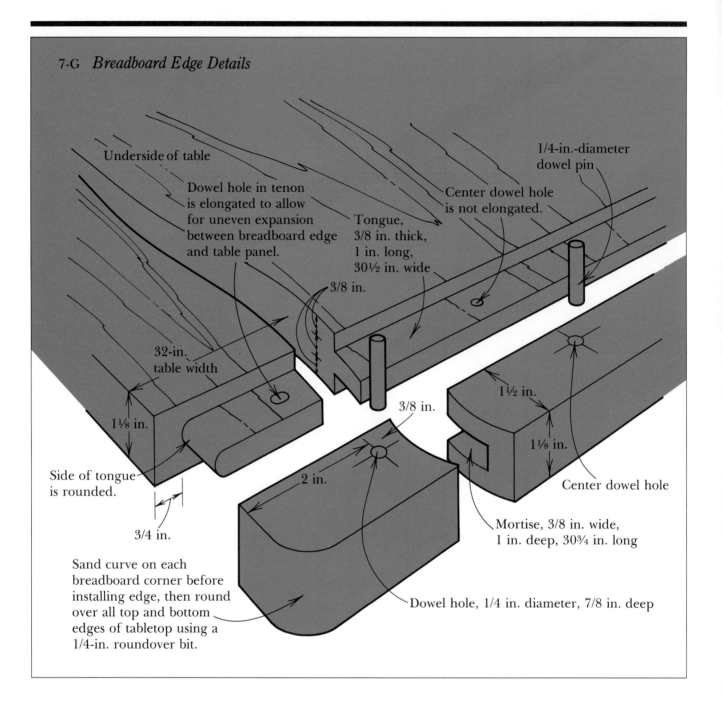

Underside of table

Dowel hole in tenon
is elongated to allow
for uneven expansion
between breadboard edge
and table panel.

Tongue,
3/8 in. thick,
1 in. long,
30½ in. wide

Center dowel hole
is not elongated.

1/4-in.-diameter
dowel pin

3/8 in.

32-in.
table width

1⅛ in.

Side of tongue
is rounded.

3/4 in.

3/8 in.

2 in.

1½ in.

1⅛ in.

Center dowel hole

Mortise, 3/8 in. wide,
1 in. deep, 30¾ in. long

Sand curve on each
breadboard corner before
installing edge, then round
over all top and bottom
edges of tabletop using a
1/4-in. roundover bit.

Dowel hole, 1/4 in. diameter, 7/8 in. deep

tail joints. When my drawer fronts are flush with their openings,
the sides extend 20⅜ in. into the table. I glue and nail a small
wood cleat to each drawer runner to act as a stop.

Finishing Up the Top

By now, I've had a chance to remove the clamps from the
cherry panel I glued up and give both sides of the panel a good
smoothing over. I start with a medium-grit belt on the belt sander
and switch to a fine-grit belt (for the top side of the panel) as
soon as excess glue and ridges at joint lines have been removed.

7-21 I mill the tongue for the tabletop's breadboard edge using the router and a 1/2-in. straight bit. A straightedge clamp, positioned across the width of the top and parallel with the tongue's shoulder line, guides the router as I make cheek cuts.

Panel ends need to be squared off, giving the panel a finished length (not including breadboard edges) of 77½ in. I make these 2 cuts with my circular saw. To guide the saw base for a straight, square cut, I position a straightedge clamp across the panel.

Now I can work on the breadboard edges. This traditional edge treatment is popular on tabletops because it covers the end grain at both ends of the tabletop, while also reducing the likelihood of warping. Each edge piece is usually grooved to fit over a tongue that is milled along the ends of the boards that make up the tabletop (*drawing 7-G*).

Each tongue needs to be 3/8 in. thick, 1 in. long, and 30½ in. wide. To mill this part of the joint, I chuck a 1/2-in.-diameter straight bit in the router and adjust bit depth to 3/8 in. Then I position my straightedge clamp across the panel top to guide the base of the router. I make the first pass at the end of the tongue, then make 2 more overlapping passes, the last one at the shoulder line (*photo 7-21*). Using this same technique, I mill both tongues to their final thickness of 3/8 in.

Instead of showing in the finished tabletop, the tongues are trimmed at the corners of the table so that they'll remain hidden inside the breadboard edges. Using a dovetail saw, I trim off 3/4 in. from the corners of each tongue (*photo 7-22*). Then, with a rasp, I round the sides of each tongue so that the tongue will fit into its mortise.

7-22 Using a dovetail saw, I trim the tongues at the corners of the table.

7-23 I mill the groove in each breadboard edge on the router table using a 1/2-in. straight bit. A featherboard, clamped to the table, helps to hold the stock firmly against the fence. Working inside the layout lines for the groove, I lower the edge down over the blade and then make a full pass before lifting the opposite end free of the bit.

7-24 The tongue-and-groove joint between each breadboard edge and the table panel is pinned with 3 dowels, rather than glued. The dowels are installed from the underside of the table so that they don't show from above. To allow for unequal movement between the edge and the end grain of the tabletop, I elongate the dowel holes near the corners of the top, using a fine rasp.

The breadboard edges are 1⅛ in. thick, 1½ in. wide, and 32 in. long. To mill the groove in each edge, I set up a 3/8-in.-diameter straight bit in the router table. The router table's fence should be positioned 3/8 in. from the bit. On the router table, I make 2 lines (perpendicular to the fence) to show the bit's cutting diameter so that I can keep track of the bit location as I lower the edge blank down over the bit.

Since cherry is fairly hard, it's safer to use 2 or more passes to complete each groove. For the first pass, bit height is kept at 1/2 in. Gripping the blank firmly, I slowly lower it down over the bit so that the bit enters the wood about 5/8 in. from the end of the blank (*photo 7-23*). Feeding the blank through the bit steadily, I raise the blank free when the bit reaches within 5/8 in. of the opposite end. Repeating this process with the bit raised a full inch above the table completes the groove.

I test-fit each breadboard edge over its tongue to make sure that it fits properly. Then I spend a couple of minutes at the drill press, using the drum sander to ease the outside corners of each piece.

Because end grain and edge grain will expand and contract at different rates, it's not a good idea to glue the breadboard edges in place. Instead, I peg them to the tongues, using three 1/4-in.-diameter dowels for each edge. The dowels are installed from underneath the table to keep them out of sight. Centers for the holes should be located 3/8 in. from the inside edge of the breadboard edge. The outer dowels should be 2 in. from the long edges of the table.

With a pipe clamp holding the breadboard edge tight against the shoulders of the tongue, I drill out the dowel holes, using tape on my drill bit to limit each hole's depth to 7/8 in. After all 3 holes are drilled, I remove the edge and elongate the outer holes using a round rasp (*photo 7-24*). This is an important step, because it will allow the panel and edge to move independently while the dowels still lock the edge in place.

To install each edge, I clamp it in place and spread a little glue on the part of each dowel that will end up just inside the wood, near the underside of the table. This will keep the dowel in place, without letting the glue get into the tongue-and-groove joint. A few gentle taps with the mallet should seat each dowel in its hole (*photo 7-25*). The dowels should be long enough to stand proud of the surface so they can be sanded flush after the glue dries.

Edges all around the table need rounding over. I chuck a 1/4-in. roundover bit in the router and go over both bottom and top edges. Now sanding is the only work that remains before applying finish. With a penetrating oil finish, the cherry tabletop can be a real showpiece, but only if you do a thorough sanding job. I like to use my random-orbit sander for this kind of work, but a conventional orbital sander will also work fine. It takes me about an hour to get the supersmooth surface I'm looking for, finishing up with 220-grit sandpaper (*photo 7-26*).

7-25 With the breadboard edge clamped firmly in place, I install the 1/4-in.-diameter dowel pins. Only the upper section of the dowel is dabbed with glue.

7-26 The cherry top deserves a generous amount of sanding in order to show off its tawny color and distinctive grain.

Chapter Eight

Chippendale Mirror

PROJECT PLANNING
Time: 2 days

Special hardware and tools:

(1) pint contact cement

(1) piece 24-in. x 30-in. high-pressure plastic laminate

(1) 14½-in. x 19-in., 1/4-in.-thick mirror

Wood:

(1) 5-ft 1x12 mahogany

Cut in half, planed to a 5/16-in. thickness, and then edge-glued to make a panel approximately 22¼ in. x 30 in. for fretwork.

(1) 8-ft 1x3 mahogany

Frame and overlay molding

(1) sheet 15-in. x 19½-in. 1/4-in.-thick plywood

Mirror backer piece

THIS ornate mirror is a good example of the Chippendale style of furniture that came to the United States from England around the middle of the eighteenth century. Like the Gothic-style houses popular in that era, Chippendale furniture is characterized by elaborate decoration. With patterns, curves, and other highly worked details, Chippendale furniture was a status symbol for well-to-do families on both sides of the Atlantic.

At Historic Deerfield, in western Massachusetts, I found an antique Chippendale mirror to serve as an authentic model for my own design. The intricately curved fretwork panels contrast nicely with a fairly simple frame. Like many Chippendale antiques, the Deerfield mirror is made from mahogany, a wood that lends itself well to carving and curved details because is has a consistent, knot-free grain.

Though this project focuses on making a mirror frame and fretwork, you could easily use many of these techniques to make a picture frame, with or without the fretwork.

My first task in this project is to make a panel from which the fretwork can be cut. Setting up my thickness planer, I run a mahogany 1x12 through the planer repeatedly to produce a board that's 5/16 in. thick. When making multiple passes like this, it's important to remove an equal amount of material from each side of the board.

After cutting my 5-ft board in half and jointing the 2 mating edges, I glue the boards together, making a panel about 22¼ in. wide and 30 in. long. When the glue dries, I remove the clamps, scrape hardened glue from around the joint, and give both sides of the panel a good sanding.

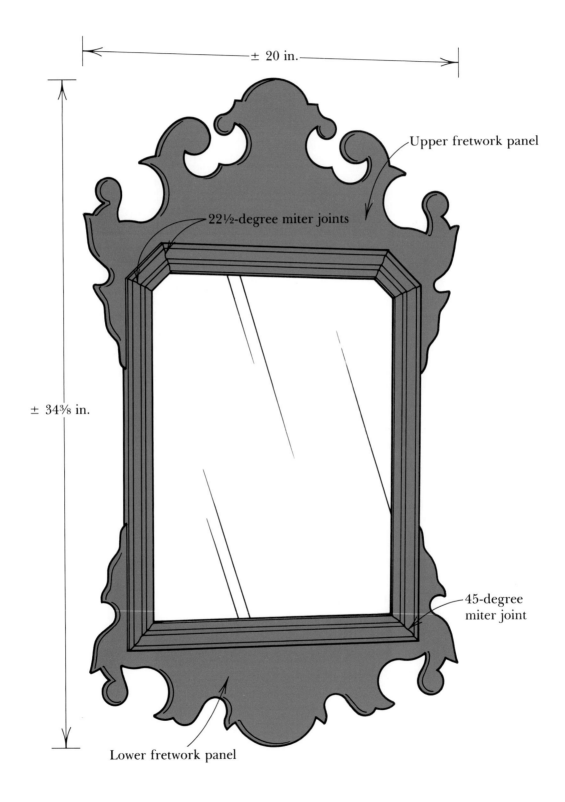

± 20 in.

Upper fretwork panel

22½-degree miter joints

± 34⅜ in.

45-degree
miter joint

Lower fretwork panel

Note: Miter cuts for angled upper corners are laid out
from outside edges of frame, before rabbets are milled.

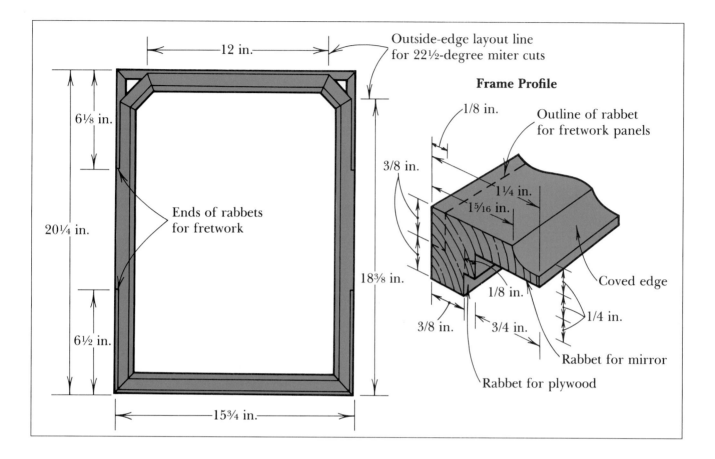

Making the Frame

As shown in drawing 8-B, the frame has a cross section that is
"stepped" at the back and delicately coved at the front. The
stepped back has 2 rabbets — one that will hold the 1/4-in.-thick
mirror and one for the plywood backer piece that covers and pro-
tects the mirror.

To make the frame members, I joint one edge of an 8-ft-long
1x3 and then rip out a board that's 1⁹/₃₂ in. wide. After jointing
the freshly sawed edge, the stock should have a final width of 1¼
in. I take this piece over to the router table to mill a very slight
cove along one edge of the piece. To do the milling, I set up a
1/2-in. cove bit in the router table and attach a wood auxiliary
fence to the standard fence. Apart from being higher than the
standard fence, the auxiliary fence enables me to install a vertical
featherboard, which does a good job of holding the stock down
against the table as I mill the cove. A horizontal featherboard,
clamped to the table, holds the stock against the fence during the
milling operation.

8-2 The coved side of the frame member runs against the table saw's rip fence as I make 2 vertical cuts. The first is 3/4 in. deep; the second is 7/8 in. deep.

8-1 The first step in making the mirror frame is to mill a slight cove along one edge of the frame blank. The router table is fitted with a wood auxiliary fence, and I do the milling using only part of a 1/2-in. cove bit's profile. Featherboards hold the blank against the fence and the table.

8-3 To complete the stepped profile on the back side of the frame, I make 2 more cuts. For these cuts, the rip fence guides the coved edge of the frame member.

In order to get the delicate cove shown in the frame profile (*drawing 8-B*), I expose only the top part of the bit above the table. To fine-tune bit height and fence position, I run some scrap stock (3/4 in. thick and 1¼ in. wide) through the setup, making adjustments until the profile is right. Then I run the 8-ft length through the setup (*photo 8-1*).

To cut the double rabbets at the back of the mirror frame, I go back to the table saw. It takes 4 separate cuts to complete the profile. For the first cut, I set the fence 1/4 in. away from the saw blade and adjust blade height to 3/4 in. A featherboard, clamped to the saw table, helps to hold the coved side of the stock against the fence as I make a vertical cut.

For the second cut, I raise the blade to a height of 7/8 in. and move the fence so that it's 1/2 in. away from the blade. Assisted by the featherboard, I once again run the coved side of the piece against the rip fence to make a vertical cut that's parallel with the first cut (*photo 8-2*).

To complete the rabbet for the mirror, I adjust blade height to 1/2 in. and set the rip fence 3/4 in. from the far edge of the blade. I make this cut with the coved edge of the stock facing up and held against the rip fence. Then I lower the blade to a height of 1/4 in. and reposition the rip fence so that it's 7/8 in. from the far edge of the blade. To complete the rabbet for the plywood back, I run the piece through this setup with its coved edge facing up and against the rip fence (*photo 8-3*).

Building the Frame

My strategy for building the mirror frame is unconventional but effective. I actually cut and assemble the frame with 4 square corners, then I "transform" the upper corners by adding a pair of short, angled sections.

The first step in this process takes place at the motorized miter box (*photo 8-4*). With the saw adjusted for a 45-degree-angle cut, I

8-4 On the motorized miter box, I miter the corners of all 4 frame members, taking care to cut each miter about 1/8 in. longer than necessary.

8-5 Using a picture framer's trimmer, I trim the frame members to final length. The razor-sharp knife on the trimmer slices off a thin shaving each time I pull the lever.

8-6 After spreading glue on the miter joints, I clamp the frame together, using a set of picture-frame clamps. By tightening wing nuts on the threaded rods, the square angles are pulled closer together.

cut a pair of sides (20⅜ in. long) and top and bottom pieces (15⅞ in. long.) These lengths are 1/8 in. longer than necessary. (*For finished lengths, see drawing 8-B.*)

By purposely cutting the 4 frame members slightly long, I leave room for trimming each joint down on my picture framer's trimmer. This special tool is the mainstay of any picture-framing shop. Its chief moving parts are 2 razor-sharp knives designed to remove the thin shaving from the end of any frame member positioned against one of the tool's 2 adjustable fences. Holding each frame member in place, I pull the lever to actuate the trimming knife, working my way toward the line in tiny increments (*photo 8-5*). In addition to promoting exceptional accuracy, this technique leaves a mirror-smooth miter that will make each joint nearly invisible. For this reason, I make sure to trim a little from both ends of each frame member.

I use a picture-frame clamp to assemble the frame. There are quite a few different types of picture-frame clamps. Mine consist of four 90-degree aluminum angles connected to one another by lengths of threaded rod. By turning wing nuts at each corner, I can force the angles together. To do a preliminary adjustment on my corner clamp, I dry-fit the 4 frame members together. Then I spread some glue on each joint, position the frame members inside the clamp, and gradually clamp the frame tight and square (*photo 8-6*).

Fretwork

While the glue in the frame is setting up, I can make the top and bottom fretwork panels that embellish the frame. This part of the project is an interesting mix of tradition and technology. My fretwork design is just like the fretwork on the antique mirror, but I've enlarged the pattern about 1½ times. Behind this authentic shape, I use a layer of plastic laminate to add much-needed strength and stability to both thin mahogany panels. I glue the laminate to the back of the panel, or blank, before cutting out both patterns. The thin (1/16 in.) layer of laminate won't be visible in the finished mirror, but it will help the fretwork survive with a high resistance to warps or cracks.

To prepare the 5/16-in.-thick blank for laminating, I go over it one last time with the belt sander, smoothing out any surface irregularities that might stand in the way of a good bond between wood and laminate. When I'm done sanding, I brush off the back of the blank to remove loose sawdust.

No matter how careful you are, contact cement is messy to work with. I protect my workbench with a large sheet of paper placed beneath the fretwork blank. Pouring a thick trail of cement onto the blank, I use a scrap piece of laminate to spread the material uniformly over the surface (*photo 8-7*). The back of the laminate sheet gets the same treatment.

8-7 Using a scrap piece of laminate, I spread contact cement evenly over the back surface of the plastic laminate sheet. The back of the fretwork blank has just received its thin layer of cement.

8-8 After joining the cemented surfaces together, I roll out any bubbles or gaps beneath the laminate. Using heavy pressure, I work from the center of the panel toward the edges.

8-9 Working with a stiff cardboard pattern, I trace the upper and lower fretwork curves onto the blank.

Depending on temperature and humidity, the contact cement should lose most of its tackiness after about 15 minutes. When my finger can no longer stick to the cement on the blank or laminate, I know that the adhesive is ready to do its work. I lift the laminate up over the blank and adhere one corner first. Bowing the laminate down slightly, I gradually flatten it out onto the blank, working away from the adhered corner. To work out any bubbles or gaps between substrate and laminate, I go over the laminate with a rubber "J" roller (*photo 8-8*).

After turning the blank over so that its good side faces up, I use patterns to trace the outlines of both fretwork sections onto the wood (*photo 8-9*). Drawing 8-C shows scaled-down versions of both fretwork pieces. When both patterns have been traced onto the blank, I cut the blank in half on the table saw, separating the top and bottom fretwork pieces. This will make it easier to maneuver the stock as I cut out the intricate patterns.

In the old days, a cabinetmaker would have cut out these intricate patterns by hand, using a coping saw. Here in the workshop, I'm fortunate to have a scroll saw, a power tool that excels at cutting tight curves. Held tightly between the pins of a U-shaped arm, the scroll saw's tiny blade moves up and down through the material being cut. By turning a dial, I can adjust the speed, or strokes per minute, to match the thin blade I'm using with the thickness and hardness of the material I'm cutting. To cut the intricate curves, I use a slow feed rate, moving the blank around on the table to keep the blade on the cutting line (*photo 8-10*). I cut the sharp corners last, after most of the waste has been removed.

Both fretwork panels are sized so that their straight inside edges will fit in rabbets that are milled along the outer-back edge of the frame. The 1/8-in.-deep, 3/8-in.-wide rabbets extend fully along the top and bottom of the frame but only partially up and down the sides. To confirm the rabbet layout shown in drawing 8-B, it's a good idea to place each fretwork panel over the frame and check where the rabbets in frame sides should stop.

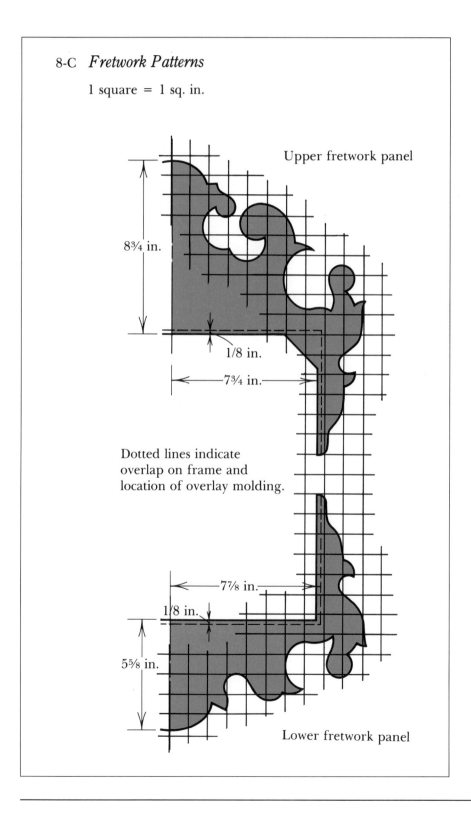

8-C *Fretwork Patterns*

1 square = 1 sq. in.

Upper fretwork panel

8¾ in.

1/8 in.

7¾ in.

Dotted lines indicate overlap on frame and location of overlay molding.

7⅞ in.

1/8 in.

5⅝ in.

Lower fretwork panel

8-10 The intricate curves of the fretwork pieces require quite a bit of careful cutting on the scroll saw.

Before the rabbets are milled, it's important to lay out the 22½-degree-angle cuts that will later be made as the square upper corners of the frame are transformed to angled corners. As shown in drawing 8-B, the angled cuts in the top frame member are laid out 6 in. from the frame's vertical centerline. The angled cuts in frame sides are laid out 18⅜ in. from the bottom corners of the frame.

To mill the rabbets, I set up a 1/2-in. straight bit in the router table. Only 1/8 in. of the bit should show beyond the fence, and bit height should be 3/8 in. A gauge block, clamped to the fence and aligned with the trailing edge of the bit, shows me where to make the plunge cut to start 2 of the 4 side rabbets. The 2 remaining side rabbets require the side to be slid free of the bit, so for these cuts I align the gauge block with the bit's leading edge. The top and bottom rabbets are simply milled all the way across (*photo 8-11*).

The end of each side rabbet needs to be squared up to hold the corner of the fretwork panel. I cut this short shoulder line with a sharp utility knife and then use a chisel to pare out the waste.

Top-Corner Treatment

I remove the clamps from the frame when the glue has dried. To add an extra measure of strength, I use my pneumatic brad driver to drive a 1-in. brad into each miter joint. The brad should be driven within 1/4 in. of the back side of the frame. Hammering these brads in place might jar the joints loose, but this isn't a problem with my pneumatic brad driver.

The next step is to transform the square top corners of the

8-11 To mill the small rabbets in the frame that will hold the fretwork panels, I use a 1/2-in. straight bit in the router table. Bit height is adjusted to 3/8 in., and the fence is positioned to show just 1/8 in. of the bit. A gauge block, clamped over the bit, helps me to start and stop the rabbets on frame sides.

frame into 45-degree corners. As shown in drawing 8-D, the back portions of the "original" top corners will remain intact, holding the frame together even while I alter its top corners. After I remove the 1/4-in.-thick top section of each upper corner, I'll replace it with a short, angled section of molding. The first step in altering the corners is to make a pair of 22½-degree miter cuts on either side of each top corner.

With my motorized miter box adjusted for a 22½-degree cut, I position the frame carefully on the saw table and against the fence. Then I make a shallow cut just inside 2 of the 4 layout lines, allowing the blade to penetrate only 1/4 in. into the frame. To make the remaining 2 cuts, I swing the saw 22½ degrees on the other side of zero (*photo 8-12*).

To remove the waste between each pair of saw kerfs, I chuck a

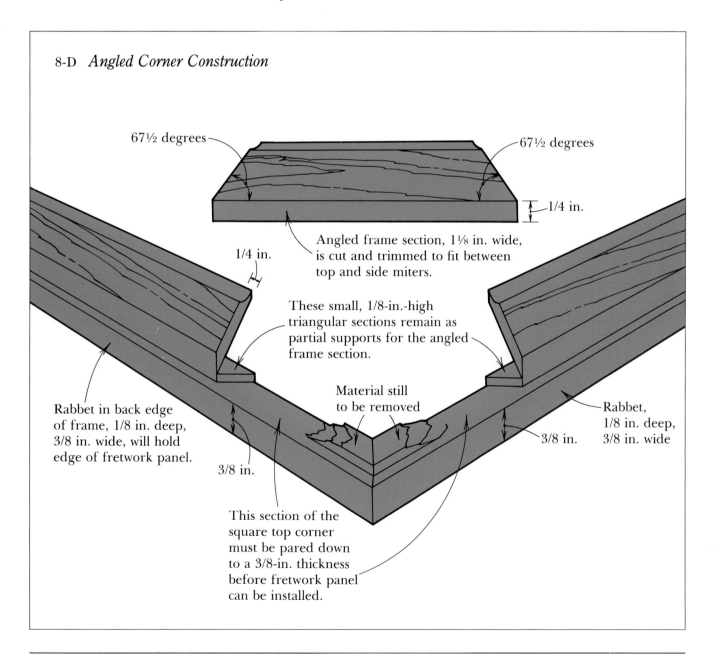

8-D *Angled Corner Construction*

67½ degrees

67½ degrees

1/4 in.

Angled frame section, 1⅛ in. wide, is cut and trimmed to fit between top and side miters.

1/4 in.

These small, 1/8-in.-high triangular sections remain as partial supports for the angled frame section.

Material still to be removed

Rabbet in back edge of frame, 1/8 in. deep, 3/8 in. wide, will hold edge of fretwork panel.

Rabbet, 1/8 in. deep, 3/8 in. wide

3/8 in.

3/8 in.

This section of the square top corner must be pared down to a 3/8-in. thickness before fretwork panel can be installed.

8-12 To create the angled treatment at the top corners of the frame, I start at the motorized miter box. With the saw adjusted for a 22½-degree-angle cut, I cut just 1/4 in. into the frame member. I make a pair of cuts at each top corner.

8-13 With a mortising bit chucked in the router, I remove the waste between each pair of kerfs at the top corners of the frame.

8-14 I use a sharp chisel to pare away the waste that remains in each corner of the frame.

8-15 The short pieces that fit into the frame's cutout sections have 22½-degree end cuts. After trimming on the picture framer's trimmer, each piece is glued in place.

mortising bit in the router and adjust bit depth to 1/4 in. Then I carefully "freehand" the router over each corner, taking care to keep the bit within the kerfs (*photo 8-13*). Any waste that remains in the corner can be removed using a sharp chisel (*photo 8-14*).

Now I can cut the short, angled pieces. First I take the remaining piece of frame molding over to the table saw to cut off the stepped back portion. Setting the fence 1/4 in. away from the blade, I make a rip cut, holding the flat section (with the coved edge) against the fence. Then I readjust the rip fence to remove 1/8 in. from the width of the molding. I make this cut with the coved edge against the rip fence, leaving the molding 1⅛ in. wide (*drawing 8-D*).

The short frame sections for the "new" angled corners are mitered on the motorized miter box and then trimmed to final length on the picture framer's trimmer. As with the other frame members, I leave about 1/16 in. of excess to be shaved from each end on the trimmer. Taking each corner piece from the trimmer to the frame and back again, I fine-tune the fit by paring away thin shavings. When both pieces fit exactly, I glue them in place (*photo 8-15*).

Before the fretwork panels can be installed, there is a small amount of trimming to be done in both top corners. As shown in drawing 8-D, the square sections of the top corners are 1/8 in. higher than they should be, even after the angled corner pieces are installed. Calling again on my chisel, I pare out this waste.

Instead of using conventional wood glue to join the fretwork panels to the frame, I use hot-melt adhesive. This type of glue sets quickly, so I don't have to set aside the assembly while the glue dries. With the frame placed on the workbench, I run a bead of hot-melt glue in the rabbeted sections of the frame, then quickly set the panels in their rabbets (*photo 8-16*). For added strength, I use my pneumatic brad driver to drive several 5/8-in. brads through each fretwork panel and into the frame.

Now fretwork and frame need a thorough sanding. I use a fine-grit disk on my random-orbit sander to go over the entire front of the mirror. I pay particular attention to the joints where the fretwork meets the frame. It's important for these areas to be flat, since they'll be covered by a thin overlay of molding.

Making and Installing the Molding

The decorative overlay molding starts out rectangular in section. Taking what remains of my 1x3 stock, I rip and joint a piece 3/4 in. thick and 7/8 in. wide. To achieve the final profile, shown in drawing 8-E, I begin with the router table, using a 1/4-in. ogee bit. To get the right profile out of my ogee bit, I need to run my stock through the bit at an angle, using a couple of beveled guide boards. I tack a guide board to the fence, with its 30-degree bevel

8-16 I fasten the fretwork panels to the frame with hot-melt glue. Using the hot-melt gun, I run a bead of the adhesive in the rabbeted section of the frame. I'll have to join the panel to the frame quickly, before the glue starts to set.

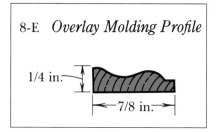

8-E *Overlay Molding Profile*

1/4 in.

7/8 in.

8-17 I mill the curved profile of the molding on the router table, using an ogee bit. To achieve the proper orientation between blank and bit, I build a jig from a couple of beveled boards. Positioned with its square edges against the auxiliary fence and the table is a board with a 30-degree bevel. A board with a 60-degree bevel is clamped to the table. Together, these guides form a 90-degree angle.

8-18 To remove a sharp inside edge on the molding, I run it through the jointer. The jointer's fence is set up to show only about 1/8 in. of the knives, as if I were milling a small rabbet. To complete the profile, I'll use the table saw to rip the molding to a final thickness of 1/4 in.

facing out and its square edge resting on the table. A second guide board with a 60-degree bevel is positioned to meet the first board. Together, the boards form a right-angled cradle for the stock, tilting it at a 30-degree angle to the bit. This setup, shown in photo 8-17, includes a vertically positioned featherboard that helps to hold the stock down against the guide boards.

To check the height of the bit and the position of each guide board, I run some scrap pieces through the setup, comparing the results to the shape of the final profile I want. When the setup checks out, I mill the mahogany blank.

My work on the router table doesn't quite complete the molding profile. I still need to remove a sharp section along what will become the inner edge of the molding. To do this, I set up the fence on my jointer as if I were going to mill a very narrow (1/8-in.-wide) rabbet. With the fence this far over on the jointer table, there's not much horizontal surface to guide the stock. So I carefully run the inner edge of the molding against the fence, letting the planer blades mill a small flat section (*photo 8-18*).

Finally, I rip the molding to a finished thickness of 1/4 in. This is done on the table saw, using the rip fence to guide the waste edge of the stock.

Now the overlay molding can be installed. To cut and fit these miter joints, I use the same procedure that I followed when building the frame. The initial miter cuts are made on the motorized miter box, allowing for a very slight excess to be shaved off on the picture framer's trimmer. It's best to take measurements for side, top, bottom, and corner molding pieces directly from the completed frame. In the finished mirror, the outer edge of the overlay molding should overlap the joint between frame and fretwork by about 1/8 in. Miter joints in the overlay molding should align exactly over miter joints in frame members. Working my way around the frame, I attach each molding piece with glue and 5/8-in. brads driven into the thickest part of the frame, also gluing miter joints together (*photo 8-19*).

At the top corners of the assembly, the back of the fretwork may need to be trimmed so that the mirror can fit into its recess. I use a router and a 1/4-in. carbide-tipped straight bit to trim these small triangular sections before setting the mirror into the back of the frame.

With the mirror in place, I cut and install the 1/4-in.-thick plywood back (*photo 8-20*). The back should slip into its rabbeted recess easily; avoid a snug fit, since this could cause problems if the back expands. Once the back is in place, I secure it by driving a couple of 1/2-in. brads into each side and end. I take care to angle each brad away from the mirror when driving it.

8-19 The molding covers the joints between fretwork panels and frame members. After cutting and trimming the molding pieces, I glue them to the frame and to each other. Using my pneumatic brad driver, I secure each piece with a few 5/8-in. brads.

8-20 The frame is designed to hold a 1/4-in.-thick mirror and a 1/4-in.-thick plywood backer panel. With the frame facedown, I install the plywood backer panel over the mirror.

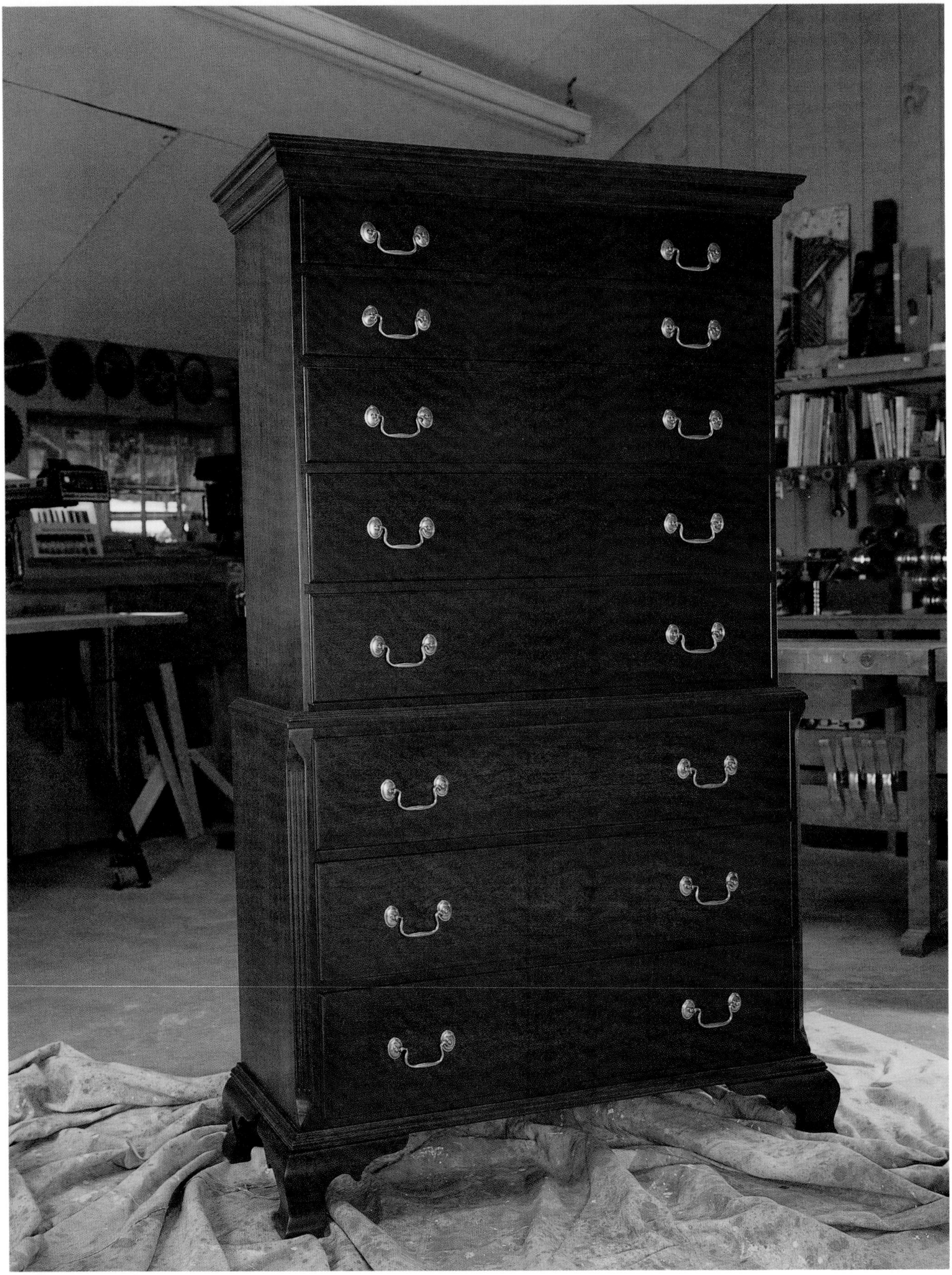

Chapter Nine

Chest on Chest

T HE traditional chest on chest is a storage solution that has stood the test of time. Long before master-bedroom suites and walk-in closets came into style, this king-size piece of furniture could be found in many a home.

At Historic Deerfield, in western Massachusetts, I found the model for my version of this classic piece. I learned that the antique Deerfield chest on chest had been made by a local craftsman over a century ago. I admired the dovetail joints between chest rails and sides and also noted that the drawer sides had been dovetailed to the drawer fronts. This fellow did a fine job of creating moldings and shaping the curved legs. And of course, the cherry he used to build the piece has gained a deep, rich color over the years.

Panel Work

I need a total of 4 cherry panels — a pair for the upper chest and a pair for the lower chest. I also need 4 pine panels, which will become the tops and bottoms of individual chests. It takes me the better part of an afternoon to cut stock to length (see the wood list for this project), orient the boards in each panel (selecting a good side of each cherry board to face out, while maintaining an alternating end-grain pattern in the panel), joint board edges, mill biscuit joints, and, finally, glue and clamp the panels together.

Each of the 4 panels for the upper chest are made from a 1x8 board and a pair of 1x6 boards. So the rough width of all panels is about 18 in. The cherry side panels for the upper chest need to have a rough length of 36 in. The pine top and bottom panels for the upper chest should be about 40 in. long before trimming. I make the cherry side panels for the lower chest about 30 in. long. The

PROJECT PLANNING

Time: 5 days

Special hardware and tools:

(16) large-size bale pulls (brass or brass-plated)

Wood:

(all wood is cherry unless otherwise noted)

for the upper chest

(1) 6-ft 1x8
(1) 12-ft 1x6

Sides. Cut two 36-in.-long 1x8 boards and four 36-in.-long 1x6 boards, then glue up 2 side panels, using a single 1x8 and two 1x6s for each panel.

(1) 8-ft 1x8 pine
(1) 14-ft 1x6 pine

Top and bottom. Cut two 40-in.-long 1x8s and four 40-in.-long 1x6s, then glue up 2 panels (two 1x6s and one 1x8 for each) approximately 18 in. wide and 40 in. long.

(1) 10-ft 1x6

Rails

(1) 7-ft 1x10
(1) 6-ft 1x8
(1) 7-ft 1x6

Drawer fronts and runners

(1) 12-ft 1x8 pine
(1) 6-ft 1x8 pine
(1) 12-ft 1x6 pine

Drawer sides and backs. Plane this stock to a 1/2-in. thickness and refer to cutting list (with drawing 9-G) for sizing.

(1) 7-ft 5/4 x 6

Cornice molding (top and bottom profiles)

(1) 6-ft 1x3 pine

Backer board for cornice

153

pine top panel for the lower chest has a rough length of about 48 in., and I make it from three 1x6s. I glue up the pine bottom panel for the lower chest from two 1x6s and a single 1x8. It also has a rough length of about 48 in.

Fortunately, I have enough pipe clamps in the shop to glue up all the panels at once. When I come back the next morning, I remove the clamps and scrape hardened glue from both sides of all the panels. With a fine-grit sanding belt in the belt sander, I give the "good" sides of all the cherry panels a thorough sanding. The cherry and pine panel sides that will be unseen in the finished piece can do with just a once-over sanding.

To cut the panels to their finished sizes, I start out by jointing an edge of each panel. This gives me a straight, square edge to run against the table saw's rip fence as I cut the panels to width. But instead of matching the distance between the rip fence and the blade to finished panel widths, I allow for an extra 1/32 in. This way, I can go back to the jointer and mill these freshly sawed edges smooth and square. Final panel widths (without the extra 1/32 in.) are as follows. For the upper chest: cherry sides, 16⅝ in.; pine top and bottom, 16¼ in. For the lower chest: cherry sides, 17 in.; pine top, 15¼ in.; pine bottom, 17¾ in.

Using my panel cutter on the table saw, I square the ends of all the panels while cutting them to their final lengths. The upper chest cherry sides are 35½ in. long, while the pine top and bottom panels are 39 in. long. The lower chest cherry sides are 28 in. long; pine top and bottom panels are 41¼ in. long.

The back edges of all 4 cherry sides need to be rabbeted to hold a 1/4-in.-thick plywood back. I do this milling on the table saw, using the dado cutter. The cutter's width should be adjusted to 3/4 in. By fastening a wood auxiliary fence to the rip fence, I can expose only 3/8 in. of the dado cutter to the stock. The remaining width of the cutter is covered by the wood fence. Cutter height should be 3/8 in. Running the back-inside edge of each side through this setup gives me 4 rabbets, each 3/8 in. wide and 3/8 in. deep (*photo 9-1*).

9-1 With the dado cutter set up in the table saw, I rabbet the back edge of a cherry panel. This rabbet, which will hold the plywood back of the chest, is 3/8 in. wide and 3/8 in. deep. A wood auxiliary fence covers all but 3/8 in. of the dado's cutting width, also guiding the edge of the panel.

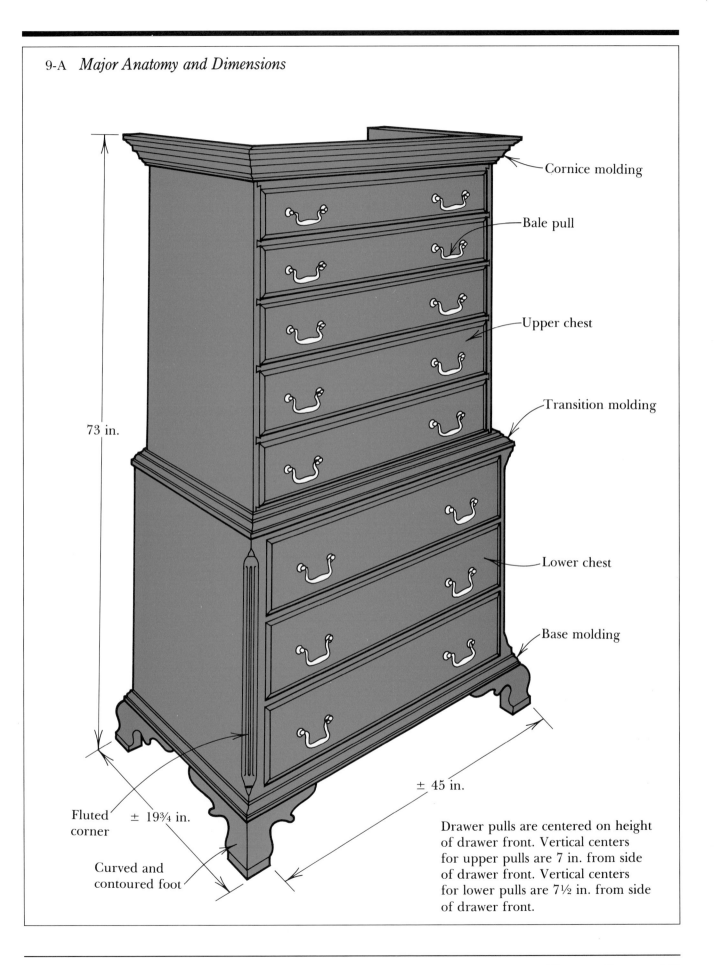

Cornice molding

Bale pull

Upper chest

Transition molding

Lower chest

Base molding

73 in.

Fluted corner

± 19¾ in.

Curved and contoured foot

± 45 in.

Drawer pulls are centered on height of drawer front. Vertical centers for upper pulls are 7 in. from side of drawer front. Vertical centers for lower pulls are 7½ in. from side of drawer front.

Before replacing the dado cutter with a saw blade, I adjust the fence to expose the full 3/4-in. thickness of the cutter. With this setup, I can rabbet the top and bottom edges of the lower-chest cherry sides to receive top and bottom panels. These rabbets should be 3/8 in. deep and 3/4 in. wide.

Making the Upper Chest

The upper chest has 6 rails, which separate the drawers and also help to hold the chest together. I use dovetail joints where the rails meet the sides. The 4 central rails join the sides with full dovetails; the top and bottom rails join the sides with half-dovetails (*drawing 9-B*).

On the inside face of each side, I lay out the locations of the rails and the drawer runners. I mark the 3/4-in. thickness of the rails on the sides and extend the line for the top edge of each rail to mark where the top edge of the drawer runner should go. Then I make a mark across these layout lines, 2⅝ in. in from the front edges of the sides. This gives me the length of the slots that will be milled to join the rails to the sides.

I could mill each slot in a single pass with my 3/4-in. dovetail bit, but because cherry is fairly hard, it's better to make an initial pass with a straight bit to remove most of the waste from the slot. I chuck a 3/8-in. straight bit in the router and adjust bit depth to 3/8 in. Then I use my straightedge clamp to guide the edge of the router base as I mill each slot. The clamp must be positioned across the side and parallel with the slot layout. Centering the bit between the marks for each 3/4-in.-thick rail, I mill six 2⅝-in.-long slots in each side (*photo 9-2*).

When I've milled all 12 slots, I replace the 3/8-in. straight bit with a 3/4-in. dovetail bit and simply repeat the milling operation, using the straightedge clamp as before (*photo 9-3*). The depth of the dovetail bit should be 7/16 in.

Now the rails can be cut to size and milled so that rail ends will

9-2 (*below left*) Using a 3/8-in. straight bit in the router, I mill 2⅝-in.-long slots in an upper-chest side. Bit depth is set at 3/8 in., and I use a straightedge clamp to guide the router base.

9-3 (*below right*) After removing most of the waste with the straight bit, I use a 3/4-in. dovetail bit to mill the dovetail slots in chest sides. Bit depth is 7/16 in.

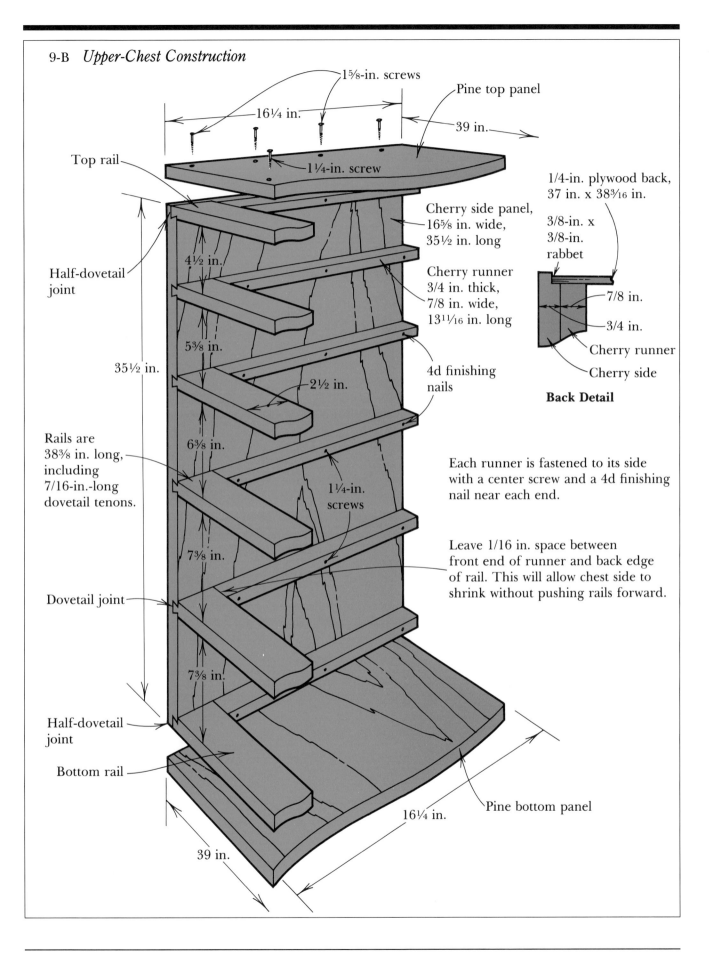

1⅝-in. screws

16¼ in.

Pine top panel

39 in.

1¼-in. screw

Top rail

Half-dovetail joint

4½ in.

5⅜ in.

35½ in.

2½ in.

6⅜ in.

Rails are 38⅜ in. long, including 7/16-in.-long dovetail tenons.

1¼-in. screws

7⅜ in.

Dovetail joint

7⅜ in.

Half-dovetail joint

Bottom rail

39 in.

16¼ in.

Pine bottom panel

Cherry side panel, 16⅝ in. wide, 35½ in. long

Cherry runner 3/4 in. thick, 7/8 in. wide, 13¹¹⁄₁₆ in. long

4d finishing nails

1/4-in. plywood back, 37 in. x 38³⁄₁₆ in.

3/8-in. x 3/8-in. rabbet

7/8 in.

3/4 in.

Cherry runner

Cherry side

Back Detail

Each runner is fastened to its side with a center screw and a 4d finishing nail near each end.

Leave 1/16 in. space between front end of runner and back edge of rail. This will allow chest side to shrink without pushing rails forward.

9-4 With the 3/4-in. dovetail bit set up in the router table, I mill dovetails on the ends of each upper rail. A high wood auxiliary fence makes it easy to hold the rail vertical during the milling process. Each dovetail tenon requires 2 passes through the setup, except the top and bottom rails, which require one pass on each end.

mate snugly with the dovetail slots in the sides. I rip and joint my rail stock to a final width of 2½ in., then I cut 6 rails to a finished length (including dovetail tenons) of 38⅜ in.

To mill the dovetail tenons in the rails, I chuck the same 3/4-in. dovetail bit in the router table and adjust bit height to 7/16 in. To give me a greater vertical surface for guiding the sides of each rail during the milling operation, I attach a tall wood fence to the router table's standard fence. Only a small area of the dovetail bit should extend beyond the fence, so I cut a small opening in the fence that's just large enough to provide clearance for the "hidden" part of the bit.

The position of the auxiliary fence relative to the dovetail bit is critical. If too much of the bit shows beyond the fence, the dovetail will be too narrow for the slot. Too little of the bit, and the dovetail will be too broad. I use some scrap stock (identical in thickness to the rails) to fine-tune the position of the fence. When my sample dovetails fit nice and snugly in the sides, I can run the ends of the rails through the setup. Each dovetail takes 2 passes to complete (*photo 9-4*), except for the half-dovetails on top and bottom rails, which need only one pass. (Be certain to mill the half-dovetails on the same side of the rail.)

Now I can assemble the upper chest. I dry-fit a couple of rails partway into their slots, just to keep the sides upright on the workbench while I attach the top and bottom. These pine panels are glued and screwed (with 1⅝-in. screws) into top and bottom edges of the sides. The front edges of the pine panels should be flush with the front edges of the cherry sides. I predrill and countersink the screw holes, taking care not to drive screws within 2⅝ in. of the front edges of the panels, since this might interfere with the half-dovetail joints.

When the top and bottom are joined to the sides, I install the rails. After spreading glue on each rail's dovetails, I tap the rail in place using my shot-filled mallet (*photo 9-5*). The front edge of each rail should be flush with the front edges of the sides. The top and bottom rails are also glued and screwed to the top and bottom panels. I drive 1¼-in. screws through the pine panels and into the rails after predrilling and countersinking the screw holes. At each top and bottom corner of the chest, I also drive a 1⅝-in. screw through the pine and through the half-dovetail joint into a cherry side. (These screw holes are also predrilled and countersunk.)

Drawer runners go in next. There are 12 in all. Each runner measures 3/4 in. thick, 7/8 in. wide, and 13¹¹/₁₆ in. long. As shown in drawing 9-B, the runners extend horizontally across the width of the sides. I install them with their top (7/8-in.-wide) edges flush with the top edges of the rails. The uppermost pair of runners guides the top of the upper drawer instead of the bottom, preventing it from tipping downward as it's opened.

9-5 After spreading glue on a rail's dovetails, I tap it into place. The front edges of the rails should be flush with the front edges of the sides. The pine top and bottom have already been fastened to the sides of the upper chest.

Over time, the potential for shrinkage is greater across the width of the side than along the length of the runner. To accommodate this movement, I allow 1/16 in. of space between the back edge of each rail and the front end of the runner. Also, I attach each runner by driving a 1¼-in. screw near the center of the runner and a 4d finishing nail near each end (*photo 9-6*). I dab a spot of glue at the screw location, but I don't glue the ends of the runners to the sides. This strategy should secure the runners without interfering with side movement in response to temperature and humidity changes.

When all the runners have been installed, I turn the chest over on the workbench so that the rails are facing down. In this position, it's easy to test the chest for squareness before the back goes on. Using my tape measure, I check to see if the diagonal measurements across opposite corners are equal. If necessary, I can rack the chest slightly to square it up. Then I glue and nail the 1/4-in.-thick plywood back in place. I spread glue in the side rabbets and on the edges of the top and bottom pine panels, fastening the back in place by driving 3/4-in. brads with my pneumatic brad driver.

Ornate Corner Posts

The lower chest is broader and deeper than the upper chest. With its curved feet and fluted corners, it's also more ornate. I start this part of the project by making the decorative corner posts. From some 8/4 cherry, I cut a pair of blanks to a finished length of 28 in. Using the table saw and jointer, I make each blank 1⅝ in. thick and 1¾ in. wide.

Dimensions and details of the corner posts are shown in draw-

9-6 Drawer guides for the upper chest are 3/4-in. by 7/8-in. cleats. I install each cleat so that its top edge is flush with the top of the rail. I screw and glue only the center of the cleat to the side. The ends of the cleat are nailed.

9-7 Using a cradle to hold the corner-post blank at a 45-degree angle, I cut the outside bevel and scallop detail on the band saw.

ings 9-C and 9-D. The back side of each post is rabbeted to fit against the chest side. I cut the rabbets on the table saw, using the rip fence to guide the blank through the blade. For the first rabbet cut, I raise the blade to a 3/4-in. height and position the fence 1/2 in. from the far edge of the blade. To complete the rabbet, I lower the blade to a 1/2-in. height and adjust the fence so that it's 3/4 in. from the far edge of the blade. For this cut, the 1⅝-in. wide edge of the blank runs against the rip fence.

The top and bottom of each post are rectangular in section. But 3/4 in. from the top end of the post, and 1½ in. from the bottom end, the profile changes, giving way to a beveled, fluted edge. The bevel starts and ends with short, curved cuts that I trace onto the stock from a pattern (*drawing 9-C*). When the curves and straight bevel line are marked on each piece, I go over to the band saw to do the cutting. I use a cradle-type jig with an angled cutout to hold the post blank at a 45-degree angle to the blade. Guiding the post in the jig, I follow the curved layout line to start the cut, then I push the post along the cradle, following the straight layout line for the bevel (*photo 9-7*). When I get close to the curve at the opposite end, I shut off the saw, move the cradle to the opposite side of the blade, restart the saw, and complete the cut.

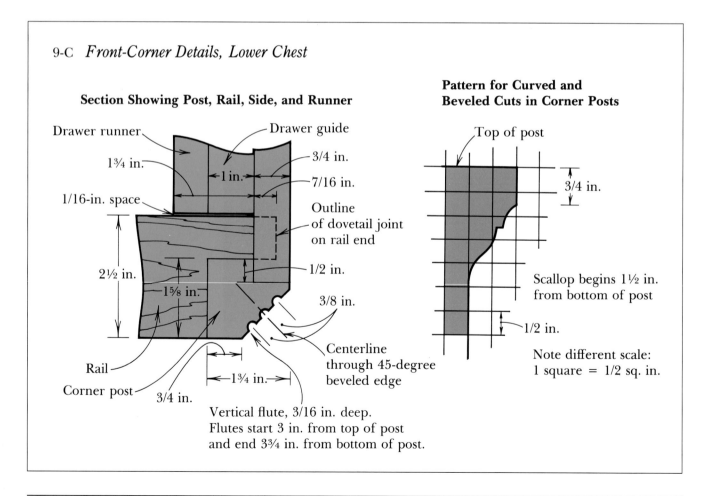

9-C *Front-Corner Details, Lower Chest*

Section Showing Post, Rail, Side, and Runner

Drawer runner
Drawer guide
1¾ in.
3/4 in.
1 in.
7/16 in.
1/16-in. space
Outline of dovetail joint on rail end
2½ in.
1/2 in.
1⅝ in.
3/8 in.
Rail
Corner post
3/4 in.
1¾ in.
Centerline through 45-degree beveled edge

Vertical flute, 3/16 in. deep.
Flutes start 3 in. from top of post
and end 3¾ in. from bottom of post.

Pattern for Curved and Beveled Cuts in Corner Posts

Top of post
3/4 in.
Scallop begins 1½ in. from bottom of post
1/2 in.
Note different scale:
1 square = 1/2 sq. in.

When I've cut both corner posts this way, I use the sanding drum in my drill press to remove saw marks and smooth out the edges that have just been cut. A 100-grit or 120-grit sanding drum does a good job of smoothing out any irregularities that have been left by the band saw blade.

The fluting comes next. Each corner post gets 3 flutes. The flutes are laid out on centerlines, and the middle flute should run down the center of the bevel. The centerlines for the 2 outer flutes are 3/8 in. from the middle flute's centerline (*drawing 9-C*). The flutes start 3 in. from the top end of the corner post and end 3¾ in. from the bottom end.

I mill the flutes on my overarm router, using a 1/4-in. round-nose bit. To hold the beveled section of each corner post horizontal, I use the same cradle that guided the stock on the band saw. I adjust the overarm router's fence so that when the cradle is held against the fence the roundnose bit is centered over a flute's lay-out line. I adjust the bit's plunge depth to 3/16 in., then I turn on the machine, plunge the bit into the stock, and mill the full length of the flute by moving the post along the cradle. I repeat this technique for each flute after repositioning the fence to align the bit (*photo 9-8*).

9-8 I mill the flutes in the corner posts using a 1/4-in. roundnose bit in the overarm router. The angled cradle is positioned against the fence as I move the post in the cradle to mill the full length of each flute.

Notched Rails

Like the rails for the upper chest, the lower rails are also 2½ in. wide. But only the 2 center lower rails are dovetailed into the sides of the lower chest (*drawing 9-D*). I mill the dovetail slots in the sides as I did earlier, when I was working on the upper chest (*photos 9-2 and 9-3*). The lone difference is that the slots for the lower chest need only be 1½ in. long.

The 2 center rails for the lower chest have a finished length of 41⅜ in., which includes the dovetail tenons at rail ends. Like the upper-rail tenons, the lower-rail tenons are 7/16 in. long, and I mill them on the router table using the 3/4-in. dovetail bit (*photo 9-4*).

In order to install the corner posts, the 2 center rails and the top and bottom panels for the lower chest must be notched to fit around the blocks. I dry-fit the 2 center rails in their slots and trace the outline of the corner post onto each rail end. To do this layout, the front edge of the rail should be flush with the square front edge of the corner post, as shown in drawing 9-C. It takes 2 cuts to complete each notch. I make the cross-grain cuts on my motorized miter box. Then I take the rails over to the band saw for the rip cuts (*photo 9-9*).

Now I glue the center rails in their slots, dry-fitting the corner blocks to make sure that the front edges of the rails will be flush with the front edges of the blocks. The center rails will hold the sides upright while I lay out the notches that need to be cut in the

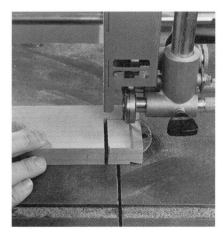

9-9 The 2 center rails for the lower chest must be notched at their ends to fit around the corner posts. After making a cross-grain cut on the motorized miter box, I cut out the notch on the band saw.

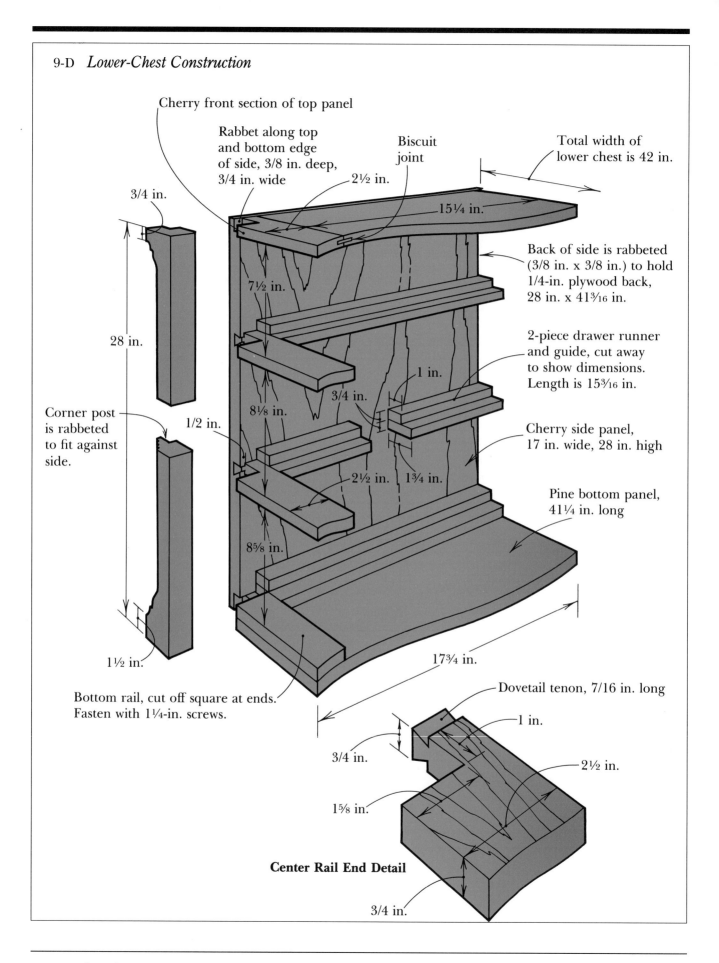

Cherry front section of top panel

Rabbet along top and bottom edge of side, 3/8 in. deep, 3/4 in. wide

Biscuit joint

Total width of lower chest is 42 in.

2½ in.

3/4 in.

15¼ in.

Back of side is rabbeted (3/8 in. x 3/8 in.) to hold 1/4-in. plywood back, 28 in. x 41³⁄₁₆ in.

7½ in.

28 in.

2-piece drawer runner and guide, cut away to show dimensions. Length is 15³⁄₁₆ in.

Corner post is rabbeted to fit against side.

1 in.

1/2 in.

3/4 in.

Cherry side panel, 17 in. wide, 28 in. high

8⅛ in.

Pine bottom panel, 41¼ in. long

2½ in.

1¾ in.

8⅝ in.

1½ in.

17¾ in.

Bottom rail, cut off square at ends. Fasten with 1¼-in. screws.

Dovetail tenon, 7/16 in. long

1 in.

3/4 in.

2½ in.

1⅝ in.

Center Rail End Detail

3/4 in.

bottom panel. I cut these notches with my jigsaw, then I glue and screw the bottom panel to the sides, driving 1⅝-in. screws in pre-drilled, countersunk holes. The bottom rail is glued and screwed to the bottom panel, so I don't bother to notch it for a fit around the corner posts.

The joinery is a little different at the top of the lower chest. The top rail is notched to fit around the corner posts, with the rail ends fitting in the rabbets that are milled in the top edges of the sides (*drawing 9-D*). The back edge of this rail is glued to a pine panel 15¼ in. wide and 41¼ in. long. I use biscuit joints to strengthen the edge-to-edge joint between the top rail and the pine panel.

When all these horizontal members are attached to the sides, it's finally time to install the corner posts. I spread glue on all the notched areas and along the rabbet at the back of each block. Then I tap the blocks in place (*photo 9-10*) and clamp them to the lower chest until the glue dries.

The drawer runners for the lower chest are 2-part assemblies designed to guide the side as well as the bottom of the drawer. As shown in drawing 9-D, the runners are made from 3/4-in.-thick cherry. The lower part of each runner is 1¾ in. wide, while the upper part is 1 in. wide. The length of both parts is 15³⁄₁₆ in. After gluing and nailing the runners together, I fasten them to the chest sides, using a single screw and two 4d finish nails per runner. The runner is glued to the side only at the center, near where the 1¼-in. screw is driven (*photo 9-11*). This is the same method that I used to attach the upper-chest runners. The top face of the 1¾-in.-wide piece should be flush with the top face of the rail. The front ends of the runners should be spaced 1/16 in. from the back edges of the rails to allow for expansion and contraction of the sides.

9-10 After spreading glue on the rabbeted back edge of a corner post and on the notched members it will fit against, I tap the post in place.

9-11 I fasten a 2-piece drawer runner to a lower-chest side, using a screw at the center of the runner and nails near the runner ends.

9-12 The 1/4-in. plywood back goes on after I've checked the lower chest for squareness. I glue the back to the rabbeted sides and top and bottom pine panels, and nail it down with 3/4-in. brads, using my pneumatic brad driver.

Once the runners are installed, I turn the chest over on the workbench with its back facing up. I compare corner-to-corner measurements across the back of the chest to make sure it's square, then I glue and nail the back in place (*photo 9-12*).

Making the Feet

The feet for the lower chest have graceful curves and contours. Despite the ornate appearance, these support members aren't that difficult to make. I rough out the contoured profile first, working on an 8/4 cherry board that's 5⅞ in. wide and about 5 ft long. I trace the profile's shape onto the end of the board (*drawing 9-E*). This shows how much wood has to be removed to achieve the final contour.

To remove the waste in the curved section of the profile, I use a 1/2-in. roundnose bit in my router, making numerous passes along the length of the board. The router's edge guide runs against the edge of the board to guide the bit. After each pass, I

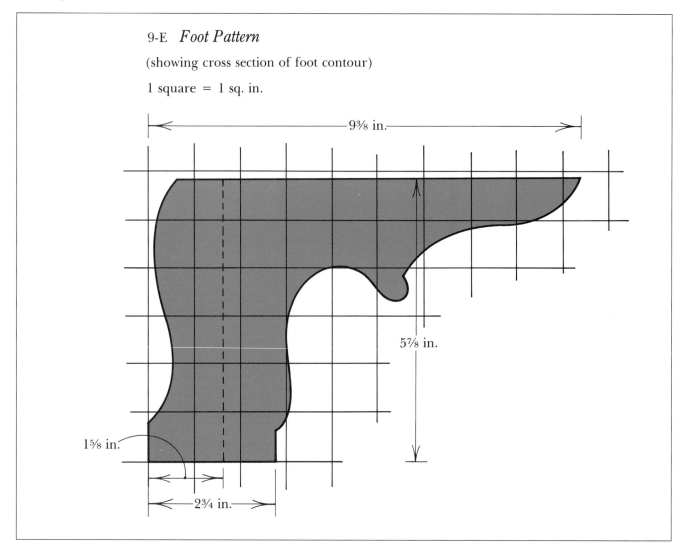

9-E *Foot Pattern*

(showing cross section of foot contour)

1 square = 1 sq. in.

9⅜ in.

5⅞ in.

1⅝ in.

2¾ in.

9-13 *(left)* To rough out the profile of the foot, I make numerous passes along the length of an 8/4 blank, using the router and a 1/2-in. roundnose bit. The edge guide keeps each pass straight. I adjust bit depth to remove as much waste as possible, following the profile traced on the end of the board.   **9-14** *(right)* Placing a pattern of the foot on the flat back of the blank, I trace out 3 left feet and 3 right feet to be cut on the band saw.

adjust the edge guide and the bit depth to remove a little more waste (*photo 9-13*).

The triangular section of waste at the corner of the board is easier to remove on the table saw. After adjusting the blade angle to match the approximate angle of the profile, I use the rip fence to guide the flat side of the board as I rip out this piece.

From now on, it will be easier to work with individual foot pieces. There are 6 in all. The front feet are made from a pair of pieces that are mitered together. The rear feet are made from single pieces. Using a cardboard pattern, I trace the outlines of 3 left feet and 3 right feet onto the flat side of the board, putting them as close together as possible (*photo 9-14*). On the radial-arm saw, I cut the board into 6 rectangular sections, each containing a single foot pattern. Then I go over to the band saw to make the curved cutouts, using a 1/4-in. blade.

There's still quite a bit of shaping work to be done on each foot piece. To smooth the tight curves that I've just cut on the band saw, I chuck a 1-in.-diameter sanding drum in the drill press (*photo 9-15*). Then I switch to a 2-in.-diameter sanding drum to shape the more gradual contours that I roughed out with the router. Finally, I use a stationary belt sander to shape the gentle outside curves on the feet (*photo 9-16*).

The 2 rear feet can simply be square-cut to a final length of 9⅜ in. The paired feet for each front corner need to be mitered (the length of each piece, after mitering, is also 9⅜ in.). I make

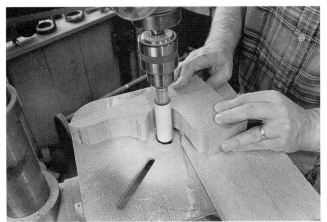

9-15 To smooth the tighter curves along the edge of each foot, I use a 1-in.-diameter sanding drum in the drill press.

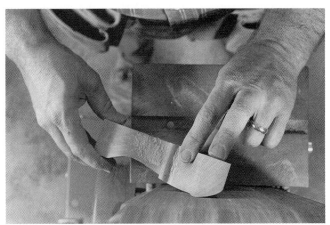

9-16 The stationary belt sander does a good job of smoothing the outside curves on each foot piece.

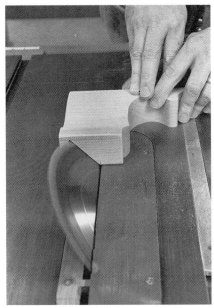

9-17 Using the table saw's miter gauge to guide the stock, I miter the edge of each front foot piece.

9-18 To make the feet at the front of the chest, mitered halves are glued and screwed together. I back up the miter joint with a corner block, which enables me to pull the joint tight with screws, driven through both exposed edges of the block. I also clamp the miter joints together until the glue dries.

these 45-degree-angle cuts on the table saw. The miter gauge is set at 90 degrees, while the blade is tilted 45 degrees (*photo 9-17*).

Now I can glue the mitered pieces together. To strengthen each miter and provide additional support at the front corners, I back the miter up with a short length of pine that's 3/4 in. thick, 1 in. wide, and 5⅞ in. long. I glue and screw the 1-in.-thick side of the pine piece against the back edge of one miter, driving 1¼-in. screws in predrilled, countersunk holes. Then I spread glue on

the miter and on the adjacent side of the backer piece before assembling the foot.

Holding the joint tight, I drive a pair of 1⅝-in. screws through
the backer piece and into the adjoining foot piece (*photo 9-18*). I
use a wooden hand-screw clamp to hold each miter joint tight until the glue dries. After removing the clamps, I do some additional sanding to even up the joining contours and smooth the
miter joint. I go over each leg first with the 2-in.-diameter drum
sander (chucked in the drill press), then I switch to the palm
sander for final sanding.

To install the feet, I also rely on pine support pieces and
braces. Each front foot gets 2 support pieces that are glued and
screwed (1¼-in. screws) to the back of the foot, their top edges
flush with the top edge of the foot. I cut the support pieces from
3/4-in.-thick, 1½-in.-wide pine. Each support piece has a square
end, which butts against the pine backer piece. The opposite end
is curved to keep the pine out of sight behind the curve of the
foot.

Once the front feet have their supports, I can glue and screw
them to the front corners of the lower chest. Photo 9-19 shows
how the support pieces are used in attaching the front feet. I predrill and countersink the screw holes before driving screws
through the bottom edges of the support pieces and into the bottom of the chest. Shorter screws can be driven into the narrower
contoured sections of the support pieces, but at least 1 in. of every screw should extend into the bottom of the chest.

Photo 9-19 also shows how I attach the rear foot, using a single
support piece and a diagonal brace. The brace is fastened to the
foot with glue and a pair of biscuits. I use a single biscuit joint
and a single screw to strengthen the glue joint between the brace
and the chest bottom.

9-19 Feet are attached to the
chest with glue and screws. The
screws are driven through pine
support pieces and into the chest
bottom. The rear foot is fastened
to the bottom using a single support piece and an angled support
block.

9-20 I use an ogee-type bit in the router table to mill both the base molding (shown here) and the upper cornice molding. Horizontal and vertical featherboards help to hold the stock as I feed it through the bit.

9-21 The transition molding gets its profile on the table saw. I use a molding head, equipped with a cove-bead combination cutter, to mill the front edge of the molding.

The upper and lower chests can now be joined together. The sides and front of the upper chest should be 1½ in. inside the top of the lower chest. I fasten the 2 chests together by driving 1¼-in. screws through the bottom of the upper chest and into the lower chest's top.

On most types of traditional furniture, moldings are used to create a graceful transition where one part or section ends and another begins. The chest on chest has 3 separate molding details — a base molding that runs along the bottom edge of the lower chest, a transition molding at the juncture of upper and lower chests, and a cornice at the very top of the piece (*drawing 9-F*). The cornice is actually made from 2 different moldings that are installed one on top of the other. Each molding "course" extends around the sides and front of the piece, with side pieces mitered to front pieces.

Solid-cherry moldings aren't stocked at the lumberyard, so for this project I make my own in the shop, using several tools. With an ogee-type bit in the router table, I can mill the base molding from a 5/4 cherry "stick" that's 7/8 in. thick and 7 ft long. As shown in photo 9-20, I use vertical and horizontal featherboards to keep the molding stock aligned as I run it through the bit. By adjusting the position of the horizontal featherboard, I can also mill the upper cornice molding. This profile is milled in a 7-ft-long, 5/4 board that I rip and joint to a width of 1⅞ in. It takes several passes to make each of these moldings. I raise the bit slightly after each pass so that I can avoid removing too much material in a single pass. In addition to being safer, this strategy prolongs the life of the bit and produces smoother contours.

To complete the profile of the base molding, I round over the edges that will be just above the legs, first using a block plane, then some fine-grit sandpaper. Next, I use my motorized miter box to cut miter joints where the side molding pieces meet the front molding piece. I glue all 3 pieces to the top edges of the legs and to one another (at the mitered corners). I nail the molding against the chest, driving 4d finishing nails with my pneumatic nailer.

The transition molding starts out as a 7-ft-long piece of 5/4 cherry that's 1⅝ in. wide. To mill its profile, I set up the molding head in my table saw. The knife I use in the molding head produces a cove-bead combination (*drawing 9-E*). I mill the contour by running the 1⅝-in.-wide edge of the board against the rip fence. As on the router table, I make several passes to complete the profile, raising the cutter slightly after each pass. A featherboard, clamped to the saw table, helps me to hold the stock against the fence (*photo 9-21*).

Before I cut the miter joints and install the transition molding,

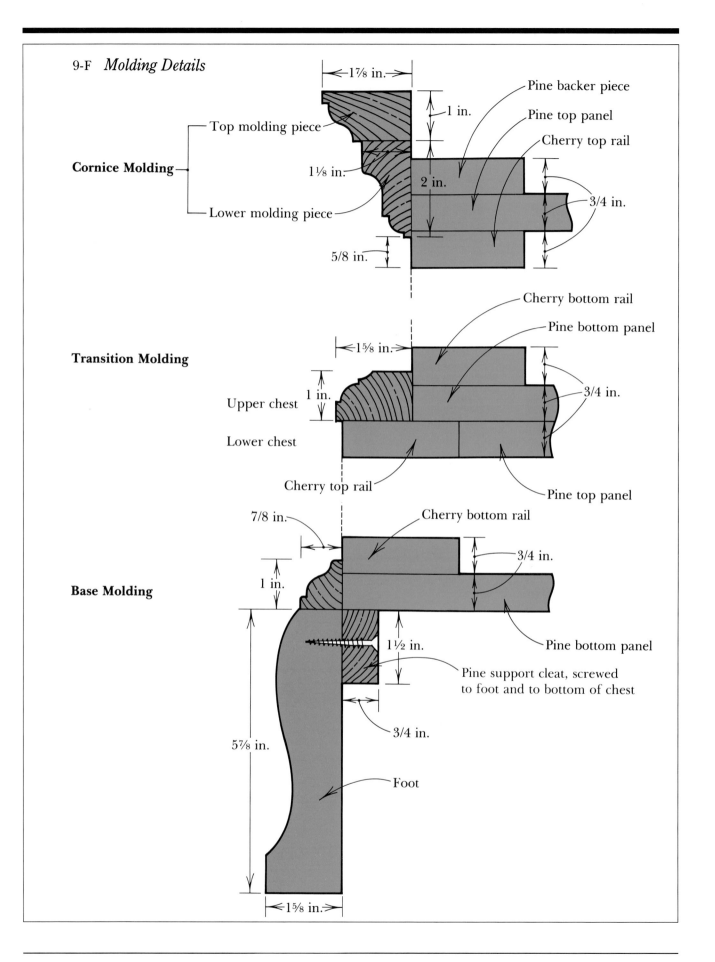

9-F *Molding Details*

Cornice Molding

1⅞ in.

1 in.

Top molding piece

1⅛ in.

Lower molding piece

2 in.

5/8 in.

Pine backer piece

Pine top panel

Cherry top rail

3/4 in.

Transition Molding

Cherry bottom rail

Pine bottom panel

1⅝ in.

1 in.

Upper chest

Lower chest

Cherry top rail

3/4 in.

Pine top panel

Base Molding

7/8 in.

Cherry bottom rail

3/4 in.

1 in.

1½ in.

3/4 in.

Pine bottom panel

Pine support cleat, screwed
to foot and to bottom of chest

5⅞ in.

Foot

1⅝ in.

9-22 Using a 1/2-in.-diameter cove cutter in the shaper, I mill a broad cove as part of the lower-cornice-molding profile.

9-23 With a 5/16-in.-diameter beading cutter in the shaper, I mill a bead along the lower edge of the molding. It's important to use featherboards and hold-down attachments when milling stock on the shaper.

I use some fine-grit sandpaper to round the sharp edges along the front of the molding. When cutting the miter joints, I make the front molding piece 1/16 in. longer than necessary. This allows me to leave a 1/32-in. space between the side molding pieces and the sides of the upper chest. Though barely detectable to the eye, this space will allow for some movement between upper and lower chests. If the transition molding is too tight around the upper chest, it may buckle or crack should the top of the lower chest shrink slightly.

After cutting the miters, I nail the molding to the top of the lower chest, gluing only the miter joints together. I avoid gluing the molding to the upper chest, since this would make it impossible to take the piece apart when moving it from room to room or house to house.

The lower molding section for the cornice is milled from a cherry blank 1⅛ in. thick, 2 in. wide, and 7 ft long. The profile for this molding consists of a broad cove with a beaded lower edge. I mill the cove first, using a 1/2-in. cove cutter in the shaper, and making several passes to achieve the full depth of the cove (*photo 9-22*). When this part of the profile is cut, I install a 5/16-in. beading cutter in the shaper, adjusting the height of the cutter so that the bead will be milled along the lower corner of the cove (*photo 9-23*). For both shaper operations, it's important to use featherboards and hold-downs to control the position of the stock as it's run through the cutters.

Before installing the cornice moldings, I screw backer boards to the top of the upper chest. These 1x3 pine pieces are installed flush with the front and side edges of the top. Once the backer pieces are installed, I can fasten the lower molding sections of the cornice to the chest. The front piece, which I install first, should overlap the top rail of the chest by 1/8 in. I nail it to the top of the chest and to the backer piece, driving 4d finishing nails with my pneumatic nailer (*photo 9-24*). The 2 side pieces can be installed the same way. In addition to gluing the miter joints together, I drive a couple of 1-in. brads into each joint.

The 3 upper molding pieces go on last. Miter joints in this 3-part assembly should align directly over the lower molding miters, and the back edges of both molding courses should be flush (*drawing 9-F*). I glue and nail the top molding pieces to one another (at miter joints) and to the lower cornice molding.

Drawers

Building the drawers calls for quite a bit of repetitive work. There are plenty of parts to cut, mill, and keep track of. Fortunately, all 8 drawers are built the same way (*drawing 9-G*). You can make this part of the project go smoothly by keeping the parts of each drawer together as they're cut and milled.

9-24 The bottom edge of the lower cornice molding should overlap the top rail by 1/8 in. I nail this molding to the top rail and to a 3/4-in.-thick pine backer board that's fastened along the side and front edges of the top.

Dimensioning the drawer parts isn't difficult if you apply a few rules. First, all 5 upper drawers should have the same depth and width. The same is true of the lower drawers. It's the height of the drawer openings that changes, and this determines the heights of drawer fronts, sides, and backs.

Drawer fronts are made to overlay their openings along top and side edges. To allow for this overlay, I dimension each drawer front so that it's 1/8 in. higher than the opening and 3/8 in. wider than the opening. Side height should be 1/8 in. less than the height of the opening. If your upper and lower chests have the same dimensions as mine, then you can use the cutting list shown in drawing 9-G to dimension all fronts, sides, backs, and bottoms. If your chests are slightly different in size from mine, you'll have to apply the aforementioned rules, also adjusting back and bottom dimensions accordingly.

After cutting all the parts to size, I begin working on the drawer fronts. First, I rabbet the side and top edges of the fronts, which will overlay the drawer openings. Each rabbet needs to be 1/4 in. wide and 7/16 in. deep. To do this milling, I set up the dado head in the table saw, adjusting cutter height to 7/16 in. and cutter width to about 3/8 in. To guide the edges of the fronts and also cover all but 1/4 in. of the dado's width, I screw a wood auxiliary fence to the rip fence.

Next, I mill the half-blind dovetail joints that will be used to connect fronts and sides. Following the directions for my dovetailing jig, I clamp each drawer front horizontally in the jig so that the template fingers are aligned over one rabbeted side. With a 1/2-in. dovetail bit and a collar mounted in the router, I mill this half of the joint. When I've finished milling the tails in all the drawer fronts, I mill the pins in the sides, again using the jig and 1/2-in. dovetail bit with its collar. For this operation, the sides are clamped vertically in my jig.

The front edges of the drawer fronts need to be rounded over,

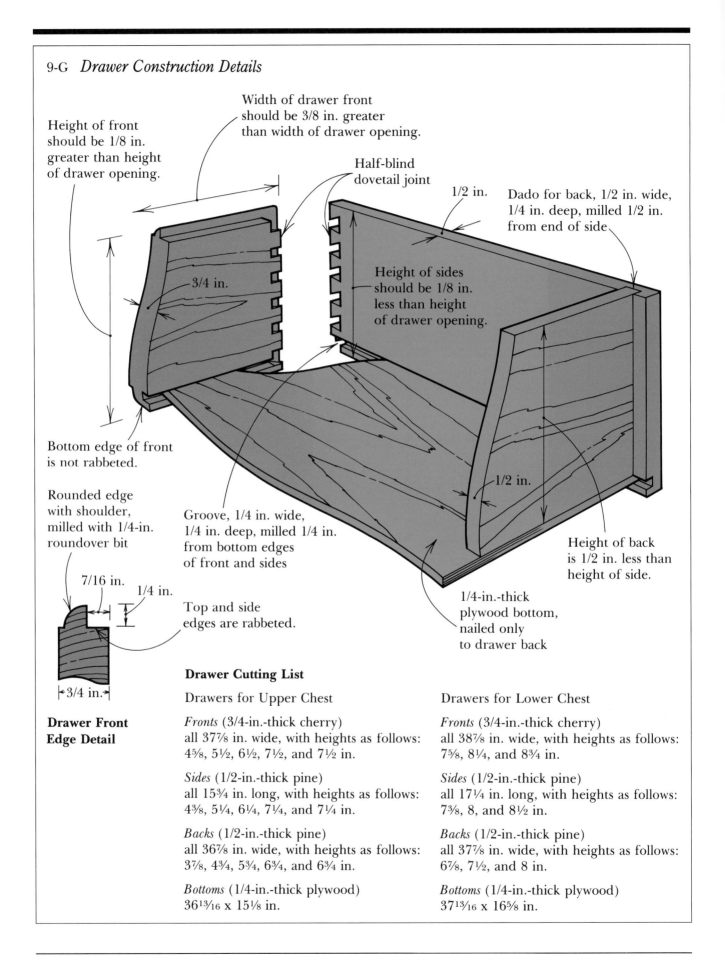

9-G *Drawer Construction Details*

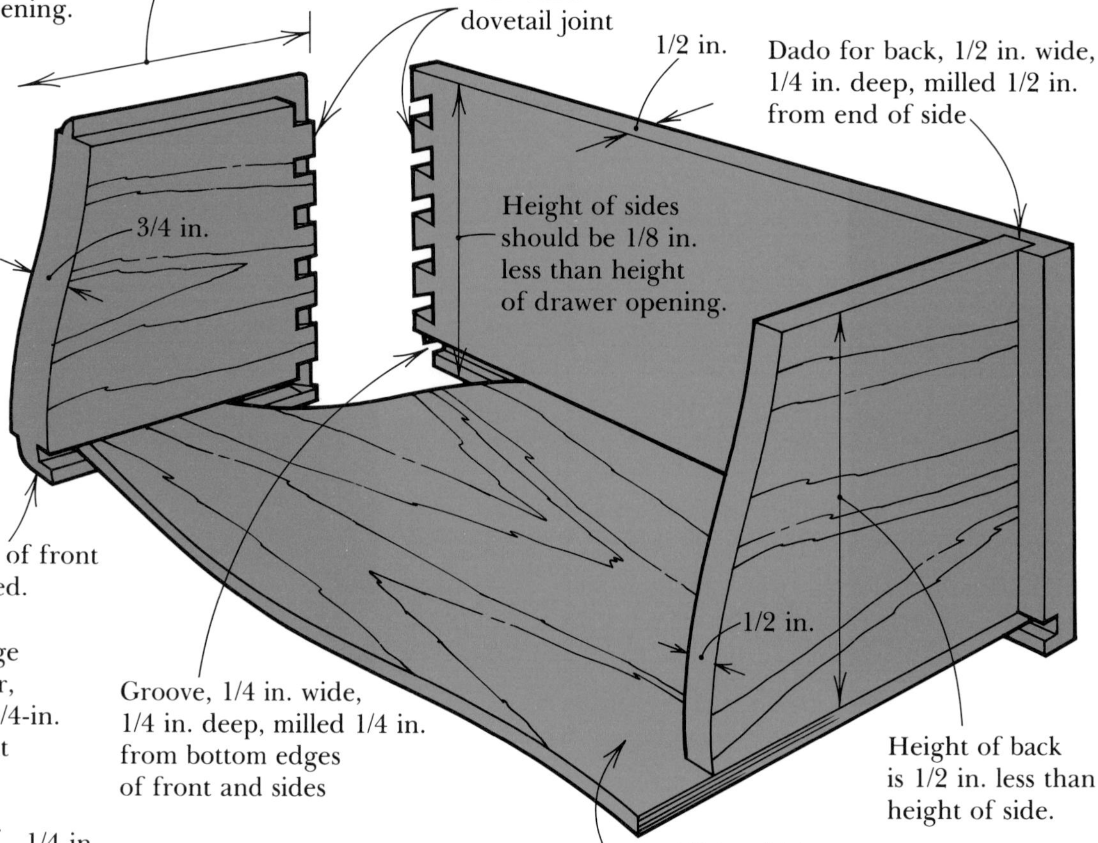

Width of drawer front
should be 3/8 in. greater
than width of drawer opening.
Height of front
should be 1/8 in.
greater than height
of drawer opening.
Half-blind
dovetail joint
1/2 in.
Dado for back, 1/2 in. wide,
1/4 in. deep, milled 1/2 in.
from end of side
3/4 in.
Height of sides
should be 1/8 in.
less than height
of drawer opening.
Bottom edge of front
is not rabbeted.
1/2 in.
Groove, 1/4 in. wide,
1/4 in. deep, milled 1/4 in.
from bottom edges
of front and sides
Height of back
is 1/2 in. less than
height of side.
1/4-in.-thick
plywood bottom,
nailed only
to drawer back

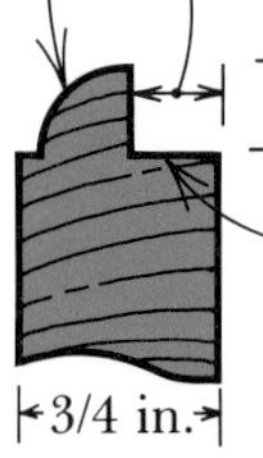

Rounded edge
with shoulder,
milled with 1/4-in.
roundover bit
7/16 in.
1/4 in.
Top and side
edges are rabbeted.
3/4 in.

Drawer Front Edge Detail

Drawer Cutting List

Drawers for Upper Chest

Fronts (3/4-in.-thick cherry)
all 37⅞ in. wide, with heights as follows:
4⅝, 5½, 6½, 7½, and 7½ in.

Sides (1/2-in.-thick pine)
all 15¾ in. long, with heights as follows:
4⅜, 5¼, 6¼, 7¼, and 7¼ in.

Backs (1/2-in.-thick pine)
all 36⅞ in. wide, with heights as follows:
3⅞, 4¾, 5¾, 6¾, and 6¾ in.

Bottoms (1/4-in.-thick plywood)
36 13/16 x 15⅛ in.

Drawers for Lower Chest

Fronts (3/4-in.-thick cherry)
all 38⅞ in. wide, with heights as follows:
7⅝, 8¼, and 8¾ in.

Sides (1/2-in.-thick pine)
all 17¼ in. long, with heights as follows:
7⅜, 8, and 8½ in.

Backs (1/2-in.-thick pine)
all 37⅞ in. wide, with heights as follows:
6⅞, 7½, and 8 in.

Bottoms (1/4-in.-thick plywood)
37 13/16 x 16⅝ in.

and I do this work on the router table, using a 1/4-in. roundover bit. Because of the rabbeted edges, I can't rely on the pilot bearing to guide the bit. Instead, I set up the fence to guide the stock. I also adjust bit height so that a very slight decorative shoulder is milled just below the rounded profile (*photo 9-25*). To avoid chipping out the corners of the fronts, I mill first across the grain, then with the grain.

To finish off the drawer fronts, I need to mill grooves in the fronts to hold the drawer bottoms. Each groove is located 1/4 in. from the bottom edge of its drawer and should be 1/4 in. wide and 1/4 in. deep. I mill the grooves on the table saw, using the dado cutter. Cutter width and height are both 1/4 in., and the rip fence needs to be positioned 1/4 in. away from the cutter. The drawer sides also need to be grooved to hold the bottoms, and I run the sides through this same setup when I've finished grooving the fronts.

Finally, I dado the sides to receive the backs. I adjust dado width to 1/2 in., maintaining cutter height at 1/4 in. Guiding each side against the miter gauge, I mill each dado 1/2 in. from the back end of the side. A short gauge block, clamped to the rip fence on my side of the blade, helps me to align each side for its dado.

With so much cutting and milling behind me, it's a pleasure to assemble the drawers. I work on one drawer at a time, always joining the sides to the front first. A small brush is a helpful tool for spreading glue in the half-dovetail joints between these parts. After tapping these joints tight with my shot-filled mallet, I glue the back of the drawer into the side dadoes (*photo 9-26*). The bottom goes in last. It should float in the side and front grooves, being fastened only at the back. I use my framing square to brace one side at a right angle to the front while nailing through the plywood drawer bottom and into the bottom edge of the back.

The drawer pulls shouldn't be installed until after the chest on chest has received its final coat of finish, but it's a good idea to lay out and drill the installation holes. A pair of holes are required for each pull, so it's a good idea to make up a small template as an aid in laying out the holes. All installation holes are centered horizontally on drawer fronts. The vertical center for each upper pull is 7 in. from the side of the drawer. The vertical center for each lower pull is 7½ in. from the side of the drawer.

9-25 I use a 1/4-in. roundover bit in the router table to give the front edges of the drawer a decorative treatment. At this stage, fronts have already been rabbeted and half-dovetail joints have been milled to hold drawer sides. The roundover bit has a pilot bearing, but for this operation the wood auxiliary fence on the router table guides the edge of the drawer as the profile is milled.

9-26 After gluing the sides of the drawer to the front, I spread some glue in the side dadoes and join the back to the sides.

Chapter Ten

Garden Bench

PROJECT PLANNING
Time: 4 days

Special hardware and tools:

(1) small unit 2-part Resorcinol glue

Wood:

(teak unless otherwise noted)

(1) 6-ft 12/4 x 6

Back legs. Cut into two 36-in. lengths

(1) 8-ft 12/4 x 5

Front legs and armrests

(1) 8-ft 6/4 x 8

Front rail, lower end rails, seat rails, and seat supports

(1) 6-ft 6/4 x 8

Upper back rail, lower back rail

(1) 6-ft 6/4 x 5

Back slats. Rip the board in half, in both directions, yielding 4 strips about 5/8 in. thick, 2⅛ in. wide, and 6 ft long. Then plane to a 1/2-in. thickness

(5) 6-ft 5/4 x 4s

Seat slats. Plane to a 7/8-in. thickness.

(3) 3-ft lengths 3/8-in.-diameter maple dowel

Pins for mortise-and-tenon joints

THE English garden bench has earned a worldwide reputation for its durability, beauty, and comfort. Having made a brief visit to England, I can appreciate the wet conditions that native garden benches must endure. In the heart of London, I found a fine model for the New Yankee Workshop version of this classic piece.

Like its English counterpart, my bench is made entirely from teak, one of the best outdoor woods you'll find anywhere. Teak is highly resistant to mildew, rot, and wood-boring insects. It's also strong and very stable, so you can expect little or no warping or cracking over time. Teak is easy to work, though its high silica content tends to dull thickness-planer blades quickly. Once outdoors, teak's nicely figured grain will weather to a light shade of gray.

All these benefits have a hefty price tag, however. Teak is very expensive, and very few lumberyards have it in stock. If you have to put in a special order, as I did, be sure to inquire about the type of teak available. Plantation-harvested teak comes from managed forests, so its use doesn't contribute to rain forest depletion.

My teak arrived roughsawn, still bearing the saw marks and surface roughness from its initial run through the sawmill. It took me about an hour to run all my boards through the planer, getting surfaces smooth and thicknesses equal. The armrests, front legs, and back legs of the bench are made from 12/4 stock, which I plane to a finished thickness of 2¾ in. The rails and seat supports are cut from 6/4 boards with a final thickness of 1⁷/₁₆ in. I plane the back slats to a 1/2-in. thickness and the seat slats to a 7/8-in. thickness (see the wood list for this project).

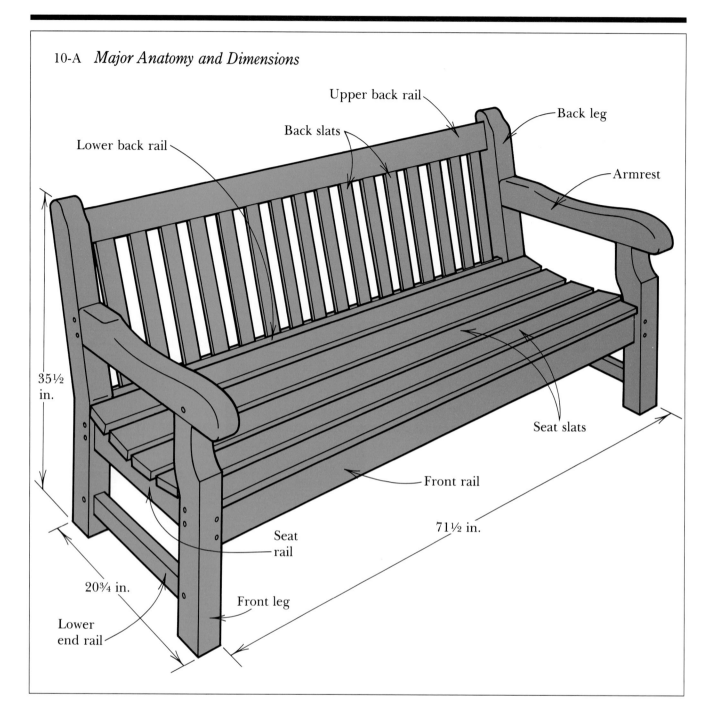

Upper back rail

Back slats

Back leg

Lower back rail

Armrest

35½ in.

Seat slats

Front rail

71½ in.

Seat rail

20¾ in.

Front leg

Lower end rail

Cutting Curves

Both ends of the bench are identical, and I build these subassemblies first. Each end consists of a front leg, a back leg (which extends to support the back of the bench), a lower end rail, a seat rail, and an armrest. Except for the lower end rails, all the parts in the end subassemblies require curved cuts. At this stage, I just need to cut out the back legs, front legs, and armrests. Patterns for these parts are shown in drawing 10-B. The back legs take the most time to lay out because in addition to being curved (at the top of each leg), the part that holds the backrest leans back at an

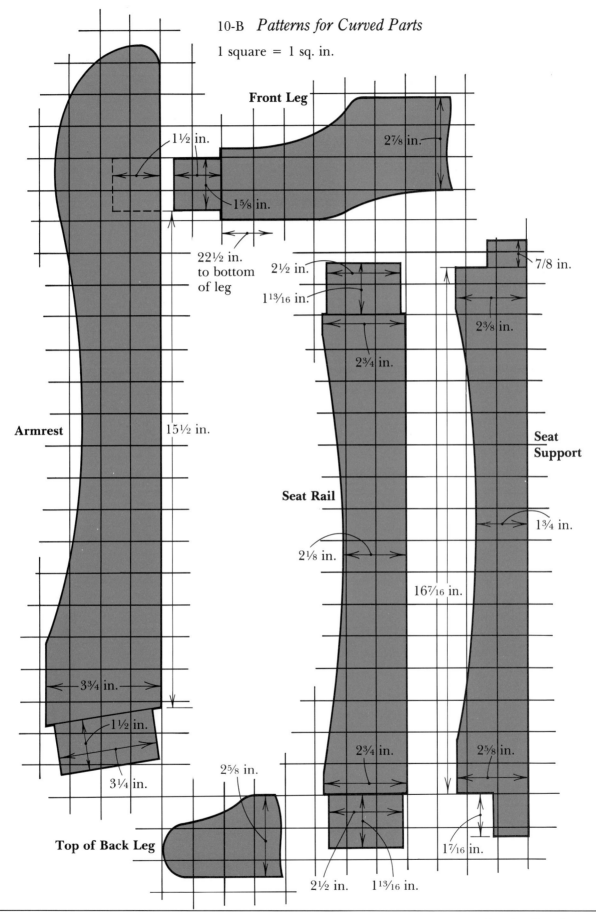

10-B *Patterns for Curved Parts*

1 square = 1 sq. in.

Front Leg

1½ in.

2⅞ in.

1⅝ in.

22½ in. to bottom of leg

2½ in.

1¹³⁄₁₆ in.

7/8 in.

2¾ in.

2⅜ in.

Armrest

15½ in.

Seat Support

Seat Rail

2⅛ in.

1¾ in.

16⁷⁄₁₆ in.

3¾ in.

1½ in.

3¼ in.

2¾ in.

2⅝ in.

Top of Back Leg

2⅝ in.

2½ in.

1¹³⁄₁₆ in.

1⁷⁄₁₆ in.

angle, also tapering slightly toward its top. Layout information for the back legs is shown in drawing 10-C.

I cut out the front legs, back legs, and armrests on the band saw. Given the thickness of the wood and the curved layout lines, I make sure to have a sharp 1/4-in. blade in the band saw. As I cut all the pieces, I try to keep the blade on the outside edge of the layout line (*photo 10-1*).

Once they're cut, these curved parts need a good smoothing to remove saw marks and other surface irregularities. I square, straighten, and smooth the 2 front edges of each back leg on the

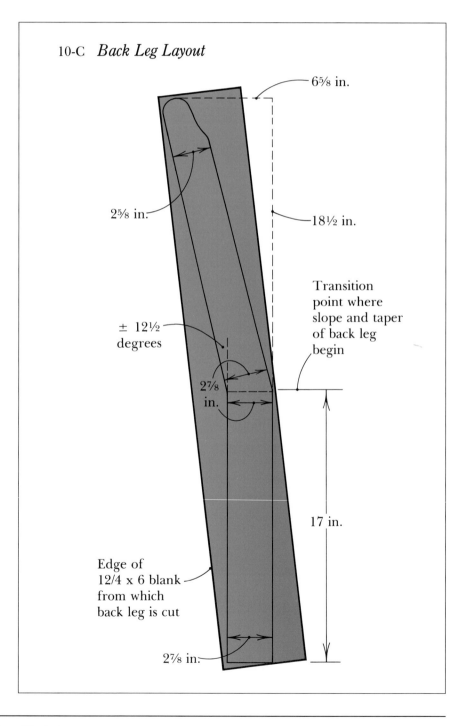

10-C *Back Leg Layout*

6⅝ in.

2⅝ in.

18½ in.

Transition point where slope and taper of back leg begin

± 12½ degrees

2⅞ in.

17 in.

Edge of 12/4 x 6 blank from which back leg is cut

2⅞ in.

jointer. Then I clamp both legs together in my bench vise, with jointed edges flush and facing down. This enables me to sand the back edges of the legs flush with one another, making these 2 parts as identical as possible. For this work, I use my belt sander and a 100-grit sanding belt (*photo 10-2*).

To smooth the curved tops of the back legs, as well as all the curves on front legs and armrests, I use a 2-in.-diameter sanding drum in the drill press. Fitted with 100-grit sandpaper, this drum does a great job of smoothing all the curved edges on these parts (*photo 10-3*).

Mortising Work

The entire bench goes together with mortise-and-tenon joints. Glued with waterproof adhesive and pegged with dowel pins, these joints should keep the bench strong and stable for many years. There are a total of 9 mortises that need to be made in each end subassembly, so mortising work takes a while to complete. Fortunately, there are a few rules that apply to all the mortises that have to be made in the front legs, back legs, and armrests. This makes layout and cutting work a little easier. First, all mortises are centered on an edge or side of the stock, and every mortise is 3/4 in. wide. Using my combination square, I can quickly lay out mortises that are located on a 2¾-in.-thick edge. I adjust the square so that exactly 1 in. of blade shows beyond the body of the tool. Then I lay out mortise cheeks by marking against the end of the blade while moving the square body of the tool against the edge of the stock. This same technique applies as I lay out mortise cheeks on the 2⅞-in.-wide faces of the legs, except that I have to extend the blade 1¹⁄₁₆ in. beyond the body of the square. To mark the ends of each mortise, I extend the blade

10-1 (*above left*) Using a sharp 1/4-in. blade in the band saw, I cut out an armrest from a block of 2¾-in.-thick teak.

10-2 (*above right*) After jointing the front edges of the back legs, I clamp both legs together in the workbench. Front edges are flush and facing down, so that I can sand the back edges even with each other.

10-3 Using a 2-in.-diameter sanding drum in the drill press, I smooth the curved edges on all the parts I've cut out on the band saw.

10-4 With a 3/4-in.-diameter Forstner bit chucked in the drill press, I rough out a mortise by drilling a series of overlapping holes.

10-5 I pare out the waste on the cheeks of the mortise using a 1- or 1¼-in.-wide chisel. The bevel of the chisel should face into the mortise.

across the width or thickness of the piece. For specifics on mortise location, depth, and length, see drawing 10-D.

Cutting the mortises is a 2-step operation. First, I drill out most of the waste on the drill press, using a 3/4-in.-diameter Forstner bit. With its flat bottom and sharp edges, the Forstner bit is ideal for roughing out mortises. It doesn't wander as it cuts into the wood, and it leaves the bottom of the mortise flat.

I adjust the plunge depth of the bit to match the planned depth of the mortise. Then I align the bit inside the layout lines for the mortise and hold the piece firmly in place while plunging the bit into the wood. I didn't use a fence as an aid in positioning the pieces on the drill-press table, but you might find it helpful to do so. To complete the roughing out process for each mortise, I drill overlapping holes, always keeping the bit inside the layout lines for each mortise (*photo 10-4*).

Paring out the remaining waste is the second step in the mortising operation. I take the drilled-out parts over to my workbench and get out a couple of sharp chisels. To pare away waste along the cheeks of each mortise, I use a 1- or 1¼-in.-wide chisel. Teak is so easy to work that I can simply use hand pressure to slice down toward the bottom of the mortise, removing shavings of waste. It's best to do this paring with the bevel of the chisel facing into the mortise (*photo 10-5*). I take care to pare each cheek flat and perpendicular to the face of the mortise.

To square up the ends of the mortise, I switch to a 3/4-in.-wide chisel. Some of this trimming calls for paring with the grain, but there's also some cross-grain cutting required, and for this I need to hammer the chisel down into the joint. With the chisel's bevel facing in, I carefully square up the corners of the mortise, chiseling only to a depth of about 1/8 in. Once the mortise opening is square, I can concentrate on cleaning out the lower corners of the mortise until they're square with those at the opening (*photo 10-6*).

10-6 I use a 3/4-in. chisel to square up the corners of the mortise. To cut across the grain, the chisel needs a little help from the hammer.

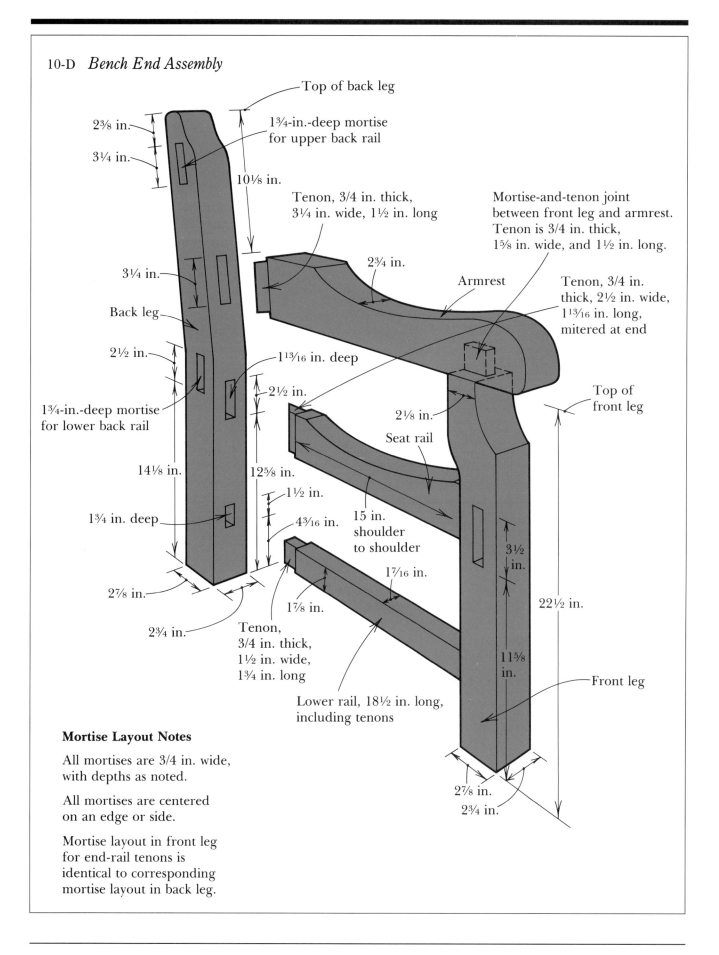

Top of back leg

1¾-in.-deep mortise
for upper back rail

2⅜ in.

3¼ in.

10⅛ in.

Tenon, 3/4 in. thick,
3¼ in. wide, 1½ in. long

2¾ in.

Mortise-and-tenon joint
between front leg and armrest.
Tenon is 3/4 in. thick,
1⅝ in. wide, and 1½ in. long.

Armrest

Tenon, 3/4 in.
thick, 2½ in. wide,
1¹³⁄₁₆ in. long,
mitered at end

3¼ in.

Back leg

2½ in.

1¹³⁄₁₆ in. deep

2½ in.

1¾-in.-deep mortise
for lower back rail

2⅛ in.

Top of
front leg

Seat rail

14⅛ in.

12⅝ in.

1½ in.

1¾ in. deep

4³⁄₁₆ in.

15 in.
shoulder
to shoulder

1⁷⁄₁₆ in.

3½
in.

22½ in.

2⅞ in.

1⅞ in.

11⅝
in.

2¾ in.

Tenon,
3/4 in. thick,
1½ in. wide,
1¾ in. long

Lower rail, 18½ in. long,
including tenons

Front leg

Mortise Layout Notes

All mortises are 3/4 in. wide,
with depths as noted.

All mortises are centered
on an edge or side.

Mortise layout in front leg
for end-rail tenons is
identical to corresponding
mortise layout in back leg.

2⅞ in.

2¾ in.

Now it's time to cut the tenons on lower end rails, seat supports, front legs, and armrests. I start off with the lower end rails and the seat rails. Each lower rail is 1⅞ in. wide and 18½ in. long, including a pair of 1¾-in.-long tenons. The seat rails need to start out 2¾ in. wide and 18⅝ in. long, including a pair of 1¹³⁄₁₆-in.-long tenons. Tenon thickness is 3/4 in.

To cut the shoulders along the sides of each lower end rail, I adjust blade height to 11/32 in. and check the miter gauge to make sure it's set at 90 degrees. Then I clamp a short gauge block to the rip fence, positioning it on my side of the blade. I adjust the fence so that tenon length will be 1¾ in. when I align the shoulder cut by butting the end of the rail against the gauge block. I make the long shoulder cuts first (*photo 10-7*), then, after lowering the blade to a height of 3/16 in., I cut the shoulders at the top and bottom of the tenon (*photo 10-8*).

I use the same technique to make the shoulder cuts in the seat rails. For these cuts, the rip fence and gauge block must be readjusted so that tenon length will be 1¹³⁄₁₆ in. Blade height for shoulder cuts along the sides of the seat rails is 11/32 in. To make the shoulder cuts along the edges of the seat rails, I set blade height at 1/8 in.

To make the cheek cuts along the sides of the tenons, I use the tenon-cutting jig designed for use in my table saw. With this accessory, I can clamp each rail in a vertical position while making the cheek cuts. I adjust blade height so that the top of the blade just reaches the shoulders of the tenon. The jig must also be adjusted horizontally so that the blade will remove the exact amount of waste with each cut. After checking the jig's setup on some scrap stock (also 1⁷⁄₁₆ in. thick), I make a pair of cheek cuts in each rail end (*photo 10-9*).

I finish up the lower-end-rail and seat-rail tenons on the band saw. I set up the band saw's fence to guide the edges of the lower end rails so that I can trim just 3/16 in. from the top and bottom

10-7 (*below left*) To cut the shoulders for a rail tenon, I clamp a gauge block to the table saw's rip fence and adjust the miter gauge for a 90-degree cut. The gauge block is positioned to align the rail for its shoulder cut when the end of the rail butts against it. Blade height for cutting the side shoulders is 11/32 in.

10-8 (*below right*) For the shoulder cuts along rail edges, blade height is changed to 3/16 in. The gauge-block position is the same.

of each tenon. Then I adjust the fence so that when each seat rail runs against it, I remove 1/8 in. from the top and bottom of each tenon (*photo 10-10*).

Now I spend a few more minutes at the band saw, cutting out the curved top edge of each seat rail. The pattern for this curve is shown in drawing 10-B. I follow up my band saw work with some smoothing on the drill press, using a 2-in.-diameter sanding drum. To finish up the seat rails, I take them over to the motorized miter box. The ends of the seat-rail tenons will penetrate into crossing mortises for front- and back-rail tenons, so these tenons need to be mitered to provide clearance for long-rail tenons. Adjusting the saw for a 45-degree-angle cut, I miter the ends of each seat-rail tenon.

In order to lay out the tenons in armrests and front legs, I dry-fit the end subassembly joints that I've completed so far. Seat-rail tenons and lower-end-rail tenons are fit snugly in front- and back-leg mortises. With the subassembly square and flat on the workbench, I can now position the armrest across (and on top of) both legs. The bottom edge of the armrest should be 10 in. from the bottom edge of the seat rail, and the armrest mortise should be centered over the front leg. When the armrest is in this position, I can lay out the angled shoulder for the armrest tenon simply by marking against the front edge of the back leg. I can also mark the shoulder line for the front-leg tenon. I use my combination square to transfer these shoulder lines around all 4 sides of each armrest and front leg.

Because the front legs are curved and the armrest tenons have an angled layout, it would be difficult to cut these tenons on the table saw. Instead, I use the radial-arm saw, replacing the blade with a dado cutter. The cutter should be adjusted close to its maximum width, since I'll be "nibbling" away at the stock, milling the tenons by making a series of passes to complete one tenon cheek at a time. I also adjust the saw's depth of cut. The armrests and legs are 2¾ in. thick, so the dado should make a 1-in.-deep cut on either side of the tenon to leave it with a final thickness of 3/4 in.

I mill the front-leg tenons first, with the saw adjusted for a straight, or right-angled, cut. Each leg must be positioned with its straight front edge against the radial-arm saw's fence. The curved section of the leg next to the tenon isn't supported by the fence, so it's important to brace the leg firmly to prevent the saw from pulling the curved section back toward the fence. I complete each cheek by making a series of overlapping passes with the dado cutter. I usually make the shoulder cut last. This is the one that has to be lined up most carefully.

It takes a little more time to mill the tenons on the armrests. I adjust the angle setting on my radial-arm saw to match the shoulder angle marked on the armrest (which for the bench I built is 12½ degrees). Then, holding the straight edge of the armrest

10-9 I use the tenon-cutting jig to make 2 cheek cuts in each rail tenon. The position of the jig relative to the saw blade determines the thickness of the tenon.

10-10 Using the band saw's fence to guide rail edges, I trim each rail tenon to its final width.

against the fence, I make a series of cuts to remove the waste and reveal the tenon cheek. I make the shoulder cut last. After cutting out a single tenon cheek on each armrest using this angle adjustment, I swing the radial arm the same number of degrees on the other side of its zero setting. Then I make a second series of passes to complete the remaining 2 tenon cheeks (*photo 10-11*).

I trim the front-leg and armrest tenons to their final widths on the band saw. The front-leg tenons should be 1⅝ in. wide, while the armrest tenons should be 3¼ in. wide. I lay out the top and bottom trim cuts for each armrest tenon so that they're perpendicular to the side shoulders of the tenon. I also trim the end of the armrest tenon so that it's parallel with the side shoulders. Armrest-tenon length is 1½ in.

The last step before gluing up the end subassemblies is to sand the subassembly parts and round over the upper edges of the armrests. I go over the parts with my pad sander, using fine-grit sandpaper. Then I chuck a 1/2-in. roundover bit in the router and mill rounded edges along the top and front of each armrest (*photo 10-12*). I stop this roundover treatment just after the bit reaches the straight edge on the underside of the armrest. Then I feather the rounded edges into the square edges using a fine rasp and some sandpaper. When doing this, I'm careful not to file or sand where the front leg will meet the armrest.

Gluing Up the End Subassemblies

The glue I use to assemble the bench comes in 2 parts that must be mixed together just before application. It's messy stuff to use, but it forms a strong bond that's impervious to water and most chemicals. Before mixing up the glue, I test-fit the armrest, legs, and rails for each end subassembly, making sure that the joints all fit together well. Then I glue the parts together, using a brush to spread glue on tenons as well as in mortises. The glue is dark in color, so it's a good idea to have a damp rag handy to wipe away excess that squeezes out of joints.

10-11 (*below left*) To cut the arm tenons, I use a dado cutter in the radial-arm saw. Height adjustment is set to leave a 3/4-in.-thick tenon after the dado removes the waste from both tenon cheeks. These tenons require angled shoulder cuts, so the radial arm is adjusted to match the angle of the rear leg. Making overlapping passes, I work my way to the tenon shoulder.

10-12 (*below right*) With a 1/2-in. roundover bit chucked in the router, I go over the top and front edges of each arm.

10-13 Pipe clamps pull the legs against the rails while I drill 3/8-in.-diameter holes through each mortise-and-tenon joint. A stop collar on the bit limits hole depth to 2¼ in.

Placing scrap-wood blocks between the clamping feet and the stock, I tighten pipe clamps across the legs to pull these tenons tight in their mortises. Then I drill out the joints for dowel pins, which will augment the holding power of the glue. Each lower-rail tenon gets a single pin. Its hole is centered 3/4 in. from the joint line, or tenon shoulder, and also centered across the width of the tenon. Each seat-rail tenon gets a pair of pins. These are centered 3/4 in. from the joint line and 5/8 in. from the top and bottom of the tenon. Each armrest tenon also gets 2 pins that are centered 3/4 in. from the joint line and 5/8 in. from the top and bottom of the tenon. I use a single pin in each armrest-to-front-leg joint. This pin is centered along the width of the tenon and 3/4 in. from the joint line.

I use a 3/8-in.-diameter brad-point bit to bore all these dowel holes in the outside face of each end subassembly. I fasten a depth stop on the bit to limit the depth of each dowel hole to 2¼ in. (*photo 10-13*). This will allow the dowel pins to penetrate all the way through the tenon and into the opposite cheek of the mortise.

After boring each hole, I spread some waterproof glue in it, using a nail. Then I tap a 2½-in.-long dowel into the hole with my shot-filled mallet (*photo 10-14*). After the glue dries, I'll sand the protruding 1/4-in. length of dowel flush with the surface of the teak. When all the joints in the end subassemblies have been drilled and pegged, I can remove the clamps and set them aside while I work on the back of the bench.

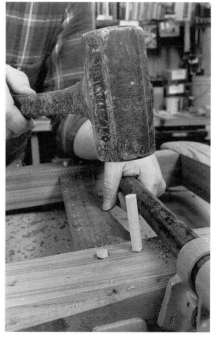

10-14 After spreading some waterproof glue in each hole, I tap a 2½-in.-long dowel into the hole until it bottoms out. After the glue dries, the maple dowels will be sanded flush with the teak.

Long Rails and Slats

The end subassemblies are joined together by 3 long rails — an upper back rail, a lower back rail, and a front rail (*drawing 10-A*).

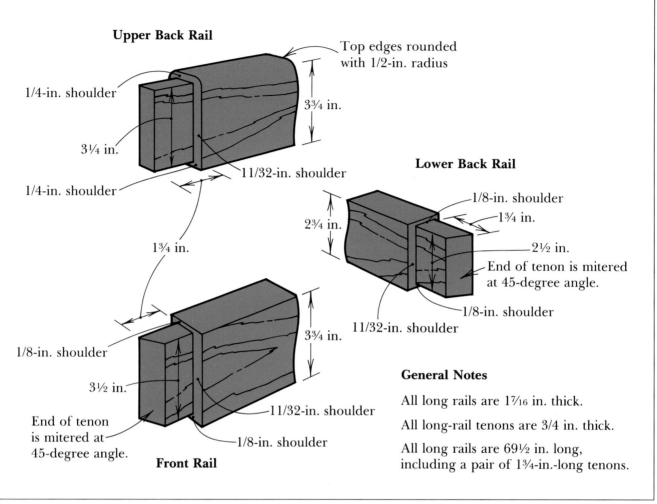

Upper Back Rail

Top edges rounded with 1/2-in. radius

1/4-in. shoulder

3¼ in.

1/4-in. shoulder

3¾ in.

11/32-in. shoulder

1¾ in.

Lower Back Rail

1/8-in. shoulder

1¾ in.

2¾ in.

2½ in.

End of tenon is mitered at 45-degree angle.

1/8-in. shoulder

11/32-in. shoulder

1/8-in. shoulder

3½ in.

3¾ in.

End of tenon is mitered at 45-degree angle.

11/32-in. shoulder

1/8-in. shoulder

Front Rail

General Notes

All long rails are 1⁷⁄₁₆ in. thick.

All long-rail tenons are 3/4 in. thick.

All long rails are 69½ in. long, including a pair of 1¾-in.-long tenons.

Each rail is 69½ in. long, including a pair of 1¾-in.-long tenons (*drawing 10-E*). I use the table saw and jointer to rip and joint the rails to their finished widths: 3¾ in. for the upper back rail and front rail, 2¾ in. for the lower back rail.

I cut the tenons in these rails on the table saw, the same way that I cut the tenons on the lower end rails and seat rails (*photos 10-7 and 10-8*). To make the shoulder cuts along the sides of the rails, I adjust blade height to 11/32 in. I also move my rip fence and gauge-block setup so that the gauge block is 1¾ in. from the far edge of the saw blade. I run each rail through this setup, guiding first one edge against the miter gauge, then the other. To align every cut, I butt the end of the rail against the gauge block. For the shoulder cuts along the edges of the upper back rail, I adjust the height of the saw blade to 1/4 in. Blade height should be 1/8 in. for the shoulder cuts along the edges of the front rail and the lower back rail.

Thanks to the high ceiling in my shop, I can again use the

tenon-cutting jig in the table saw to make the cheek cuts in the long rail tenons. Jig position and blade-height adjustments can remain the same as when I cut the cheeks on the lower-end-rail and seat-rail tenons. With each tall member clamped in the jig, I cut first one cheek, then the other.

On the band saw, I cut the tenons to their final widths, using the fence to guide the edges of the rails. The upper-back-rail tenons are 3¼ in. wide. Front-rail tenons are 3½ in. wide, and the width of the lower-back-rail tenons is 2½ in. When I'm done trimming the top and bottom of each tenon, I go over to the motorized miter box and miter the ends of the tenons on the lower back rail and front rail.

My next job is to mill the mortises for the slats in both back rails. There are a total of 16 slats, each 1/2 in. thick, 2 in. wide, and 15½ in. long. In the back subassembly, the slats will float in mortises milled in upper and lower back rails (*drawing 10-E*).

I mill the mortises in the upper rail first, using a 1/2-in. hollow-chisel mortising setup in the drill press. On the bottom edge of the upper back rail, I lay out 2-in.-wide mortises, spacing the mortises 2 in. apart. I adjust the fence of the mortiser to center the bit over the 1⅞₁₆-in.-wide edge; I also adjust the bit's plunge depth to 1 in. Holding the rail against the fence, I make a series of overlapping cuts, lowering the bit inside the mortise layout lines to complete each mortise. A roller stand comes in handy as a support for the free end of the rail as I mill the first and last few mortises (*photo 10-15*).

Unlike the upper back rail, which is oriented parallel with the slope of the bench back, the lower back rail is installed vertically. This means that the lower mortises have to be milled at an angle. This angle should match the angle of the shoulder cuts I made earlier when milling the armrest tenons. With a few wedges, positioned on the drill-press table, I can secure the lower rail at the correct angle while milling all 16 mortises. As shown in photo 10-16, I use 3 different wedges to form an angled channel for the lower back rail. All 3 are about 14 in. long, and I cut them on the table saw. I temporarily tack one wedge to the wood part of the mortiser's fence. The second wedge (beveled and also ripped to a width of 1⅞₁₆ in.) rests on the drill-press table. And the third wedge is clamped to the table surface, locking the second wedge in position. I slide the lower back rail along this angled channel as I mill each mortise.

Before assembling the back of the bench, I chuck a 1/2-in. roundover bit in the router and go over the top edges of the upper back rail. This is also a good time to ease the edges of all the long rails with some sandpaper. I give them a quick once-over just to take the sharpness off the corners.

Now I can fit the back slats between the back rails. First, I use my shot-filled mallet to drive the slats into the top-rail mortises.

10-15 I use my hollow-chisel mortiser in the drill press to mill slat mortises in both rear rails. Here, a roller guide is set up level with the drill-press table to support one end of the upper back rail.

10-16 Slat mortises in the lower back rail have to be angled to match the slope of the bench's back. I use 3 wedges to form an angled channel for the rail as I mill these mortises.

10-F *Back Slat Installation*

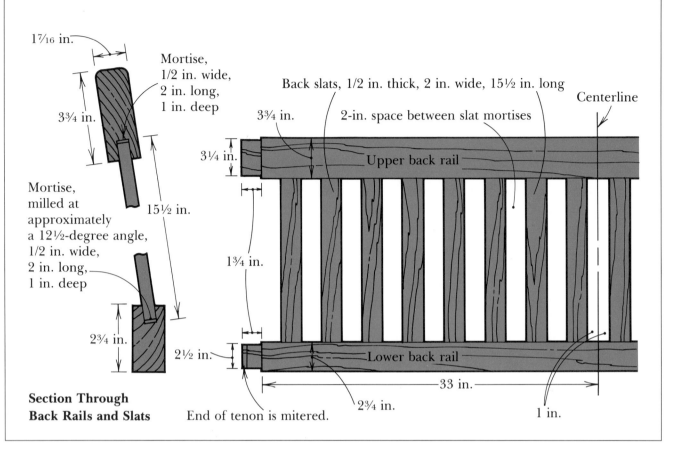

1⁷⁄₁₆ in.

Mortise,
1/2 in. wide,
2 in. long,
1 in. deep

3¾ in.

Mortise,
milled at
approximately
a 12½-degree angle,
1/2 in. wide,
2 in. long,
1 in. deep

15½ in.

2¾ in.

2½ in.

**Section Through
Back Rails and Slats**

End of tenon is mitered.

Back slats, 1/2 in. thick, 2 in. wide, 15½ in. long

3¾ in.

2-in. space between slat mortises

Centerline

3¼ in.

Upper back rail

1¾ in.

Lower back rail

33 in.

2¾ in.

1 in.

10-17 I use my shot-filled mallet to coax the back slats into lower-rail mortises.

These slats aren't tenoned, and the rail ends just float in their mortises. Next, I clamp the lower back rail in my workbench, with its mortises facing up. I complete the back subassembly by tapping down on the upper back rail while engaging each slat in its lower mortise (*photo 10-17*). To facilitate joining the back rails to the end subassemblies later, I use my mallet to adjust the distance between upper and lower tenons (in the back subassembly) to match the distance between corresponding mortises in the end subassemblies.

The front rail still needs some work before I can assemble the complete bench frame. There are 2 mortises that need to be made in this piece for 2 seat supports that extend from the front rail to the lower back rail. Each mortise is located 21⅜ in. from a tenon shoulder. The mortises are 3/4 in. wide, 1¼ in. long, and 7/8 in. deep (*drawing 10-G*). I lay out each mortise as shown in the drawing, so that its bottom edge is 2⅜ in. from the top edge of the rail. It takes me a few minutes to mill the mortises on the drill press, using the hollow-chisel mortiser (*photo 10-18*). Rather than set up the fence to align these 2 mortises, I position the rail freehand. This calls for extra care in positioning the rail so that the chisel stays square with and inside the layout lines.

I cut the shoulders and cheeks of the seat-support tenons on the table saw, using the miter gauge, the gauge block, and the tenon-cutting jig as I did when making the other tenons. I cut

10-18 Using the hollow-chisel mortiser, I mill mortises in the front rail for the seat supports.

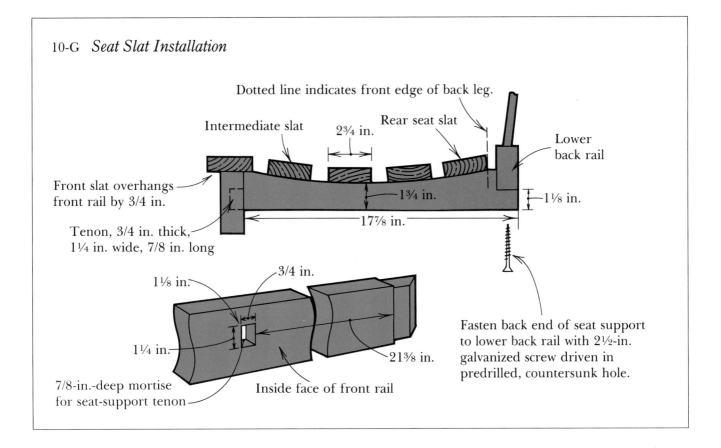

10-G *Seat Slat Installation*

Dotted line indicates front edge of back leg.

Intermediate slat

2¾ in.

Rear seat slat

Lower back rail

Front slat overhangs front rail by 3/4 in.

1¾ in.

1⅛ in.

Tenon, 3/4 in. thick, 1¼ in. wide, 7/8 in. long

17⅞ in.

1⅛ in.

3/4 in.

1¼ in.

21⅜ in.

7/8-in.-deep mortise for seat-support tenon

Inside face of front rail

Fasten back end of seat support to lower back rail with 2½-in. galvanized screw driven in predrilled, countersunk hole.

10-19   After spreading waterproof glue on the joining parts, I fit the back-rail tenons in their mortises.

10-20   To complete the bench frame, I fit the mortises in the opposite-end subassembly over the tenons of the 3 long rails. The next step will be to clamp the bench ends tight against the long rails while pinning the mortise-and-tenon joints with dowels.

each seat-support tenon to its final 1¼-in. width on the band saw. Then I stay at this workstation to cut out a notch in the opposite end of each seat support. This 1⅛-in.-deep, 1⁷⁄₁₆-in.-wide notch will fit against the bottom edge of the lower back rail. Finally, I use a pattern to trace the curve of the seat support's top edge onto both of the pieces I've been working on. Then I cut out the curves on the band saw and smooth the sawed edges on the drill press, using my 2-in.-diameter sanding drum.

Assembly

After dry-fitting the long rails in their mortises to make sure these joints will go together smoothly, I mix up another batch of waterproof glue. Then I spread some glue in the mortises for the 2 back rails and on the back-rail tenons that will fit into them.

With the end on the floor, I fit the back subassembly in place, tapping the tenons home with my shot-filled mallet (*photo 10-19*). Once the front rail has been glued to this end of the bench, I can spread glue on and in the remaining joints and fit the opposite end of the bench over the three remaining tenons (*photo 10-20*). I pull the ends tight against the long rails with 3 pipe clamps, then peg each mortise-and-tenon joint with two 3/8-in.-diameter dowel pins. At all 6 joints, dowel holes are centered 3/4 in. from the joint line and 5/8 in. from the top and bottom of the tenon.

The seat supports can be installed next. I spread some glue in the mortise and on the tenon before fitting the seat support in place (*photo 10-21*). To secure these mortise-and-tenon joints, I peg each one, gluing a 2¾-in.-long dowel in a hole bored into the top edge of the front rail (1/2 in. from the inside edge of the rail). I fasten the rear of the support to the lower back rail with a single 2½-in. galvanized screw, driven up through the bottom edge of the support and into the bottom edge of the rail (*photo 10-22*). Before driving the screw, I predrill and countersink the screw hole, making sure that the support is perpendicular to the lower back rail.

When both seat supports are fastened to the frame, I can install the seat slats. Each slat is 7/8 in. thick and 2¾ in. wide. I cut the front slat to a length of 66 in. The rear slat and the 3 intermediate slats are 71½ in. long. Each slat is fastened with four 1¼-in. galvanized screws — one at each seat-rail location and one at each seat-support location. Each screw is centered across the width of its slat. I predrill for each screw, using a bit that makes a 3/8-in.-diameter counterbore.

I install the front and rear slats first. The front slat should

10-21 I glue each seat-support tenon in a front-rail mortise.

10-22 After predrilling and countersinking the screw hole, I drive a 2½-in. screw through the notched back of the seat support and into the bottom edge of the lower back rail.

overhang the front rail by 3/4 in. The back edge of the rear slat should butt against the front edges of the back legs. Once these 2 slats are in, I space the 3 intermediate slats evenly between them, using a spacer block to keep neighboring slats equidistant from one another (*photo 10-23*).

Now the counterbore holes need to be filled with wood plugs. For the sake of appearance, these plugs should be as inconspicuous as possible. The best way to ensure this is to make the plugs from teak. After chucking a 3/8-in.-diameter plug cutter in my drill press, it takes me a couple of minutes to bore out 20 plugs in

10-23 I use a spacer block as a guide when installing the 3 intermediate seat slats. Each seat slat gets a single screw at each seat rail and seat support. I predrill and counterbore the screw holes, centering each hole along the width of the slat.

a piece of scrap teak. I break the plugs loose from the block with a straight screwdriver. Each plug gets a dab of waterproof glue before I tap it in its hole (*photo 10-24*). Once the glue has dried, I sand the plugs flush and give the entire bench a final sanding before setting it out in the weather (*photo 10-25*). With no finish at all, this bench will be a garden showpiece for years to come.

10-24 Counterbore holes are filled with teak plugs that I make on the drill press, using a plug cutter. I dab some waterproof glue on each plug before tapping it in place.

10-25 Once the glue has dried, I use my random-orbit sander to sand the plugs flush.

Chapter Eleven

Entertainment Center

PROJECT PLANNING

Time: 3 days

Special hardware and tools:

(4 pairs) brass-plated, semi-concealed cabinet hinges

(4) 6-ft adjustable shelf standards, with clips

(4) 1¼-in.-diameter brass knobs

(4) magnetic catches

Wood:

(2) sheets 4x8, 3/4-in.-thick cherry-veneer plywood

For the sides: Crosscut one sheet 72 in. long x 4 ft wide. Then rip this sheet into 2 pieces 23⅝ in. wide and 72 in. long (finished dimensions).

For the fixed shelves: Rip one sheet into a piece 23¼ in. wide and 96 in. long, then cut this sheet into 3 pieces 31¾ in. long (finished dimensions).

For the adjustable shelves: Rip the remaining 96-in.-long piece to a width of 22¼ in., then cut this into 3 pieces 30⅞ in. long (finished dimensions).

Note: An extra adjustable shelf (22¼ in. wide, 30⅞ in. long) can be made from the piece that remains after the sides are cut, but this shelf will have its grain running in the wrong direction.

(1) sheet 4x8, 1/4-in.-thick plywood, with a cherry face veneer on one side only

For the back: Crosscut panel to a length of 71¾ in., then rip to a 31⅝-in. width.

(2) 10-ft 1x6s cherry

Cut one 6-ft-long piece and rip it in half to make *face-frame stiles.* Use remaining piece to make *middle and bottom face-frame rails.*

THE entertainment center is one project that I had to design without an antique prototype. But I wanted this piece of furniture to have a traditional appearance in spite of the electronic equipment it's meant to hold. At the Essex Institute's Crowninshield-Bentley House in Salem, Massachusetts, I found a couple of antiques with details that I could incorporate into my entertainment center. In the kitchen, I admired the angled cornice molding and cutout toe-kick on a pine cupboard. I also liked the convenience of the cupboard's upper and lower compartments. This antique would be a little too rustic for the living room, however. My search for more formal details took me upstairs, where I found a combination bookcase and desk with raised-panel doors. These traditional doors were just what the entertainment center needed.

Like the kitchen cupboard at the Crowninshield-Bentley House, my entertainment center has upper and lower compartments separated by a fixed center shelf. The upper set of doors cover cabinet space designed to hold a full-size (19-in.) television and, above it, a VCR and compact disc player. The lower compartment is for VCR tapes, compact discs, and other smaller items. A pair of shelf standards are dadoed into each side of the cabinet so that shelves in each compartment are adjustable.

Assembling the Carcass

The body, or carcass, of this cabinet is made from 3/4-in.-thick plywood with cherry face veneers. Plywood is stronger and more stable than solid-wood panels, so it's a good choice for a large cabinet that will hold heavy items. And once the cabinet is finished,

Cut remaining 10-ft-long 1x6 to a 90-in. length and use to make *base molding*. The remaining 30-in. piece will be used to make the *top face-frame rail*.

(2) 8-ft 1x6s cherry

Each 8-ft piece makes *door stiles and rails* for one side of the cabinet.

(2) 10-ft 1x6s cherry

Cut each 10-ft board into two 36-in.-long pieces and two 20-in.-long pieces. Edge-glue each pair of boards into a panel to make *raised panels*.

(1) 8-ft 1x4 cherry

Cornice molding

(1) 8-ft 5/4 x 3 cherry

Edges for adjustable shelves

you won't be able to see any edge plies, so the plywood will actually look like edge-glued, solid-cherry boards.

Full-size sheets of plywood are difficult to handle, but I'm fortunate to have plenty of room for maneuvering these sheet goods in the workshop. I also have some useful accessories that make it easier (and safer) to cut 4x8 panels down to size on my table saw. If you don't, as I do, have extension tables for your table saw and a couple of roller stands, then you'll need a helper to guide the plywood as you cut it. You might also consider cutting sheets roughly to size with a circular saw, making only the final cuts on the table saw. Still another option is to have your lumber dealer handle the major plywood cuts on a panel saw.

Finished dimensions for the sides, fixed shelves, and adjustable shelves are given in the wood list for this project. I cut out the sides by first cutting a full sheet down to a length of 72 in. I then rip this large piece in half lengthwise. I set up roller stands for both of these cuts, first along the side of the saw, then at its outfeed end (*photo 11-1*). To rip the sides to their final width, I adjust the rip fence so that it's 23⅝ in. from the blade.

All 3 fixed shelves can be cut from a piece of plywood 8 ft long and 23¼ in. wide. Using my panel cutter, I cut each of these shelves to a finished length of 31¾/4 in. The 3 plywood panels that I use to make the adjustable shelves need to be 22¼ in. wide and 30⅞ in. long. To finish up my sheet-cutting work, I cut out the back of the cabinet. This piece, which should measure 31⅝ in. by 71¾ in., is cut from a 1/4-in.-thick sheet of plywood with a cherry face veneer on one side only.

Once these parts are all cut to size, I can begin the carcass joinery work, which consists of rabbets and dadoes that are made in the sides. The fixed center shelf and fixed bottom shelf are both dadoed into the sides, while the top shelf (which could also be called the top of the carcass) is rabbeted into the sides (*drawing 11-B*).

I often mill rabbets and dadoes on the table saw, using my dado cutter. But it's difficult to make crosscut dadoes in long pieces, even if they're guided by the rip fence. So to mill these joints, I keep the sides stationary and do the work with my router. On both sides, I lay out the locations of rabbets and dadoes using my framing square. Then I chuck a 1/2-in. straight bit in the router and adjust bit depth to 3/8 in. To guide the router base and keep the bit within the layout lines for each dado, I use a pair of straightedge clamps. Each clamp guides the base of the router for a shoulder cut, so I can complete the 3/4-in.-wide dado in 2 passes (*photo 11-2*). If you don't have straightedge clamps like mine, you can do the same work with a couple of straight guide boards. Just use some clamps to hold the boards in position while you mill the dado.

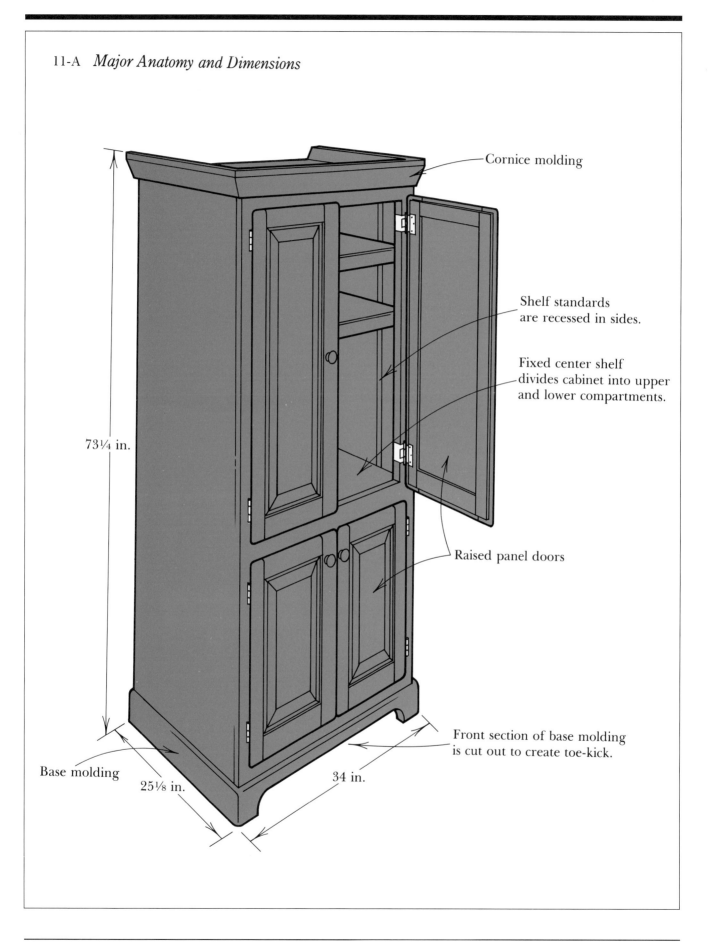

Cornice molding

Shelf standards
are recessed in sides.

Fixed center shelf
divides cabinet into upper
and lower compartments.

Raised panel doors

73¼ in.

Front section of base molding
is cut out to create toe-kick.

Base molding

25⅛ in.

34 in.

11-1 Extension tables and outfeed rollers provide important additional support for solo cutting of plywood sheets on the table saw. Here I use the rip fence to guide the plywood as I cut the sides from a 72-in.-long sheet.

11-2 I mill dadoes and rabbets in the carcass sides using my router and a 1/2-in. straight bit. A pair of straightedge clamps, positioned parallel with the joint layout, guide the base of the router. Bit depth is 3/8 in.

To mill the rabbet along the top edge of each side, I use just one straightedge clamp to guide the router base. Two passes are required to complete each rabbet, just as with the dadoes.

Each side needs a pair of dadoes that extend from top to bottom, to recess the shelf standards. Unlike the joints that I've just milled, these dadoes run along the length of the sides. I can thus mill them easily on the table saw, since the rip fence will guide each piece. I replace the blade with a dado cutter, adjust the width of the cutter to 5/8 in., and raise it 3/16 in. above the table. Then I position the rip fence 2⅜ in. away from the cutter. Turning on the saw, I run the long edges of each side against the rip fence, taking care to mill the dadoes on the same side of each piece where the dadoes and rabbets are located.

To finish up the sides, I rabbet the back edge of each side to hold the plywood back panel. The back of the cabinet is just 1/4 in. thick, but I make the rabbet 3/8 in. deep to keep the back out of sight in the finished piece. The width of the rabbet is also 3/8

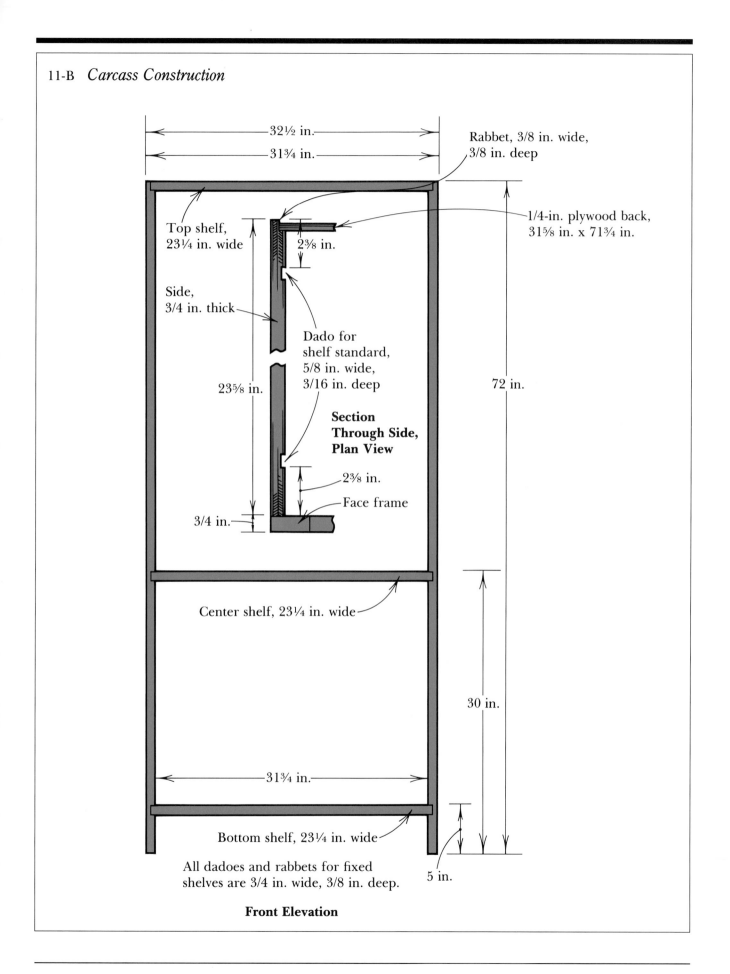

32½ in.

31¾ in.

Rabbet, 3/8 in. wide, 3/8 in. deep

Top shelf, 23¼ in. wide

1/4-in. plywood back, 31⅝ in. x 71¾ in.

2⅜ in.

Side, 3/4 in. thick

Dado for shelf standard, 5/8 in. wide, 3/16 in. deep

23⅝ in.

72 in.

Section Through Side, Plan View

2⅜ in.

Face frame

3/4 in.

Center shelf, 23¼ in. wide

30 in.

31¾ in.

Bottom shelf, 23¼ in. wide

All dadoes and rabbets for fixed shelves are 3/4 in. wide, 3/8 in. deep.

5 in.

Front Elevation

in. I mill these rabbets using a 3/8-in. rabbeting bit in my router. Bit depth should be adjusted to show 3/8 in. of the cutter.

Now I can assemble the carcass. With one side flat on the workbench, I use a small brush to spread glue along its rabbet and dadoes. Then I fit the 3 shelves into place. The important thing when joining the sides and shelves is to keep the front edges of all parts flush. This will ensure a good fit for the face frame. Leaning underneath the side, I drive a few 4d finishing nails into each joint, using my pneumatic nailer (*photo 11-3*). This holds all 3 shelves in position while I fit the remaining side over the upturned edges of the shelves. Again, I glue these joints together and hold them fast with 4d finishing nails that I drive with my pneumatic nailer.

The back goes on next. Despite its light weight, the back effectively braces the carcass. So before attaching it, I have to make sure that the sides and shelves are square with one another. With the carcass placed facedown on the workbench, I test it for squareness by taking diagonal measurements (from top corners to bottom corners). When these measurements are equal, I spread glue on the side rabbets and along the back edges of the shelves before fitting the back (*photo 11-4*). Making sure that the sides are straight, I fasten the back down by driving 3/4-in. brads into sides and shelves.

The Face Frame

Composed of vertical stiles and horizontal rails, the face frame covers the front edges of the carcass and forms the openings for the upper and lower compartments. I cut this face frame from

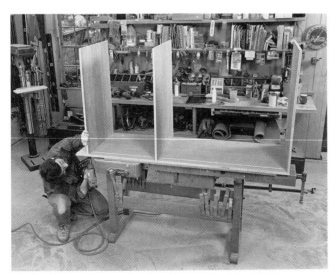

11-3 After gluing all 3 shelves to a side, I use my pneumatic nailer to drive 4d finishing nails through the sides and into shelf edges.

11-4 Installing the back completes the carcass. I spread glue along the rabbets in the sides and along the back edges of the shelves before slipping the back in place and nailing it with 3/4-in. brads.

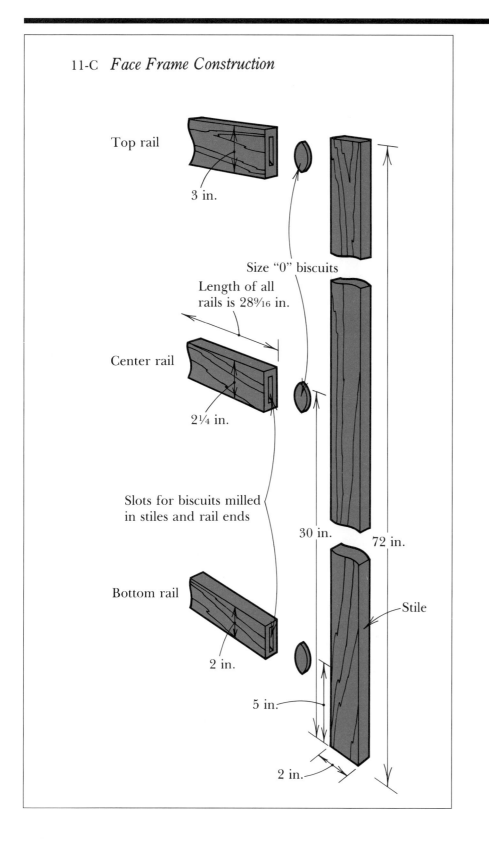

11-C *Face Frame Construction*

Top rail

3 in.

Size "0" biscuits

Length of all
rails is 28⁹⁄₁₆ in.

Center rail

2¼ in.

Slots for biscuits milled
in stiles and rail ends

30 in.

72 in.

Bottom rail

2 in.

Stile

5 in.

2 in.

3/4-in.-thick cherry. There are 2 stiles, each 2 in. wide and 72 in.
long. The bottom rail is 2 in. wide, the center rail is 2¼ in. wide,
and the top rail is 3 in. wide. Length of all 3 rails is 28⁹⁄₁₆ in.
(*drawing 11-C*). I use the table saw and jointer to rip and joint

11-5 Using my biscuit joiner, I mill slots for biscuits in a stile. The ends of the rails will receive corresponding slots so that the entire face frame can be assembled with biscuits.

11-6 After gluing and clamping the face frame together, I glue and nail it to the carcass. Clamps can remain attached until I've secured the face frame by driving 4d finishing nails into the front edges of the carcass.

these members to their final widths, then I cut them to length on the motorized miter box.

The traditional way to attach stiles to rails is with lap joints or mortise-and-tenon joints. But for this project, I use biscuit joinery to assemble the frame. (For more on biscuit joinery, see the Introduction.) Using glue in combination with the biscuit-shaped spline at each stile-to-rail connection makes an extremely strong joint, and it's far quicker and easier than milling mortises and tenons (*drawing 11-C*). I dry-fit the face frame together and make a mark across each joint (centered on the width of the rail) to align the biscuit joiner. Then I use the tool to mill a slot on the end of each rail and along the edges of the stiles (*photo 11-5*). I mill slots to hold the smallest-size biscuits ("0").

Once all the slots have been cut, I spread glue on each joint, including the biscuits, and assemble the frame. I tighten a pipe clamp across the width of the frame at each rail location. With the frame secure and square, I can install it now, rather than wait for the glue to dry. I place the carcass on a pair of sawhorses, with its back facing down. After spreading some glue on the front edges of the carcass, I lift the face frame and clamps together and align the frame over the front of the carcass. Don't worry if the frame is slightly wider than the carcass — it's meant to be that way. The important thing is to align the bottom and center rails so that their top edges are flush with the top surfaces of bottom and center shelves. I also position the frame so that the stiles extend evenly beyond the sides. When this alignment is right, I use my pneumatic nailer to drive 4d finishing nails through the frame and into the front edges of the carcass (*photo 11-6*) every 6 to 8 in. The clamps can be removed as soon as all frame members have been nailed.

When the glue has had a chance to dry, I can trim the outside edges of the stiles flush with the carcass sides, using a flush-trimming bit in my router. This type of bit combines a carbide-tipped straight cutter with a pilot bearing. The bearing is located directly beneath the cutter and has the same diameter as the cutter. I adjust bit depth so that the bearing will be guided by the carcass side, allowing the bit to trim the edge of the stile flush with the side (*photo 11-7*).

Making the Cornice

The cornice for the entertainment center was actually inspired by a cornice that I admired on an antique cupboard. The finished cornice looks to be made from thick stock, but it's actually cut from a board just 3/4 in. thick and 3¼ in. wide. Clever angles create the illusion.

It takes 4 separate cuts on the table saw to rough out the profile of the cornice molding. The saw blade is tilted to a 25-degree angle for all 4 cuts. It's the position of the rip fence that has to change for each cut. If you don't have a pattern piece to help you set up the rip fence, then trace the molding profile on the end grain of the board and use this to help position the fence. The profile, along with the order of cuts, is shown in drawing 11-D.

The first 2 cuts will create a new pair of edges that will be vertical when the cornice is installed. Each of these cuts is made by running the board on edge through the blade. The rip fence is adjusted to guide first one side of the board, then the other (*photo 11-8*). There should be about 3/8 in. between the fence and the blade for the first cut. I increase this distance to about 1/2 in. for the second cut.

The last 2 cuts are made by running the edges of the piece against the rip fence (*photo 11-9*). These cuts create top and bottom edges adjacent to the "vertical" edges of the molding. The top edge should be 1/2 in. wide; I make the bottom edge 3/8 in. wide.

Making these angled cuts on the table saw leaves some saw marks that need to be planed out before I install the molding. Edge number one, the first to be cut (*drawing 11-D*), can stay as it is, since it won't be seen once the cornice is installed. To clean up edges 3 and 4, I adjust the fence on my jointer to a 25-degree angle and make 2 passes, guiding one side of the molding against the fence, then the other. Each pass removes 1/32 in. of wood from the edge, leaving it smooth and flat. When jointing these edges, it's important to check the orientation of the molding to avoid jointing an edge at the wrong angle.

Edge 2 is difficult to smooth on the jointer, so instead, I clamp the molding on my workbench and smooth this edge with my portable power plane. By holding the tool's fence against the op-

11-7 I use a flush-trimming bit in the router to trim the outside edges of the face frame flush with the sides of the carcass. Trimming action is very precise because the bearing that runs against the side has the same diameter as the cutter.

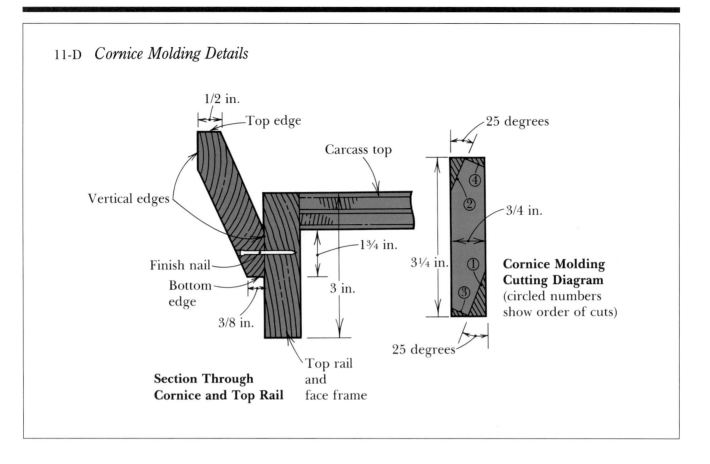

11-D *Cornice Molding Details*

1/2 in.

Top edge

Carcass top

25 degrees

Vertical edges

④
②

3/4 in.

Finish nail

1¾ in.

3¼ in.

**Cornice Molding
Cutting Diagram**
(circled numbers
show order of cuts)

Bottom
edge

3 in.

①
③

3/8 in.

Top rail
and
face frame

25 degrees

**Section Through
Cornice and Top Rail**

11-8 Guiding the side of the board against the rip fence, I make the second of 4 angled cuts to rough out the profile of the cornice molding. Blade angle is adjusted to 25 degrees.

posite edge of the molding, I can guide the plane bed at the proper angle to smooth this edge (*photo 11-10*).

Now I go over to the motorized miter box to cut this single length of molding into 3 pieces. One will fit against the top rail of the face frame, while the other 2 will be fastened to the sides. To orient the molding properly for the miter cuts, I clamp a wood fence to the saw table, which will act as a stop for the top edge of the molding. The lower part of the molding fits against the saw's fence, just as it will fit against the face frame. Using this orientation, I cut all three pieces to their finished sizes. Each side piece gets a square cut and a miter, while the front molding piece is mitered at both ends.

Before installing the cornice, I give the face frame a thorough sanding, using my random-orbit sander and some fine-grit sandpaper. Sanding by hand with fine-grit sandpaper, I also ease all edges of the face frame. Then I fasten a side piece of cornice molding to a side of the carcass, using my pneumatic nailer to drive finishing nails through the molding and into the side. The bottom edge of the cornice should be 1¾ in. down from the top edge of the carcass, as shown in drawing 11-D. The front molding piece goes on next, followed by the remaining side piece (*photo 11-11*). I glue only the miter joints where side molding pieces meet the front molding piece. For extra holding power, I also nail each miter joint with a couple of 1-in. brads.

11-9 The last 2 cuts for the cornice are made by running either edge of the board against the rip fence. Blade angle remains at 25 degrees.

11-10 I use a portable power plane to smooth one of the molding edges that's difficult to plane on the jointer. With the molding clamped on the workbench, I maintain the correct planing angle by guiding the power plane's fence with one hand.

The Base Molding

Like the cornice, the base molding is installed in 3 pieces, with miter joints where the pieces meet at the front corners of the carcass. To make the molding, I start by ripping and jointing a 90-in.-long cherry 1x6 to a finished width of 4 in. Using my motorized miter box, I cut the miter joints in side and front pieces, also cutting the sides off square at their back ends.

The front base molding has a cutout, creating a kickspace that gives the finished piece a lighter, more graceful appearance. The curved ends of the cutout start 3 in. from the mitered ends of the front molding, and each curve has a 2¾-in. radius (*see drawing 11-E*). The cutout leaves a straight center section that's 1¼ in. high.

After laying out the cutout on the front molding, I clamp the piece in my workbench vise and cut out the waste with my portable jigsaw. Then I use a sanding drum, chucked in the drill press, to smooth out the saw marks along the cutting line.

To strengthen the miter joints where side and front base-molding pieces meet, I use a couple of biscuits in each joint. My biscuit joiner has an attachment that enables me to mill slots in edges that are mitered at a 45-degree angle. I still have to make a pair of alignment marks across each joint. Then I clamp the molding in my workbench vise, position the biscuit joiner centered on my alignment marks against the miter, and plunge the cutter into the edge (*photo 11-12*).

When I've milled a pair of slots in each mitered edge, I fasten the 3 pieces of base molding to the bottom of the carcass. I glue only the miter joints, taking care to spread glue on the biscuits as well as on adjoining edges. I attach the side-molding pieces by driving 1¼-in. screws into the molding from the inside face of the

11-11 After sanding the face frame, I install the cornice molding by nailing its 3 pieces to the sides and top rail of the cabinet. I glue only the mitered corner joints.

11-12 The mitered joints between base-molding pieces are reinforced with biscuits. The front piece of base molding, with its toe-kick cut-out, has already received its slots as I mill a pair of slots in a side piece. An angled base accessory for the biscuit joiner enables me to mill slots at a right angle to the mitered edge.

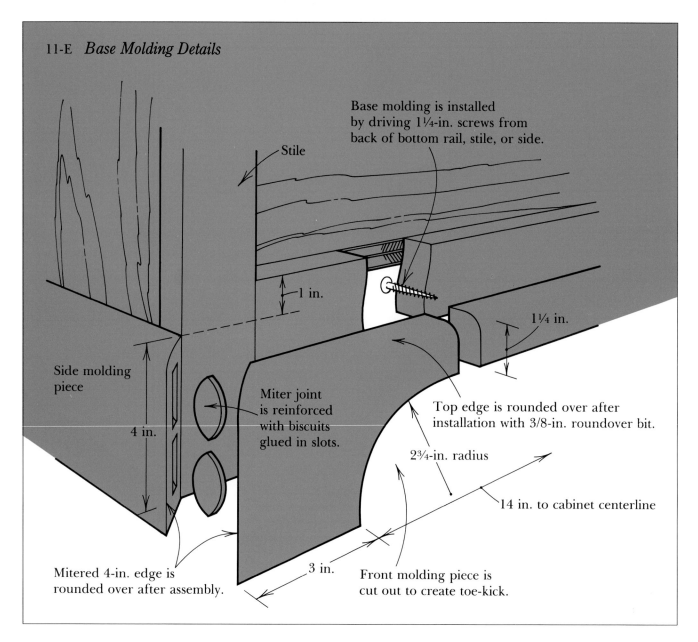

11-E *Base Molding Details*

Stile

Base molding is installed by driving 1¼-in. screws from back of bottom rail, stile, or side.

1 in.

1¼ in.

Side molding piece

4 in.

Miter joint is reinforced with biscuits glued in slots.

Top edge is rounded over after installation with 3/8-in. roundover bit.

2¾-in. radius

14 in. to cabinet centerline

Mitered 4-in. edge is rounded over after assembly.

3 in.

Front molding piece is cut out to create toe-kick.

side. The front molding is secured to the bottom rail and stiles the same way, with screws driven from the back side. I predrill and countersink these screw holes. Finally, I finish off the base molding by rounding over its top edge and its mitered corners. To do this, I chuck a 3/8-in. roundover bit in the router and run the bottom of the router base against the outside face of the molding (*photo 11-13*).

Door Construction

The doors for the entertainment center are traditional in style and construction. Each door has a stile-and-rail frame that encloses a solid-cherry panel with raised edges. The horizontal rails are coped at their ends to fit against the molded profile of the stiles. The edges of the door frames are rabbeted to overlay the door openings.

It's possible to use a router or router table to mill the contoured profiles in stiles and rails, but for repetitive milling of door parts, nothing beats a shaper. With its 3/4-in.-diameter spindle and heavy cast-iron table, the shaper can handle production work involving cutters that dwarf most router bits, and it can usually remove a lot more material too.

There are quite a few shaper cutters available for making cabinet doors. One set of cutters may mill a deeper panel grove than another, and this affects how frame members are sized. If your cutters are different than mine, you'll probably have to revise the stile and rail sizes given here.

I cut the 4 stiles for the upper doors to a length of 39⁹⁄₁₆ in. Stiles for the lower doors start out 23⁵⁄₁₆ in. long. Stile width is 2⁵⁄₁₆ in. The top rails share this 2⁵⁄₁₆-in. width, but I make the bottom rails 2¹³⁄₁₆ in. wide. Rail length is 10¾ in. You'll notice that these dimensions are 1/16 in. greater than the finished dimensions shown on drawing 11-F. I deliberately oversize the frame members slightly, because by running some scrap stock through my cutters I learned that every pass through the cutters will reduce the overall width of the piece by 1/32 in.

The stile-cutting set for my cabinet doors consists of 3 separate cutters that are stacked on the shaper's spindle. The lowermost cutter mills the bead on the inside edge of the stile. The center cutter mills the groove where the edge of the raised panel fits. The straight top cutter simply mills a square, straight edge that will be seen on the inside of the finished door. Above the top cutter, I install a circular guard, which covers the cutting area for safety purposes.

As with the router table, cutter height and fence position are crucial to create the proper profile. To make sure the setup is correct, I run some 3/4-in.-thick scrap stock through the cutters, adjusting spindle height and fence position as necessary. I also

11-13 Using a 3/8-in. roundover bit in the router, I go over the top edges and the mitered corners of the base molding.

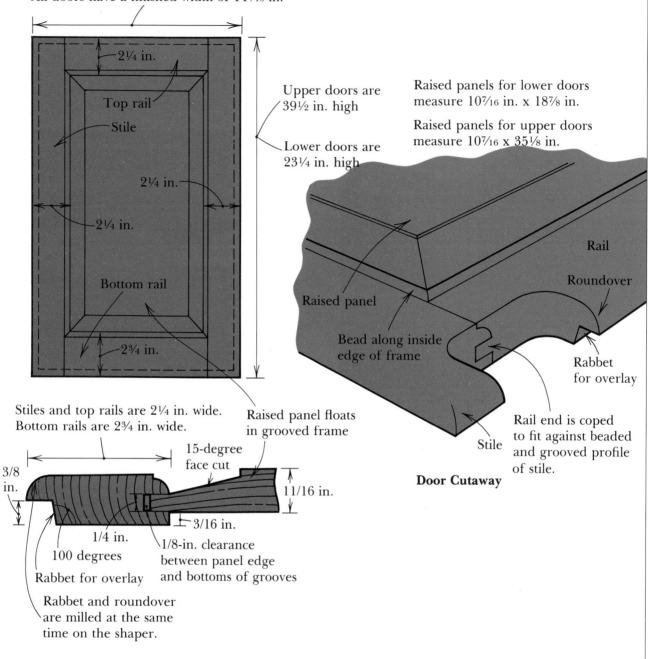

All doors have a finished width of 14⁷⁄₁₆ in.

2¼ in.

Top rail

Stile

2¼ in.

2¼ in.

Bottom rail

2¾ in.

Upper doors are 39½ in. high

Lower doors are 23¼ in. high

Raised panels for lower doors measure 10⁷⁄₁₆ in. x 18⁷⁄₈ in.

Raised panels for upper doors measure 10⁷⁄₁₆ x 35⅛ in.

Rail

Roundover

Raised panel

Bead along inside edge of frame

Rabbet for overlay

Stile

Rail end is coped to fit against beaded and grooved profile of stile.

Door Cutaway

Stiles and top rails are 2¼ in. wide. Bottom rails are 2¾ in. wide.

Raised panel floats in grooved frame

15-degree face cut

3/8 in.

11/16 in.

1/4 in.

3/16 in.

100 degrees

1/8-in. clearance between panel edge and bottoms of grooves

Rabbet for overlay

Rabbet and roundover are milled at the same time on the shaper.

position a pair of hold-downs made for the shaper. One forces the face of the board against the shaper table, while the other keeps the inside edge of the board against the fence. Like the featherboards I use on the router table, hold-downs are important for safe milling on the shaper. Once the setup is right, I run my stiles and rails through the cutters (*photo 11-14*). For safety, I use a push stick to push the back end of each piece through the cutter.

The next step is to cope the ends of the rails so that they can fit snugly against the molded inside edges of the stiles. To set up this operation, I need to install a different 3-piece set of cutters on the shaper spindle. These cutters are designed to mill a profile that's an exact opposite of the first profile. I can install them without having to adjust spindle height or fence position.

The copes are milled across the grain, so I can't use the same hold-downs that worked for the first profile. Instead, I guide each rail with a miter gauge that's set at 90 degrees, using a screw-type hold-down that prevents the stock from shifting up or away from the cutters. To prevent chipping as the cutters exit the rail end, I back up each rail with a scrap piece of wood (*photo 11-15*). There are 16 copes to be milled. For 8 of these, the cutters will exit on the contoured edge of the rail. To prevent chipping on these cuts, I back up the rail with a piece of scrap wood that has been coped *with* the grain, along a long edge.

The shaper excels at making raised panels. Each panel blank is glued up from a pair of cherry 1x6 boards. After scraping hardened glue from along the joint lines, I run each blank through my thickness planer, removing material from both sides until all panels are 11/16 in. thick. I then cut the panels to their finished sizes on the table saw. The panels for the upper doors are 10⅞/16 in. wide and 35⅛ in. long. Lower-door panels are 10⅞/16 in. wide and 18⅞ in. long. These sizes allow each panel to float in the grooves on the inside of the door frame, with between 1/16 in. and 1/8 in. of expansion space between each panel edge and the bottom of its groove.

There are quite a few panel-raising profiles to choose from. My panel-raising cutter is designed to leave a flat, 15-degree face cut and a slight shoulder in 11/16-in.-thick stock. After securing the cutter and guard to the shaper spindle, I adjust spindle height and fence position, checking my setup by making sample cuts in scrap stock. For a panel to fit in its grooved frame, panel edges should be 1/4 in. thick. I set up a single hold-down to maintain downward pressure on the stock. Then I "raise" the panel by making 4 passes through the cutter (*photo 11-16*). The first 2 passes should always be across the grain, since these passes are likely to produce some chipping out. The last 2 passes, made with the grain, will remove the chipped areas.

When all the panels have been raised on the shaper, I can assemble the doors. I use a small brush to give the coped rail ends a thorough coating of glue before joining each pair of stiles and rails together around a panel (*photo 11-17*). It's important for the panel to float in its frame, so I do my best to keep glue out of the panel grooves. A pair of pipe clamps, tightened across the width of each panel (at rail locations), holds these joints together until

11-14 With stile-cutting knives set up in the shaper, I can mill the stile's full bead-and-groove profile in a single pass. A pair of hold-downs force the stile against the table and against the fence as I mill the edge.

11-15 I cope the end of each rail to fit against the stile profile. To prevent chip-out while milling this cope, I back up the rail with a scrap piece of stock that is also coped to fit against the profiled back edge of the rail.

11-16 When raising panels on the shaper, I always make both cross-grain cuts first, then finish up by milling with the grain.

11-17 When assembling each door, I spread glue carefully on the coped joints where rails meet stiles. The panels aren't glued at all, so they can expand and contract freely within the grooved door frame.

11-18 Using a special cutter in the shaper, I can mill the complete overlay profile along the outside edge of each door. The profile includes a 100-degree rabbet, which fits against the cabinet face frame, and a rounded-over edge, which shows from outside the cabinet.

11-19 I screw the hinges to the doors first, then attach them to the face-frame stiles.

the glue dries. I use only moderate clamping pressure on these joints.

When the glue has dried, I remove the clamps from each door, scrape off any hardened glue, and return once again to the shaper. Now it's time to finish off the doors by milling overlay edges. As shown in drawing 11-F, the doors are designed to overlay their openings. The standard overlay profile includes a rabbet with a 100-degree shoulder and a rounded outer edge. The shaper cutter I use can mill the rabbet and roundover at the same time. I set up the cutter as before, topping it off with the circular guard and the locking nut. Then I use some scrap stock to check cutter height and fence position. When the setup is right, I run the door edges through, always milling the 2 rail edges first (*photo 11-18*).

To mount the doors, I use standard semiconcealed cabinet hinges. I chose brass-plated hinges for this project, since brass looks nice with cherry. I screw each hinge to the inside of the frame, aligning the leaf of the hinge with the inside edge of the rail. Once the hinges have been screwed to the doors, it takes just a few minutes to fasten the "free" leaves of the hinges to upper and lower cabinet stiles (*photo 11-19*).

Adjustable Shelves

For strength as well as appearance, I cover the front of each adjustable shelf with a solid-cherry edging. There are 2 adjustable shelves for the upper compartment and one for the lower compartment (see the wood list for this project), so 3 edge pieces are needed. I cut all 3 pieces from 5/4 stock, which has an actual thickness of about 1 in. After ripping and jointing the 5/4 board to a finished width of 1¾ in., I cut all 3 pieces to a finished length of 30⅞ in.

As shown in drawing 11-G, each edge piece is rabbeted to fit around the front edge of the plywood shelf. The rabbet is 3/8 in. deep and 3/4 in. wide. With a couple of adjustments of blade height and fence position, I can cut these rabbets on the table saw. For the first cut, I raise the blade 3/8 in. above the table and set the fence 3/4 in. from the far edge of the blade. I run each edge piece through the blade, guiding what will be the top of the edging against the fence. After cutting all 3 pieces this way, I raise the blade to a 3/4-in. height and move the fence so that it's 5/8 in. from the near edge of the blade. To finish each rabbet, I run the edging through the blade, holding the front of the edging against the fence (*photo 11-20*).

The fronts of the edge pieces need to be rounded over, and it's easiest to do this before they're attached to the shelves. I use a nonskid pad on my workbench to keep each piece steady while I go over both front corners, using a 3/8-in. roundover bit in the

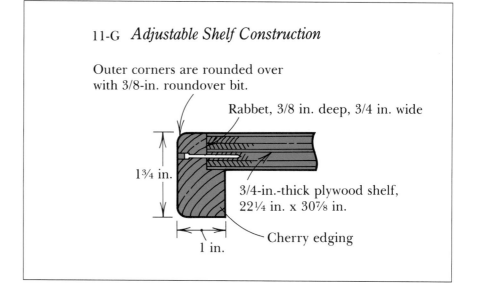

11-G *Adjustable Shelf Construction*

Outer corners are rounded over with 3/8-in. roundover bit.

Rabbet, 3/8 in. deep, 3/4 in. wide

1¾ in.

3/4-in.-thick plywood shelf, 22¼ in. x 30⅞ in.

Cherry edging

1 in.

router. Then I spread glue along the rabbeted edges and join each piece to its shelf. A few 4d finishing nails, driven with my pneumatic nailer, secure each edging piece while the glue dries (*photo 11-21*).

The shelf standards can wait to be installed until after I've applied the finish. But now is a good time to drill a hole in each door for installing the knobs. Holes for all knobs are centered on the width of inner door stiles. Holes for the lower knobs are located 3½ in. from the top edges of the lower doors. Holes for the upper knobs are 19¾ in. down from the top edges of the upper doors.

11-20 Each adjustable shelf is edged with a 1-in.-thick cherry edging that is rabbeted to fit against the plywood edge. Using the rip fence to guide the edge pieces, I complete each rabbet in 2 passes on the table saw.

11-21 After rounding over the outside corners of each edge piece, I attach it to the shelf with glue and 4d finishing nails.

Chapter Twelve

Finishing

MAKING furniture is an excellent way to improve your skill in crafting all kinds of joints. But it's also a great opportunity to learn about different finishes. The more furniture I build, the more I enjoy the challenge of applying a first-rate finish. In this chapter, you'll find descriptions of the different finish treatments used on the projects built in this book. Regardless of the finish you choose, it's important to follow a few general guidelines to ensure good results.

A good sanding job is crucial, and it's important to sand during the construction process as well as after it. Many parts are easier to sand individually, before they're joined to other pieces. While you're creating all this sawdust, you have to find a way to keep it from contaminating your finish. In the New Yankee Workshop, I'm fortunate to have a separate room that I can use just for applying finish. I keep this room as dust-free as possible, doing all my sanding in the workspace where my power tools are. Just before applying the first coat of finish, I wipe down wood surfaces with a tack rag to remove any remaining sawdust.

Application instructions vary for different finishes as well as for different effects. For example, if I want a stain to "take" lightly, I usually apply it with a rag, since this enables me to limit the amount of stain that goes into the wood. To get the maximum effect from a stain, I'll paint it onto the wood surface with a brush, keeping in mind that the longer I let it sit on the surface, the deeper the color will be. If the finish happens to turn out too dark, it's possible to lighten it slightly by wiping the wood surface down, using a rag dampened with the appropriate thinner.

I reserve my best brushes for applying solvent-based polyurethanes and final coats of paint. In any multiple-coat finish, it's important to follow the instructions on the can concerning drying time between coats and compatibility with other finishes (as when applying polyurethane over stain).

Choosing the Right Finish

Just as power tools have made joinery work faster and more accurate, modern finishes have evolved to be more durable and easier to apply than their antique counterparts. There are 2 projects, of course, that are simply left "in the raw" to weather naturally outdoors (the Adirondack chair and the English garden bench). For the remaining projects, I used a variety of stains, sealers, paints, and varnishes.

Price ranges for different brands of finish can be astonishing. Unfortunately, the range of quality is correspondingly broad. In most cases, you get what you pay for. Less-expensive finishes are usually formulated with inferior ingredients that may affect the uniformity and durability of the finish.

Like many furniture-makers, I find myself using more latex and water-based finishes. Because these finishes don't contain volatile solvents, they're environmentally safe (just the same, your finishing room should be well ventilated). They're also a pleasure to use because cleanup is so easy. Latex paints have been around for a long time, but water-based polyurethane is fairly new. I used this clear finish on quite a few projects, with good results. The brand of water-based polyurethane that I used is best applied with a foam brush. It goes on milky white in color, drying clear and very hard. It works well as a primary finish, or over a stain, but at least 2 coats should be applied. For an extra-smooth finish, I apply 3 or 4 coats, sanding the second-to-last coat lightly with 220-grit or finer "wet-or-dry" sandpaper.

Choosing paint colors can be a challenge, especially if you're searching for a hue that looks authentically antique. Instead of relying on the small squares of color in a manufacturer's brochure, you might consider visiting a museum where painted furniture is on display. My eye for Colonial colors improved greatly as I examined old furniture in museums, at antique dealers, and even in private homes. Most paint stores can custom-mix colors, so there's no need to feel limited by premixed selections.

Index